RAILROAD

Glenns Ferry

RAILROAD
Trains and Train People in American Culture

Edited by James Alan McPherson and Miller Williams

Random House/New York

This book is dedicated to the rebuilding of our roadbeds and the replacement of ties and rails so that America's trains, which are its history, will not ride on crystallized metal, rotten wood and uncertain ground.

Library of Congress Cataloging in Publication Data
McPherson, James Alan, 1943-
Railroad.

1. Railroads—United States—History. I. Williams,
Miller, joint author. II. Title.
TF23.M3   385'.0973   76-15994
ISBN 0-394-49857-7
ISBN 0-394-73237-5 pbk.

Manufactured in the United States of America
2 4 6 8 9 7 5 3
First Edition
Design concept: Ira Teichberg

Grateful acknowledgment is made to the following for permission to reprint previously published material:

John Wiley & Sons, Inc.: Diagram from *A Field Manual for Railroad Engineers* by J. C. Nagle.

Railroad Magazine: "Boomer Days," excerpted from "On the Spot" by Charles B. Chrysler from *Railroad Magazine,* Vol. 39, February 1946. Copyright 1946 by Railroad Magazine.

Brotherhood of Locomotive Engineers: "How Kate Shelley Saved the Midnight Express" from *The Locomotive Engineer,* April 4, 1975.

Columbia University Press: "Railroads Ain't No Good" from *Sticks in the Knapsack and Other Folk Tales,* collected by Vance Randolph (1958), p. 84; also "Slow Train Through Arkansas" from *Who Blowed Up the Church? and Other Ozark Folk Tales,* collected by Vance Randolph (1952), p. 7.

Philosophical Library, Inc.: "Thomas Edison Tells about His Days as a Train Butch," from pages 44–49 of *The Diary and Sundry Observations of Thomas Alva Edison,* edited by Dagobert D. Runes. Copyright 1948 by Philosophical Library, Inc.

Houghton Mifflin Company: "Carnegie Tells about Talking Over," excerpted from *Autobiography of Andrew Carnegie* by Louise Whitfield Carnegie, pages 63–64 and 69–72. Copyright renewed 1948 by Margaret Carnegie Miller.

Tudor Press: Excerpt entitled "Rascality Rides the Rails" from *The Romance of the Rails* by Agnes Laut.

Victoria Ginger (Mrs.): Condensation entitled "Eugene V. Debs and the American Railway Union" from *The Bending Cross* by Ray Ginger. Published by Rutgers University Press. Copyright 1949 by the Trustees of Rutgers College.

Harcourt Brace Jovanovich, Inc.: "A. Philip Randolph and the Brotherhood of Sleeping Car Porters," condensed from *A. Philip Randolph: A Biographical Portrait.* Copyright © 1972, 1973 by Jervis B. Anderson.

Charles Scribner's Sons and William Heinemann Ltd.: "Thomas Wolfe on the Train," from *Of Time and the River* by Thomas Wolfe. Copyright 1935 by Charles Scribner's Sons; renewed 1963 by Paul Gitlin, Administrator, C.T.A.

Sterling A. Brown: "Long Gone" from *Southern Road* by Sterling A. Brown, by permission of the author (Harcourt Brace, 1932).

Erie Lackawanna Railway Company: Material excerpted from *The Story of Phoebe Snow* and reprints of original Phoebe Snow jingles.

Farrar, Straus & Giroux, Inc., and McIntosh, McKee & Dodds, Inc.: "The Train" by Flannery O'Connor from *The Complete Stories.* Copyright 1948, © 1962 by Flannery O'Connor, renewed 1976 by Regina O'Connor.

Otto B. Salassi: "RR," reprinted by permission of the author.

Northeast/Juniper Books: "Bunk Car" by Dave Etter from Juniper Book #4 *Strawberries* by Dave Etter. Copyright © 1970 by Northeast/Juniper Books.

New Directions Publishing Corporation: "The Little Black Train" from *Collected Poems* by Kenneth Patchen. Copyright 1949 by New Directions Publishing Corporation.

Shael Herman: "Track 6: The Sunset Limited," reprinted by permission of the author.

Doubleday & Company, Inc.: "Cross Ties" from *Growing Into Love* by X. J. Kennedy. Copyright © 1964, 1967, 1968, 1969 by X. J. Kennedy.

Wesleyan University Press and Rapp & Whiting Ltd.: "A Poem Written under an Archway in a Discontinued Railroad Station, Fargo, North Dakota" from *We Shall Gather At the River* by James Wright. Copyright © 1963 by James Wright.

Poetry Now and Warren Woessner: "The Night Train" by Warren Woessner from *Poetry Now,* Issue 3, Vol. I, No. 3. Copyright © 1974 by E. V. Griffith.

The New York Times: "Conrail Born As Congress Fails to Act" Copyright © 1975 by the New York Times Company. Reprinted by permission.

Joseph T. Monroe: "Thirty Years in the Dining Car," reprinted by permission of the author.

Shenandoah: The Washington and Lee Review: "Train Windows" by David Evans. Copyright © 1974 by *Shenandoah.* Reprinted by permission of the Editor and the author.

Irv Broughton: "Short," reprinted by permission of the author.

Random House, Inc., and Robert Lescher Literary Agency: "The Midnight Freight to Portland" from pages 274–285 of *Walking the Dead Diamond River* by Edward Hoagland. Copyright © 1971 by Edward Hoagland.

Harper & Row Publishers, Inc.: "Vacation" from *The Rescued Year* by William Stafford. Copyright © 1960 by William E. Stafford.

Illinois Central Gulf Railroad: "The City of New Orleans," words and music by Steve Goodman; also "The Story of Casey Jones," adapted by Miller Williams.

Atheneum Publishers, Inc.: "The Wheels of the Trains" from *The Carrier of Ladders* by W. S. Merwin. Copyright © 1967, 1968, 1969, 1970 by W. S. Merwin.

E. P. Dutton & Co., Inc., and John Cushman Associates: "Leaving New York on the Penn Central to Metuchen" from *Halfway From Hoxie* by Miller Williams. Copyright © 1964, 1968, 1971, 1973 by Miller Williams.

Little, Brown and Company: "A Solo Song for Doc" from *Hue and Cry* by James Alan McPherson. Copyright © 1968, 1969 by James Alan McPherson; also "The Railway Train" from *Poems* by Emily Dickinson, edited by Martha Dickinson Bianchi and Alfred Leete Hampson.

William B. Hart: "And Why Not?" reprinted by permission of the author.

Random House, Inc.: "Troop Train" from *Selected Poems* by Karl Shapiro. Copyright 1943 and renewed 1971 by Karl Shapiro.

Every effort had been made to clear permission for reprinting of all material not in the public domain. If the editors have failed in any instance to find the owner or author of any material used, it is not for lack of concern or effort, and we offer our sincere apologies. Material not attributed to an author or listed as anonymous is by the editors.

The editors are grateful to all those whose names appear in the formal acknowledgments and to the individuals in the offices of the railroads, libraries, publications, and other institutions who helped to put this collection together by furnishing material and patiently engaging in what seemed to be endless correspondence. And personal thanks to Sheila Barham, Ann Burban, J. L. Charlton, Herb Fowler, Claude Gibson, Alice Greene, Linda Horne, Wade Kreie, James Santana, Leo Van Scyoc, Dorothy Douglas Wood and John Wood. "The Story of Casey Jones" is our adaptation of the chapter on Casey Jones in Carlton J. Corliss' Illinois Central history, *Main Line of America,* by permission of the Illinois Central Gulf Railroad. Thanks to the Association of American Railroads for most of the information in the "Railroad Timetable."

CONTENTS

PAY DAY HUSSEYS CAMP BO BRR

INTRODUCTION

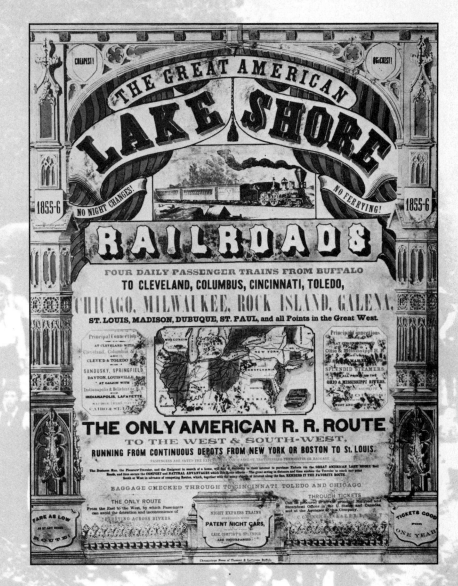

I'll die with this hammer in my hand. . . .
— John Henry

Not many young boys—maybe not any—want to grow up to be railroad engineers. There was a time when many of them did, and knew the lines they would work on and pictured the engines in their minds. Well, there aren't lines in the sense that there once were, and as passengers, we did just about lose the habit of traveling by rail. With Amtrak, we're slowly getting back into the habit. We know that we won't ever hear that whistle again, and probably there won't be any more railroad songs written—or railroad heroes to sing new songs about—but people will sit in day coaches and travel slow enough and look out the windows at something better than clouds.

This is important, and so the train is important. It carried this country a good part of the distance it's traveled, and it's no exaggeration to say that we can't understand this country if we don't know the story of the railroad. Whatever we believe our country is made of—people, songs, fables and stubborn forces—more often than not it is the people, songs, fables and force of the railroad that we remember. Or ought to.

These people we speak of were not the abstract "people" of ideology. They were human beings, pioneering human beings who regarded toughness of spirit and resilience as the most admirable of human qualities. They confronted in their daily lives the most powerful and frightening symbol of nineteenth-century American technology, and made it reflect all the values which we identify with the human personality. They did it not by taking on the personality of the machine but by taking parts and dimensions of the machine—its whistle, its sound, its coaches, its tracks, the work it required—and using these to express something about their own hopes and fears and sorrows and happiness. It is true that the railroad transformed the people; but it is also true that the people transformed the railroad. The experience has made the people no less human, nor has it made the machine any more frightening. But the experience, especially the people's articulation of it, has produced a great deal of art. This art has been what has kept things in the right perspective.

To remember the railroad as it was, and as it changed, is to know our history in special ways. It's to know the Civil War and the move West, and the development of our industry and commerce. To remember the railroad is to know the ways in which our history and the train's history are the story of laboring people—the workers who laid track and shoveled coal and waited on tables. No industry ever relied more heavily on the people who worked with their hands to keep it going—especially the Chinese and the Negroes and the Irish. No industry played so large a role in the birth and growth of labor unions, and no unions ever fought harder for the workers' share. The labor leaders Eugene V. Debs and A. Philip Randolph are as important to the history of the rails and of America as are Commodore Vanderbilt and Jay Gould. The great railroad strike of 1877 was all but a revolution.

All those people are here, and those events, and the songs and the fables. And pictures. And old and new poems and stories the railroad still hisses and whistles through. To have us remember and to have us believe again in the simple/complex truth of Emerson's 1844 prediction in "The Young American":

> Luckily for us, now that steam has narrowed the Atlantic to a strait, the nervous, rocky West is intruding a new and continental element into the national mind, and we shall yet have an American genius . . . It seems so easy for America to inspire and express the most expansive and humane spirit; new-born, free, healthful, strong, the land of the labourer, of the democrat, of the philanthropist, of the believer, of the saint, she should speak for the human race. It is the country of the Future. It is the country of the Future . . . it is a country of beginnings, of projects, of designs, of expectations.

It may happen yet that one day, with our concern now for the uses of energy and the purity of air and the pace and quality of life, a fifth-grader—boy or girl, Negro, Anglo, Chicano, Oriental, or whatever—will tell us if we ask that he or she wants to grow up to be a railroad engineer. And grow up to be one.

J. A. M.
M. W.

SOME OBSERVATIONS ON THE RAILROAD AND AMERICAN CULTURE

I really think there must be some natural affinity between Yankee "keep moving" nature and a locomotive engine . . . Whatever the cause, it is certain that the "humans" seem to treat the "engine," as they call it, more like a familiar friend than as the dangerous and desperate thing it really is.

—Mrs. Matilda C. Houstoun
in *Hesperos: or, Travels In The West,* 1850

Although they admired George Stephenson's Rocket for its smoothness of design, precision and stability, American railroad enthusiasts realized, around 1829, that the model English locomotive was ill-suited to the physical conditions of their country. Engineered originally to negotiate the flat British countryside, Stephenson's Rocket ran efficiently only along a straight line and over a level iron roadbed. The American landscape imposed sharp grades, abrupt curves, vast distances. And iron for rails was in short supply. The gauge of British tracks was standardized at four feet eight inches, according to legend the approximate width of the Roman chariot wheels which cut British roads centuries before. In America the only old roads were Indian trails. Nor did the English locomotive allow the speed, in both construction and movement, considered imperative by the Americans. Despite limited capital resources, they were motivated by an urgency to exploit commercially the Western properties beyond the reach of the natural waterways and newly dug canal systems. The problem, for Easterners, was deciding on the most economical mode of transportation to the open lands beyond the Alleghenies.

The conventional idea was that more canals would suffice. Indeed, as early as 1811 some New York merchants had begun promoting the idea of a new canal linking the fertile Mohawk Valley and Lake Erie. They had reconsidered for a while when a New Jersey inven-

When the original Illinois Central Railroad was completed in 1856, it was the longest railroad in the world. This painting by George I. Parrish, Jr., comissioned by Illinois Bell Telephone Company to commemorate the state's sesquicentennial in 1968, shows a construction scene on the 705.5 miles of "charter lines" in Illinois. On September 27, 1856, at a point near Mason, the last rail was laid and the last spike was driven in this line.—*Courtesy of Illinois Central Gulf Railroad*

tor named John Stevens stepped forward and proposed that, instead of a canal, it would be cheaper and more profitable to construct a railroad for steam locomotives. But the Erie Canal commissioners said no, finally, and continued with their project. Unperturbed, Stevens returned to Hoboken and, in 1826, constructed a model steam locomotive which he ran along a circular track on the lawn of his estate. People admired the little machine, but most considered it a toy. Meanwhile, the great Erie Canal was completed.

—Penn Central

EASTERN DIVISION.
No. 1.
P. R. R. PASSENGER AND FREIGHT
SCHEDULE.
On and after THURSDAY, January 1, 1852.

LEAVE WESTWARD.					Stations.	Miles.	LEAVE EASTWARD.				
Local Freight HARRISBURG & LANCASTER.	Local Freight PIPE'n & Rail Road.	SLOW PASSENGER.	PASSENGER.	FAST PASSENGER.			FAST PASSENGER.	SLOW PASSENGER.	Local Freight PIPE'n & Rail Road.	Local Freight LANCASTER.	Local Freight HARRISBURG.
P. M.	P. M.	A. M.	P. M.				A. M.	P. M.	A. M.	A. M.	A. M.
5 45	5 30	11 30		9 40	2 Dillerville,	11 0					
6 45	6 30	12 05	10 15	6 Mount Joy,		11 0	5 55	5 10	11 00	11 10	
7 30	7 15	12 30	10 40	7 Elizabeth'n,		6 4	5 25	4 27	9 55	10 20	
7 45	7 30	12 37	10 47	8 Conewago,		8 0	5 05	4 17	9 05	9 45	
8 21	8 06	12 55	11 05	9 Middletown,		5 5	4 58	4 05	8 40	9 25	
9 15	9 00	1 20	11 30	11 Harrisburg,		9 9	4 37	3 48	8 00	8 45	
A. M.	9 30	1 30	11 45				4 10	3 20	A. M. 7 00	8 00	A. M.
						6 4	3 50	2 55	9 00		
	6 10	1 48	12 02	Siding,		4 0	3 31	2 36	9 20		
	6 36	2 00	12 15	13 Cove,		4 0	3 21	2 26	8 00		
	7 00	2 12	12 27	14 Duncannon,		8 4	3 07	2 12	7 35		
	7 50	2 37	12 52	16 Baily's,		4 6	2 44	1 47	6 40		
	8 29	2 51	1 06	17 Newport,		5 2	2 28	1 32	6 05		
	9 05	3 06	1 21	18 Millerstown,		10 0	2 13	1 17	5 23		
	10 00	3 31	1 46	19 Tuscarora,		6 2	1 46	12 50	4 46		
	10 35	3 46	2 02	22 Mifflin,		11 8	1 30	12 35	3 46		
	10 45	4 13							3 30		
	11 44	4 48	2 30	23 Lewistown,		7 0	12 58	12 04	2 30		
	12 04										
	12 45	5 02	2 46	Anderson's Siding,		12 36	11 46	1 45			
						4 9					
	1 20	5 18	3 00	25 M'Veyton,		10 0	12 22	11 31	1 20		
	2 20	5 45	3 25	20 N. Hamilton,		3 0	11 54	11 01	12 25		
	2 45	5 54	3 34	27 Mount Union,		6 6	11 46	10 51	11 56		
	3 30	6 13	3 50	29 Mill Creek,		5 0	11 27	10 31	11 15		
	4 10	6 31	4 05	30 Huntingdon,		6 0	11 13	10 16	10 40		
	4 58	6 50	4 23	31 Petersburg,		5 0	10 50	9 53	9 53		
						5 8			9 33		
	5 35	7 09	4 40	32 Spruce Creek,		7 0	10 33	9 35	9 03		
	6 20	7 39	5 05	33 Tyrone,		6 5	10 08	9 05	8 13		
	7 02	7 59	5 22	34 Fostoria,		8 3	9 44	8 46	7 33		
	7 50	8 21	5 42	35 Altoona,		6 4	9 18	8 21	6 43		
	8 21	8 37	5 57	36 Intersection.			9 00	8 00	5 57		
P. M.	P. M.	A. M.					P. M.	A. M.	A. M.		

The passing Places are indicated by the large Type.

Westward Trains have preference of road. They are not to wait for Eastward trains, but run with great caution, if they are not found at the passing places. If Westward passenger trains are behind time, Eastward passenger trains will wait 20 minutes, then run at Schedule rate to next Station, after which, if the expected train is not passed, both trains must proceed with extreme caution, running all the curves until they meet.

If passenger trains are detained, freight trains must wait for them until they have passed, unless written orders to the contrary have been received from a responsible source.

Ballast, express, and all extra trains must give notice of the field of their operations, and make constant use of the caution and danger signals. Conductors and engineers are both held responsible for running curves, and in case of accident, both will be liable to dismissal, if any precaution has been omitted, even though the rules should not have provided for the case.

The maximum speed for Fast passenger trains is 2 minutes to a mile; for Slow passenger trains 2½ minutes, and for freight 3½ minutes, to be reduced when not consistent with safety.

Compare time daily with office clock at Harrisburg. Never leave a station until the time is fully up. Pass bridges at 6 minutes to the mile. Run slowly around curves. Report slides, accidents, detentions, defects in track, &c., to the Superintendent, with the number of the nearest mile post. Observe whistling posts and caution boards.

Freight trains, when not running exactly to schedule, and all ballast or other irregular trains, must keep out of the way of passenger trains 20 minutes when running in opposite directions, and 10 minutes when running in the same direction.

If freight trains are detained, wait 30 minutes, then proceed cautiously, both trains running curves, until the expected train is passed. Conform to rule in backing when trains meet.

If the cars of the Baltimore and Cumberland Valley roads are in sight when the time arrives for leaving, wait for them. Wait for Westward passenger trains at Dillerville until train arrives. For cars at Duncansville, three Hours.

Agents, watchmen and track repairers must not fail to report engineers who run beyond the maximum speed allowed, or leave any station ahead of time.

Train on Columbia Branch East Leaves Harrisburg at 10 30, A. M. West Columbia at 4 45, P. M. Train on Columbia Branch East Leaves Middletown at 10 55, A. M. West Middletown, 5 30, P. M. Announce name and time of stopping at each station. When waiting for another train, state how long.

* Passengers dine.   † Passengers take Supper.   ‡ Passengers take breakfast

H. HAUPT,

SCHEFFER & BECK, PRS.—HARRISBURG.   GEN'L. SUPERINTENDENT.

Other entrepreneurs demonstrated better vision. By July 4, 1829, three years after the opening of the Erie Canal, the Baltimore & Ohio Company had laid its first mile of track. It celebrated this feat by entertaining its stockholders with a newly composed piece of music, "The Carrollton March," dedicated to the Honorable Charles Carroll—a signer of the Declaration of Independence and a major stockholder in the B & O. Men like Carroll were among the first to envision that locomotives, and not wagons or canals, would dominate the market for hauling freight and passengers. They also perceived that James Watts' steam engine, and not horses or sails, would propel rail cars along the track.

But there remained the problem of engineering. George Stephenson, designer of the model Rocket, insisted that his locomotive could not round a curve with a radius of less than three hundred feet; and the fledgling B & O had already graded curves with radii of a hundred and fifty to two hundred feet. Stockholders in the new company were unwilling to invest more capital in reconciling their curves to the demands of George Stephenson's machine. But one of the stockholders, an inventor named Peter Cooper, refused to allow failure of the B & O to threaten his investments; his prosperity depended on the development of Baltimore as a railroad center. With a number of inventions already behind him, the resourceful Cooper proceeded to modify the design of the British locomotive in order to correct the problem of radii. Many years later the founder of New York's Cooper Union recalled the response to Stephenson's prediction:

> . . . the directors had a fit of the blues. I had naturally a knack of contriving, and I told the directors that I believed I could knock together a locomotive . . . I had an iron foundry, and some manual skill in working in it, but I couldn't find any iron pipes. The fact is, there were none for sale in this country. So I took two muskets and broke off the wood part, and used the barrels for tubing to the boiler . . . I went into a coachmaker's shop and made the locomotive, which I called the "Tom Thumb" because it was so insignificant. I didn't intend it for actual service, but only to show the directors what could be done.

To eliminate the problem of radii, Cooper used a shorter wheel base on his locomotive and used the "coined" wheels invented by Jonathan Wright, chief engineer of the B & O. Cooper also introduced a technique for changing rectilinear to rotary motion. Although no more than a toy, Peter Cooper's Tom Thumb had a successful trial run: it rounded curves at 15 miles per hour, negotiated grades with ease, and in flatlands achieved the tremendous speed of 18 miles per hour.

Other improvements were made as necessity dictated. The psychological problem of limiting the imagination to the known landscape was overcome by the recognition that if one mile of track could be laid, so could ten, twenty, even one hundred or more. But the assault on space and the necessity to economize in that assault created other problems. The scarcity of iron made the Americans dependent on wooden ties, which emphasized the inequities of the roadbed. To remedy this, a flat bar pinned at its center to the locomotive frame was used to distribute the shock of rough roadbeds evenly between the two wheels. This was called the "equalizer lever." But there still remained the problem of sharp curves along mountainous areas of the right-of-way. In 1831 the engineer John B. Jervis invented the swivel trunk to solve this problem. Attached by a strong pin under the front end of the boiler, this "bogie trunk" worked upon friction rollers in order to adjust more easily to the curves of the road. Similarly, the unavailability of coal required both the use of wood fuel and an engineering adjustment in order to accommodate its bulk. Thus came into existence the American wood-burning locomotive with its gigantic balloon stack.

Additional improvements were made as the railroads broke the monopoly which wagoners and canal systems had on the market for the transportation of freight and passengers. Since each new departure from established British railroad tradition created fresh problems, a new inclination toward improvisation and change was bred into American engineers. A most pressing problem was the fear aroused in people and animals by the smoke-puffing iron contraption. In 1831 the West Point, operated by the South Carolina Canal & Railroad Company, affixed a "barrier car" between the

A railway track of the seventeenth century.—*New York Public Library Picture Collection*

steam engine and the passenger section to protect people from the steam. The "barrier" was a flatcar piled high with bales of cotton. Directly behind it, especially on festive occasions, came a carful of Negro musicians. Likewise, the lack of established roadways caused tracks to be sprawled over open fields, and not confined behind walls as in England. American farmers expressed fear for the safety of their livestock. In response to this fear, Isaac Dripps designed a metal attachment for the front of the locomotive that would impale a cow on its prongs and carry it along with the engine. This early "cowcatcher" was redesigned when it was discovered that Dripps' device killed more cows than it swept aside. Soon afterwards, the Susquehanna, out of Delaware City, Delaware, added a whistle designed to "give awful notice to the locomotive's approach." People listened to it, and after a while the sound became associated with a cluster of ideas and images, the importance of which depended on the interests of individual men.

To some men the whistle might have signaled the dawning of industrial society because theirs was a pragmatic dream of manufacture and commerce. To them, the railroad was a godsend, as had been the flatboat, the steamboat, the immigrants from Europe and the imported men from Africa. The development of tools and techniques and modes of transportation, the availability of settlers and cheap labor, the growth of banks and corporations, were necessary for the clearing of the land and the growth of commerce. These men recognized that the railroads could follow the farmers into territories far beyond the reach of the natural waterways, and could be to them what the flatboats and steamboats were to the traders and planters of the Mississippi Valley. Toward this end, many new railroads sported the mythical additive ". . . and Pacific" in their titles, even though the thousands of miles between their main lines and the great Pacific remained trackless. Beginning in the 1830's the steam engine was applauded as a symbol of the new economic order. It was compared favorably with the fire-bringing Prometheus. It promised economic progress, many merchants argued, and an entirely new conception of human society based on mechanization. To those who expressed concern for the arts in such a society, the proponents of mechanization argued that all other arts rested upon the mechanical arts and that mechanization was as worthy an art as any of the fine arts.

Such arguments were not persuasive to this second category of men—those who questioned the positive effects of mechanization. Influenced by the Romantic Movement in Europe, American artists such as Hawthorne, Melville and Thoreau expressed in their writings a concern that the values engendered by the new technology would conflict with those virtues by which men raised themselves to the levels of perfection necessary for the creation of great art. Even those artists who saw in the new techniques the possible source of a new kind of culture worried that overvaluation of machinery might result in the neglect of the spontaneous and imaginative components of the human psyche. Glancing over their shoulders at the early effects of industrialization on British society, many complained that no high level of culture could be expected to develop among a people struggling to assert a national identity in a country dependent on machines and industry. To many such artists, people of highly refined sensibilities, the sound of the whistle might have been no more than a troublesome distraction from their contemplation of the arts, and of the responsibilities of the artist, in a society which seemed uneasy with established tradition.

But to a third group of people, those not bound by the assumptions of either business or classical traditions in art, the shrill whistle might have spoken of new possibilities. These were the backwoodsmen and Africans and recent immigrants—the people who comprised the vernacular level of American society. To them the machine might have been loud and frightening, but its whistle and its wheels promised movement. And since a commitment to both freedom and movement was the basic promise of democracy, it was probable that such people would view the locomotive as a challenge to the integrative powers of their imaginations. It demanded assimilation as a symbol of culture. The problem presented by such a demand was essentially aesthetic: the image of the locomotive had to be rearranged into patterns of experience invested with beauty and meaningful implication. The techniques available for solving such a problem had been developing for almost two centuries: the tradition of resilience and openness to change, the improvisational bent which characterizes life among a frontier folk. The forms created in the past, though sometimes crude, had provided ways of expressing the relationships of diverse peoples to each other, the language, and the tools and artifacts of their new environment. Such forms had patterned the human response to the necessity of creating a new identity in a radically different kind of society.

What in reality he [John Winthrop] was telling the proto-Americans was that they could not just blunder along like ordinary people, seeking wealth and opportunity for their children. Every citizen of this new society would have to know, completely understand, reckon every day with, the enunciated terms on which it was brought into being, according to which it would survive or perish. This duty of conscious realization lay as heavily upon the humblest, the least educated, the most stupid, as upon the highest, the most learned, the cleverest.

—Perry Miller
"The Shaping of the American Character"

American autumn, Starucca Valley, Erie R. Road. 1865.—*Library of Congress*

The patterns it [American folk art] evolved were not those which are inspred by ancient traditions of race or class; on the contrary, they were imposed by the driving energies of an unprecedented social structure. In their least diluted form these patterns comprise the folk arts of the first people in history who, disinherited of a great cultural tradition, found themselves living under democratic institutions in an expanding machine economy.

—John A. Kouwenhoven
The Arts in Modern American Civilization

The early relationships had been patterned in stories. These stories appeared whenever and wherever the new American techniques produced an artifact or machine upon which survival, prosperity or identity required a dependence. As early as the 1700's, for example, a new type of ax had been forged out of bar iron and cast steel. Its head was lighter, sharper and more durable than the ax heads then common in Europe. Hardiness in the ability to use it, especially on the frontiers of the old Southwest, brought a man a high reputation. A Yankee peddler might bring into New England stories about some stalwart Arkansas backwoodsman; a curious European or literate frontier gentleman might sketch an exaggerated tale about such a man; and word of mouth, travel books, or newspapers such as the old *The Spirit of the Times,* would pass these stories on to a wider audience. In another set of stories the artifact might be a weapon, such as the knife associated with James Bowie of Louisiana and Texas. Designed by either James or his brother Rezin P. and forged by some unknown frontier blacksmith, this "Arkansas Toothpick" began generating stories years before Jim Bowie died at the Alamo. The knife's appeal lay in the strong guard between its blade and handle. It was finely proportioned and balanced, with well-tempered steel and a curved point. Its original function was to protect the hand of its user while he stabbed cattle from horseback, but the reputation of the knife grew as men extended its use from animals to a variety of other functions. In the hands of Bowie, however, the "Arkansas Toothpick" prompted learned comparisons to Beowulf's battle-ax, Siegfried's Gram and Arthur's Excalibur.

But the most familiar stories were those

older ones about guns. In the 1730's and 1740's German and Swiss gunsmiths in eastern Pennsylvania perfected a gun with a barrel forty-two inches long. The bore was deliberately made small because powder and lead were scarce. This new rifle-barreled hunting tool could get as many as forty-eight bullets from one pound of lead, while the same amount of lead would make only a third as many balls for the heavier European muskets. This "long rifle" also used smaller amounts of powder and could shoot further and more accurately than, say, the flintlock muskets used by British soldiers. The celebration of this gun entered American folklore with Daniel Boone. In the novels of James Fenimore Cooper it became associated with an archetypal American hero. He could snuff a candle flame at fifty yards; hit a squirrel in the eye at sixty yards; drive a nail at a hundred yards. He also shot men.

With such a tradition already established long before the emergence of the railroad, it was probable that the same kind of assimilation would take place as people became dependent upon the new machine. It, too, had to be drawn into the felt experience of the people. Ironically, while more cultivated men debated the effects of the machine on the nation's art or turned in embarrassment from the indigenous folk creations to European styles and manners, the people on the vernacular level of American society—who had no option other than to move ahead with whatever was available—were confronting the problem of reconciling human values with the necessity of coexistence with machines. And since they were the people most enchanted by the promise of American life, the possibility of physical and class mobility, it was practically unavoidable that they would develop a fascination for the central symbol of the expanding industrial economy.

The Africans among them were slaves. They were people who had been torn away from tribal societies in which art was functional, part of the daily work process. They were used to replace Indian and white immigrant laborers as the basis of an agricultural economy. In Southern fields they worked in gangs, planting and reaping cane, rice, tobacco, cotton. To keep each other under pressure while maintaining a steady, intense rhythm of work, they created songs and hollers whose rhythms synchronized their movements into an efficient work pattern. Originating in agriculture, these work patterns anticipated the routines of factory group labor, most notably the assembly line, and conditioned in the Africans an early appreciation of the work rhythms which later came to characterize industrial society. They were also conditioned to appreciate the rhythms of the locomotive. If its movement suggested the possibility of freedom to the white laborer, to the slave the suggestion was much more meaningful. To be a slave in a society offering more freedom than any other in the history of the world made the hope of emancipation pregnant with happy implications. The image of the locomotive began appearing, strangely enough, in songs of worship—"The Gospel Train," "Get on Board, Little Children," "Every Time I Feel the Spirit":

Ain't but one train on this line
Run to heaven and back again . . .

With the help of white abolitionists the railroad began serving as a metaphor for the moral consciousness of the nation. Beginning in the 1830's, a network was developed of hearts and hands and homes running from the slave states as far north as Canada and as far west as the Indian Territory. This network of human sympathy, called the Underground Railroad, paralleled and sometimes duplicated the movement and language of its mechanical counterpart. Chief organizers, such as the Society of Friends in Philadelphia, were called "conductors"; morally committed whites who escorted slaves from home to home, or "station" to "station," were "agents"; letters moved between them as efficiently as official train schedules over telegraph wires. "Yours for the slave," the closing line in their letters, expressed forceful opposition to the hated Fugitive Slave Act. It expressed their stand on moral principle. The very successful anti-slavery song, "Get Off the Track," by the Hutchinsons, was directed at those former owners who, under authority of the hated law, sent professional slave-catchers after their runaway property. The Underground Railroad had a successful run. After the Civil War, in the late 1860's and early 1870's, the Thirteenth, Fourteenth and Fifteenth Amendments were added to the United States Constitution, conceding to the slaves a formal freedom.

Black people were not free in the same sense that whites were free, but their status had been improved enough to allow some to join the great migrations west. Removed from the debate between proponents of mechanization, they also enjoyed enough freedom to decide what their own response to the locomotive would be. They owned no capital, so to them the machine could not function strictly as a symbol of economic progress and power. Nor did they, like the immigrant farmers settling the heartlands, view the locomotive as the envoy of commercial powers which threatened the peace of a budding agricultural utopia. The freeman's relation to the pastoral ideal was shattered forever when the Reconstruction myth of "forty acres and a mule" gave way to the realities of serfdom. But some perceived that the locomotive, and especially the rhythms of its movement, offered aesthetic possibilities that might be missed by the naked eye. In this view they were close to Walt Whitman, who, almost alone among nineteenth-century poets, added the *sound* of the locomotive to his song while other artists were segregating the mechanical arts from the fine arts of music, drama, literature, poetry and painting. Whitman was not disturbed, in his "Passage To India," to hear the locomotives "rushing and roaring across the landscape." In fact, he urged the machine on: ". . . roll through my chant with all thy lawless music," the poet wrote. Many a black field hand heard this same music. And like many people at the bottom of the economic ladder, they accepted the locomotive as a meaningful symbol offering both economic progress and the possibility of aesthetic expression. This was perhaps the synthesis Whitman had in mind when, in 1851, he had suggested to a Brooklyn audience that "the steam engine is no bad symbol" for the nation.

The idea that the United States was indeed a nation was made manifest, first at Appomattox and later, on May 10, 1869, at the spike-driving ceremony at Promontory Point, Utah, joining East and West. As early as 1862 Abraham Lincoln had perceived the necessity of such an enterprise to link the two shores of the continent, to end the dangerous isolation of California and to bind some of the wounds left by the Civil War. In that year the Congress passed and Lincoln signed the Pacific Railroad Act, incorporating the Union Pacific Railroad and making grants of land and money to the building corporation. The Union Pacific was to lay track westward from a point on the Missouri River across the Nebraska plains, over the Rockies and through the Great Salt Basin until it met the tracks of an independently incorporated California railroad named Central Pacific.

Both Union Pacific and Central Pacific hired massive crews. The Union Pacific camp near Omaha drew Irish immigrants from the Eastern cities, black men from the unreconstructed South, Indians, scouts, teamsters and hunters from around Fort McPherson in Nebraska Territory. The Central Pacific used mostly Chinese labor. Just before the polished iron spike was driven at Promontory Point and its sound and the word "Done" went out over the telegraph wires, Chinese hands from the Central Pacific crew laid the last rail. Irishmen

Across the continent on the Pacific Railroad. Drawing-room of the hotel express train.—*Library of Congress*

from the Union Pacific side had put in place the one before that. Bret Harte arrived from San Francisco to write a celebratory poem. He focused on the machine: "What was it that the engines said," Harte asked, " 'pilots touching head to head"?" Perhaps only the laborers knew, but on that day officials did all the talking.

The Chinese dominated the Central Pacific work force. The directors decided early that the rate of attrition among the Irish workers was too high and began actively recruiting the Chinese, who moved into Central Pacific crews from mining towns, the Salinas Valley and the slums of San Francisco, where they had retreated after being driven from the gold fields. Central Pacific even advertised in Canton. By 1866 more than six thousand Chinese were employed. They were good workers: they worked longer hours than whites, and for less wages. They cut a rail path eastward through the solid rock of the Sierra Nevadas, dug a tunnel through Donner Summit, working long and dangerous shifts underground. Many died inside the tunnels; many others died in snowslides. In June 1867, up in the High Sierras, two thousand Chinese went on strike. They demanded a raise in pay to the level of the whites, reduction of work hours to ten per day in the open and eight per day in the tunnels. "Eight hours a day good for white man," they declared, "all the same good for Chinaman." The directors wired East for two thousand Negro replacements. The strike failed. Although they laid the last rail at Promontory Point, the Chinese were scarcely mentioned by the speechmakers.

The Irish were another story. They might have labored just as hard as the Chinese, but they are remembered as "light-hearted and gay" because their songs rose from the camps along the Union Pacific tracks. However, some of their songs came very close to the sentiment expressed by the Chinese:

In eighteen-hundred and forty-two
I left the old world for the new;
Bad cess to the luck that brought me through
To work upon the railway.

When we left Ireland to come here,
And spend our latter days in cheer,
Our bosses, they did drink strong beer,
And Pat worked on the railway.

Our boss's name it was Tom King
He kept a store to rob the men;
A Yankee clerk with ink and pen
To cheat Pat on the railway.

The famous Tom Thumb in a race with one of the early horse-drawn cars used on the Baltimore and Ohio Railroad. The race, which took place on August 25, 1830, was won by the horse. The scene shown here was painted by H.D. Stitt.—*Baltimore & Ohio Railroad photo*

The black laborers did not sing their songs at evening, gathered around the fire; they created music and sang it while they worked. The rhythms of their songs complemented the work requirement: tamping ties, spiking rails, lining track, dumping gravel—there were even songs for pulling up worn track sections, or "gandy dancing." Their work songs here, like their rowing songs and chanties on flatboats and riverboats back along the Mississippi, matched the pace of their movements:

Jack the rabbit! Jack the bear!
Can't you line him just a hair,
Just a hair, just a hair?
Annie Weaver and her daughter
Ran a boarding house on the water.
She got chicken, she got ham,
She got everything, I'll be damn.
Old Joe Logan, he gone North
To get the money for to pay us off.

They also told stories about how they lived, stories about the ways a man stood above the crowd in the rail camps. Around 1870 came a story, out of the rail camps of West Virginia, about a steel driver who had beaten the speed of a steam drill. The black laborers sang about him as they laid rails or cut tunnels. No one actually knew John Henry, but he touched something very deep in human consciousness—like Hercules performing his tasks. The songs inspired by the contest between man and machine at Big Bend Tunnel in West Virginia dramatized the relation between these two forces in American society. John Henry died soon after the epic contest, but he died affirming the subordination of the machine to man, and people seized on the story. From West Virginia to Texas, wherever men worked in gangs, songs about him were created which matched the hammers of section hands against the one used by John Henry. More than a dozen states claimed him as a native son. The development of sheet music, along with books and the minstrel stage, made his legend accessible to the new immigrants who came in waves at the beginning of the twentieth century. They absorbed his legend as quickly as they absorbed the language, because the songs and stories about him also described a toughness of spirit prerequisite for survival in America:

Cap'n said to John Henry,
"Gonna bring me a steam drill round;
Take that steam drill out on the job,
Gonna whop that steel on down."

John Henry told his captain,
"A man ain't nothin' but a man,
'Fo' I let your steamdrill beat me down,
I'll die with my hammer in my hand."

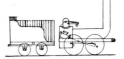

Not all the heroic figures associated with the railroad were workers. Some, like Railroad Bill, were wild-spirited and tough, as if determined to represent in their personalities the ruthless capabilities of the machine. Others, like Sam Bass, Christopher Evans and John Sontag, and the Reno, Dalton and James gangs, had influences which transcended narrow occupational definitions. In their roles as train robbers they provided a romantic outlet for the minds of many thousands of people. By the 1870's railroads had begun to transform the farmers of the Midwest and West into producers of staple crops for Eastern markets. Still faithful to the agrarian ideal envisioned by Thomas Jefferson, these small farmers found themselves dependent on the fluctuating freight rates of the railroads and the demands of markets distant from them. Besides this, the inventions of Cyrus McCormick and others were rapidly extending mechanization to the organic, substituting mechanical movement for human motion and revolutionizing agriculture. These advances were making the yeoman obsolete. Farmers drawn into the heartlands by the promises of the Homestead Act found themselves embattled by mechanization and, at the same time, competing with railroads for the best government lands. These farmers, organizing themselves into the Patrons of Husbandry, did not welcome the coming of industry into the smooth, rolling flatlands which Abraham Lincoln had affectionately called "the Egypt of the West." Their growing hostility toward mechanization and the railroads expressed itself through the wide popularity enjoyed by train robbers.

Though the protests of farmers may have influenced the passage of the Interstate Commerce Act to regulate freight rates, the legis-

HUDSON RIVER Railroad.

~~~~~~~~~~

This Company is prepared to issue **Commutation Tickets** to residents on the line of the road, at reduced prices.

Persons, commuting for 6 months or for 1 year, from Feb. 1st, and requiring 120 tickets per quarter, will be supplied at the following rates:

Between N. York & Manhattanville 10 cts. pr ticket.

"	"	Yonkers.......14	"	"
"	"	Dobbs' Ferry,..18	"	"
"	"	Tarrytown,.....22	"	"
"	"	Sing Sing,.....26	"	"
"	"	Peekskill,......34	"	"
"	"	Cold Spring,...43	"	"
"	"	Fishkill,.......48	"	"
"	"	Po'keepsie,....60	"	"

Persons commuting for the next quarter only, (February, March and April,) will be charged an advance of 20 per cent. on the above rates.

The tickets are not transferable, and are valid only during the quarter for which they are issued.

For further information, and for tickets apply at the office of the Company, 54 Wall Street.

New York, Jan. 23, 1850.

---

lation had no effect on the expansion of the railroads. The tracks simply followed the telegraph wires. By 1900 more than six hundred different railroads bound the continental United States in a network of steel rails. The presence of the railroads forced men to modify their myths, as well as their language, in order to accept the reality represented by the machine. The dream of an agrarian utopia died on the prairies; few men could find independence on an isolated plot of land. Almost every growing town along the railroad's right-of-way sooner or later named one of its streets "Railroad Avenue." People learned to make class distinctions by using as a metaphor the tracks dividing sections of a town.

But "rugged individualism" persisted for a selected few. It was evoked not only by the names Gould, Hill, Mellon, Morgan and Vanderbilt; the tracks and cars of the railroads they owned also reflected this preoccupation. No two trains were alike. Cars of connecting railroads could not be switched because their gauges were not standardized. By 1886 more than twenty-five different gauges were in use, ranging from the three feet of the Denver & Rio Grande Western to the six feet of the New York & Erie. The Chicago & Northwestern, financed by an Englishman, moved its cars on the leftmost set of its double tracks. When the New England railroad and the Union Pacific joined forces, finally, to propose standardization at the preferred four feet eight inches, most of the major railroads complied. The Louisville & Nashville, however, probably remembering the Civil War, bucked the Yankee dictate by standardizing its gauge at four feet *nine* inches.

This tension between North and South was only one of many stressful relationships which characterized the final quarter of the nineteenth century. It was a period of stark contrasts: great wealth and great poverty, concentrated political power and mass disenfranchisement; strong economic ambition and weak moral commitment; the studied flaunting of opulence and an abiding blindness to social inequities. It was a period of ruthless betrayal. In New England the heirs of the abolitionist movement were fading away. Wealth turned its eyes on European manners and styles. Even the railroads testified to this confusion of values. Newly constructed depots and the interiors of the better cars advertised an inappropriate infatuation with the ornate—those styles that were Greek or Roman or unabashedly Rococo. Luxury sleeping cars were named for mythical figures from other cultures: Attica, Hector, Hera, Pharos, Prometheus, Ulysses. But outside these luxurious cars the workers were organizing. At Pullman, Illinois, on May 11, 1894, over three thousand employees of the sleeping-car industrialist George Pullman—encouraged by the newly formed American Railway Union—went on strike to protest wage cuts and high rents in Pullman's model company town. On July 10, after a riot in Chicago and the calling out of federal troops by President Grover Cleveland, the president of the new union, Eugene Victor Debs, was indicted for inciting the workers. Debs immediately became a hero to workers all over the country, and out of his speeches and organizing emerged the basis for the American labor movement.

The importance of George Pullman, however, is much more profound than the consequences of his policies at Pullman, Illinois. In his own way, George Pullman was responsible for helping to create the tradition of the democratic industrialist. Before he began building his cars, American trains had only one passenger section, in contrast to the three or four classes common on European trains. When Pullman started advocating luxury in train travel for those who could afford it, he attempted to democratize, as far as possible, the concept of train comfort reserved traditionally for the aristocracy of European society. Pullman's model was the Train Imperial, owned by Napoleon III of France, and in 1865 he had introduced his Pioneer, designed to give luxury sleeping space to passengers who could afford fifty cents more than the normal fare. (Ironically, the very first trip of the stylish Pioneer was to bear the body of Abraham Lincoln

class passengers, the essence of drawing-room elegance. Despite the limitations imposed by caste and the introduction of sleeping cars for first-class passengers, the hotel and dining cars designed by George Pullman allowed a degree of democratic interaction between people from diverse backgrounds that still remains unsurpassed.

Perhaps it was this same democratic impulse, or a troublesome burden of conscience, that encouraged many railroad companies to express in their emblems something about the occult relation of the machine to the land itself. Many companies sponsored contests among their workers, giving prizes for the most appropriate designs. The emblem of the Santa Fe Railroad, for example—the cross within a circle found on all its cars—was derived from the Indians of New Mexico. For centuries before the Spanish converted them to Christianity, these Indians worshiped the

from Washington to his birthplace in Springfield.) Pullman anticipated only two classes of cars, and his concept of train travel has never been changed. By 1869 he had patented his line of hotel and dining cars, serviced by Negro waiters who created a system of service techniques which preserved, at least for first-

sun. Finding them reluctant to give up their religion, the Spanish missionaries compromised by enclosing their Christian cross within the Indians' Sacred Circle. The Lackawanna Railroad, when it started hauling coal, used a white woman in its emblem, expressing the very subtle mythology of black and white in American culture: "Phoebe Snow, dressed in white, rides the road of anthracite," the Lackawanna's slogan ran. The Northern Pacific adopted an Oriental symbol for its emblem; The Great Monad, Chinese symbol of eternal life, advertised the company's access to the long-sought-after trade route to the Orient. The red, white and blue shield of the Union Pacific symbolized that company's association with the federal government in construction of the road. All of these incorporations indicated the extent to which the machine was now inseparable from the myths, common experiences and history of the American people.

> *You could divide up the meat section of that menu under beef, lamb, pork, and so on, under hot and cold, or according to the way they were cooked . . . and maybe that's a service to the customer. But to multiply divisions that way in music, in my opinion, merely multiplies confusion. Fish, fowl, and meat may provide us with a parallel, but never forget that the art is in the cooking.*
>
> —Duke Ellington
> *The World of Duke Ellington*

> *The business of "quilling" (blowing train whistle) was especially dear to the Negroes and seemed to induce in every colored boy within earshot a peculiar hero worship for the engineer . . .*
>
> —Freeman Hubbard
> *Railroad Avenue*

Railroad engineers were fathers to much of American music, although the leading artist among them, Casey Jones, is remembered as the hero of a famous train wreck. In John Luther Jones' day each engineer made his own whistle and developed a distinctive tone and technique for its quilling. They pioneered in the creation of an art form. People could tell who was at the engine of a passing train by the sound of his quill. In the right hands, these homemade whistles suggested the same pitch and intonation as the human voice. "Jones," one writer says, "had a six-chime whistle formed by six slender tubes banded together, the shortest being exactly half the length of the tallest. With its interpretative tone the ballast scorcher [engineer] could make that quill say its prayers or scream like a banshee."

Jones' technique was to start his chime notes at a high crescendo, then train off into a whisper: *"Kay–Cee–Jooooooones."*

Such whistles were essential to engineers in Casey Jones' day because they functioned as "time bearers," certifying in the consciousness

Cue Feb. 26, 1938.—*New York Public Library Picture Collection*

of people along the right-of-way the reliability of railroad time. This new time had come into existence on November 18, 1883, when the major railroads initiated, over much public outcry, the division of the entire country into time zones in order to better coordinate the movement of trains. Until then people had relied on solar time, or subscribed to jewelers for "standard time." Some twenty different time zones were in use when the railroads acted. People protested; they had grown used to telling time their own way. "Damn old Vanderbilt!" some cried. "We want God's time!" Nevertheless, the time zones based on the 75th, 90th, 105th and 129th meridians west of Greenwich became established as the new time zones. Although the U.S. Attorney General issued orders that government departments not adopt the new system, they accepted the new arrangement when a number of officials began missing trains. Predictably, the Congress did not give formal recognition to the time zones until many years later: on March 19, 1918, probably in response to the coordination made necessary by World War I, it passed the Standard Time Act. But in the years before passage of the act, between 1883 and 1918, train engineers bore responsibility for gaining respect for the reliability of "train time." This explains why Casey Jones was speeding when he had his famous accident on April 30, 1900, at Vaughan, Mississippi.

Wallace Saunders, the Negro who made up the first ballad celebrating Casey Jones, must have had great respect for the engineer's quilling technique. But he was only one of many black people who had fallen in love with the engineer's whistle. This admiration might have begun when a worker looked across an open field and considered the statement made by the locomotive. To him it may have offered the same mobility and freedom it seemed to offer whites, and a belief in this promise was reflected in his spirituals. But after achieving a kind of freedom, he began contemplating what was suggested to the listening habits of his ear by the *motion* of the machine. He liked its rhythms: the regular, recurring beat of the train could sound like the patter of feet and the clapping of hands. He also liked its steady drive and thrust, its suggestion of unrestrained freedom and power, the way, in the right hands, a quilling whistle sounded. He became expert in reproducing this motion on a guitar by running his fingers rapidly along the strings, or by playing successive chords with a regularity and sound similar to that of a moving train. The lonesome sound of the whistle could be reproduced by blowing through a harmonica. Sometimes it came up from the depths of his own soul. And when the mood native to the land came over him, he found that he had a device not available to those people who, from the sixteenth century onward, could *describe* "a fit of the blues" as something like "a depression of the spirits" but could *do* very little to relieve that depression. Here, probably, was the beginning of a tradition. A man could talk directly about his metaphysical experience of the world, about the painful facts of life, by combining his narrative with the music he made and by imposing a basic twelve-bar structure on it. He could use a basic 2/2 beat, perhaps that of the train, to provide a rhythm that was fast enough for dancing. While his lyrics made a tragic statement, the music might express mocking, humorous commentary which contradicted the lyrics. The form, in its entirety, affirmed human resilience and projected a mood of comfort and well-being. The form could express a basic belief that though life was hard, it was well worth living. Musicians incorporated work songs and field hollers into this music, using the guitar, the harmonica, even the fiddle, to create an interplay between the lyrics and any sound the instrument could make that was thought appropriate and palliative to the mood. Most often the lonely sound of the train whistle provided counterpoint. In fact, in many such songs the train functioned as a metaphor for escaping the mood: "Broke Down Engine Blues," "Statesboro Blues," "Trouble In Mind," "Goin' Where the Southern Cross the Dog":

When a woman takes the blues
She tucks her head and cries.
But when a man catch the blues
He catch a freight and rides.
I got the blues,
But I'm too damn mean to cry.

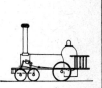

They created a whole literature of "train" blues.

They brought this music from the Mississippi Delta, from the farms and backwater towns of Georgia, Tennessee, the Carolinas, Arkansas, the bleak Texas prairies, and took it into the cities. The people were rough-mannered and tough. They were people with memorial names: Blind Lemon Jefferson, Josh White, Huddie Ledbetter ("Leadbelly"), Papa Charlie Jackson, Richard "Rabbit" Brown, Ida Cox, Ma Rainey, Big Bill Broomsley, Scrapper Blackwell—and hundreds of lesser-known ones with ever more mysterious Scotch, English and Irish names. Their music was unpolished, but in the towns and cities of early-twentieth-century America it took hold. Commercial interests helped it along because "race records" brought in steady profits for the fledgling phonograph companies. Recording agents went down South looking for such music because it was popular, and not only among black city dwellers who remembered its folk sources. Like "ragtime," and like the work songs and spirituals of the previous century, this new development in the idiom had wide appeal because it expressed a toughness of spirit and resilience, a willingness to transcend difficulties which was strikingly familiar to those whites who remembered their own history.

Innovations in blues idiom stylization were not confined to the cities along the Eastern seaboard. The migrations encouraged by the prosperity of World War I drew folk artists into all parts of the country. And out in the heartlands, in Chicago, St. Louis and Kansas City, such people were finding ways of making the piano produce sounds which before had been heard only on guitar and banjo. One new technique made more use of rising and falling chords. The bass, played with the left hand, was made to reproduce the rhythms and counter-rhythms of a high-speed train running smoothly against track. The right hand produced treble variations, perhaps the voice of the conductor, the puff of the smokestack, the moan of the whistle, which imposed a narrative over the rhythmic movement of the bass. The music was called "boogie-woogie," perhaps in commemoration of the American "bogie trunk" invented by the engineer John B. Jervis. In the hands of skilled pianists like Meade Lux Lewis, compositions such as

Parlor Car interior.—*New York Public Library Picture Collection*

"Honky Tonk Train Blues" gave impressionistic interpretations of trains moving in and out of Chicago. Together with Pine Top Smith, Lewis combined the blues idiom of the American South with the movement and sound of the great rail centers of the Midwest.

Even during the Depression years, when the rest of the nation focused on the state of the economy, the prairie states continued to reassert their old claim as the Egypt of the West. Kansas City during those years was a booming railhead, with trade in livestock and agricultural goods. It was a city of drive and momentum and fluidity and tension. It drew young men to its center (not least conspicuously, Ernest Hemingway and Walt Disney a decade before), and its center was still under the patronage of the Pendergast machine. This great mixture of commerce and corruption generated a creative tension; so it was in Kansas City that an entirely new style in the blues idiom emerged. The railroads brought innovative men into the city from Oklahoma, Missouri, Texas and the Deep South. A group of them—Ben Webster, Jimmie Lunceford, Lester Young, Walter "Hot Lips" Page, William "Count" Basie—gathered around a young bandleader named Bennie Moten, and began confronting in their music the activity and life that was Kansas City. Under Moten's leadership they took the ideas of jazz rhythms originated by Louis Armstrong and created a new ensemble style that could *swing*. The old 2/2 beat of New Orleans stylization, some elements of ragtime, and the innovations of boogie-woogie were blended into a much more complex and smoother-flowing style. This new development in the blues idiom offered infinite flexibility of expression, allowing the accent, once the basic beat had been established, to be placed anywhere. Moten's overall goal was the creation of a flowing, driving rhythm with which not even solo improvisations, or riffs, could interfere. For their creation of a musical style allowing unity within diversity, Moten and his musicians might have earned the praise of Walt Whitman. Their music expressed a fuller sense of individual freedom, and the idea that there are no absolutes save the ambiguities and tempo of human activity. It was altogether appropriate, and deliciously ironic, that the conflict between aesthetic ideals and economic realities, the old argument between opponents and proponents of mechanization, should reach artistic resolution out on the prairies where so many dreams had died.

St. Louis Iron Mountain R.R. car built in 1870.

Art is not a servile copying of objects but the discovery of a harmony among numerous relationships.

—Paul Cézanne

Although American technology has grown much more complex, the traditions which in the past encouraged aesthetic responses to the human problems created by technology are still intact. All we need do is relocate them. Perhaps a reexamination of the emergence of the American railroad will help revive memories of who we are and how we emerged as a people. Indeed, the promise of the locomotive whistle, whether perceived in economic or aesthetic terms, has to a great extent been fulfilled. Human and technological values can coexist, given the will to improvise and an openness to new ways of viewing patterns of experience. This was the major teaching of the American railroad in the nineteenth and twentieth centuries.

The American people and the American railroad are now inseparable. The responses of the one to the other have created much of American history and culture. A survey of that interrelationship demonstrates the ability of human beings to not only integrate into their imaginations what once seemed fearful but, more important, to create new relationships through that integrative process. Perhaps we will learn something more from this process, in railroad coaches and dining cars, as our railroads are revitalized.

J. A. M.

DOWN AT THE STATION HOUSE

Being the Other Side of the Story of the Tracks

When I go back as far as I can go in my memory, back before school, before bicycles and grapevine cigarettes, there is country music and there are trains. I don't know which I was aware of first: country music and trains and the music so often about trains that they seemed naturally parts of the dark, good and mysterious world. As far back as I can go I hear them, the guitar and the vulnerable lonesome voice and the train whistle. The guitar and the voice are still around, but the old whistle is gone.

The first time I heard that whistle—well, not the first time at all, but the first I can put a date on—was very early one morning in a little town in northeast Arkansas. My brother, just older than I, woke me up because he heard a noise downstairs. We crept down the staircase and saw our college-brother-come-home, watching a long black Lionel train race around an oval track on the living-room rug. It was the most magnificent thing I had ever seen. Then our brother put the whistle to his mouth and blew—a sublime, sad, incomparable sound, a real train whistle. It was two o'clock in the morning. It was Christmas Day. I had found out about Santa Claus, but it was all right.

The next train I have a date for was a freight with a great engine black as the end of the world. It passed twice a day in front of my grandmother's home outside of Swifton. Whenever we went to see her, we drove for miles alongside a track so high we couldn't see the cotton fields beyond it, and then we would turn abruptly off the highway, and the overloaded Dodge would almost upend as it growled to the top of the roadbed, bumped across the rails and coasted down the other side to an unpainted, tin-roofed house with no grass around it and a few chickens pecking near the edge of the cotton field—somebody else's cotton—that ran in careful rows toward a line of trees a long way off. There was a stream there we used to wade in.

When the train came by at night, it shook the ground and the house and woke us up with those sounds fast freight trains make.

Most of us slept on pallets. We woke up to the hard floor and it wasn't easy to go to sleep again. I could hear my grandmother turn over in her scarred spindle bed—her one material treasure—and groan.

When she fell sick she turned over and groaned for the noon train, too. It seemed to take longer going by every time it passed. My grandmother would moan and mumble Jesus' name and say how she hurt and the house would keep shaking. My mother would try to help with a cold cloth and look helpless. Sometimes I would go out when I heard the early whistle and stand on the porch to wave at the engineer. It made me feel guilty when he waved back.

My grandmother died there, with the train going by.

I took my first ride when I was seven. To Memphis. We walked through cars that were bedrooms and then we walked through a dining room and then we walked through a saloon. The bedroom was an aisle between heavy curtains. It seemed darker than it must have been, and safe and soft, where people didn't have anything to worry about, where grown-ups didn't talk about money and Mrs. Hinkle didn't teach the second grade. I didn't tell anybody how I wanted to crawl up one of the ladders and disappear behind my own curtains. A long time later I learned what that must have meant, but for me then it was a hiding place, and it was natural to want one. We didn't sleep there. The seats were comfortable enough and it wasn't a long trip. And we were in the middle of a depression.

The dining hall was white: white tablecloths and white jackets, so white you had to squint your eyes against it if the sun was right. The knives and forks and spoons my father said the waiter said were real silver. The Lone Ranger's bullet was real silver.

We carried a basket of our own food with

us—chicken and cold biscuits and a fruit jar full of buttermilk and some sugar cookies—but my father said he thought, Depression or not, we could have one breakfast in the dining car. I don't remember eating anything. I stared at the sure, quick hands of the waiter who changed the setting as if he were a magician with a table of dishes on stage at the Roxy Theater. I touched the silver. I fingered the rich cloth hanging toward my lap and rolled it up like a window shade and let it fall. The waiter called my father Sir. My father didn't believe in Negroes saying Sir to white people and the waiter was a Negro but my father didn't correct him. We had orange juice with the breakfast. I drank it slow. Outside, across the Arkansas flatlands, hundreds of Indians on horseback charged through high cotton shooting at the train with bows and arrows and yelling their Indian yells, but inside the train of course I couldn't hear them.

The best part of the trip was going from car to car. You opened a door, and it took both hands pushing hard to open it, and the sound of train came over you as if a deaf man had suddenly got his hearing back under a waterfall, and the floor slid back and forth like a carnival fun house and you knew it was dangerous and you might die there. That was the most exciting part and sometimes I stood between the cars until someone always a grownup sometimes a porter would come along and speak to me as if I were lost or frightened and ask me where I belonged.

I would go back to the seats and try to stand on one foot in the aisle with the rocking train trying to throw me off balance. It always did.

The Indians came closer to the train, racing alongside trying to grab hold of something to pull themselves on board so they could get in. I was getting sleepy and didn't care very much whether they got in or not but then we got to the Mississippi River bridge and the Indians couldn't stop and fell into the water, horses and all.

In Memphis we stayed in a hotel but it wasn't any fun.

"What's that?"
"It's a penny."
"It ain't."
"It is too."

"How come it got like that?"
"I put it ona railroad track. Train run over't."
"Didn't do no such of a thing."
"Did."
"You cain't put nothin' on a railroad track."
"I just went an' did it."
"It's aginsta law."
"Ain't."
"Is too. Police'll git you."
"Won't neither."
"Train jumpa track, police gonna git you for sure."
"Penny ain't gonna do that to no train."
"How you know it ain't?"
" 'Cause I done it before."
"Lemme look at it."
"Go do your own penny. This here-un's mine."

Missouri Pacific's Sunshine Special, photographed from the painting by William Herndon Foster.—*Photo courtesy of Missouri Pacific*

Saturday afternoon I squatted in a field of young corn near Seven Mile Creek and kept my eye on the penny I could barely make out, lying on the rust-eaten rail. I was scared. I didn't have a watch. Only fathers had watches, but I knew the train was late. It was so late I knew something was wrong. I heard a rustle in

Ten minutes for refreshments.—*Library of Congress*

the cornstalks. Somehow they knew there was a penny on the track. A metal detector. Maybe they could even tell where it was. That's why the train was stopped back at the station. I couldn't go get the penny. With field glasses you could see for miles along the track. Running through the corn would make too much noise. So I slid down into the ditch between the cornfield and the roadbed and ran through thick reeds and slime until I came to a crossing and then I ran stumbling along the gravel road toward home, making up a story about my wet shoes and overalls while behind me the Cotton Belt freight rattled past. I didn't even look back.

————————

One of the things to do was walk the rails. Jodell Bascum could walk a rail faster and farther than anybody. He could even stand on one rail and get all bent over with his knees broken and his fists stuck out behind him and swing his arms forward and jump to the other rail and land balanced. Then he'd go right on walking down that one like it was laid there for him to walk on it.

"It's 'cause I got Indian in me," Jodell said when we were swinging our legs off a trestle, trying to light ten-cent cob pipes stuffed too tight with cornsilk that was too green to burn

anyway. "Indians walk with one foot right in front of the other. 'Cause a Indian trail ain't no wider than one of them rails is. You get born with it, like colored people can sing and stuff."

I believed him. There was no way not to. He was the one that could walk the rails and he had a right to the reason why. I gave up trying to be as good as he was at it, but that night as I lay in bed waiting to be sleepy, I wondered if there was anything you get born to if you're just plain white people. I had never heard anyone mention anything. I about decided to ask my father about it, but then I heard the whistle of the train that came through at midnight and I knew he wouldn't be awake.

————————

Jodell could put his ear on the rail and tell if a train was coming and how far. I could do that about as well as he could. If we did it together a hundred yards apart we could sometimes tell which way it was coming from.

We never did it in the wintertime. There was a story about a boy that tried to lick frost off a rail and his tongue stuck and the train came along and he had to tear the top of his tongue off to keep from getting run over. I never thought it would do that to your ear but I was afraid I'd think about sticking my tongue to the cold rail and couldn't help myself. I finally told Jodell that and he said he'd thought about it too.

———————————

Later on, but in the Depression still, just before the start of World War II, I'd wait down at the station house for the passenger trains to come through on weekends and sell sack lunches on the platform. Two pieces of chicken, one dark and one light meat, with a pickle and two cold biscuits. My mother fixed the lunches, and said that I could sell them for fifty cents. I got to keep a nickel from each sack. I sold them for fifty-two cents because then most people gave me fifty-five and let me keep the three-cents change.

There were little sacks, too, with three pieces of peanut-butter fudge. These sold for a nickel and I got to keep half of that money, so every time I sold a sack of fudge I ate one.

I saw a lot of men on the tops of boxcars and in the doors of boxcars and underneath them, riding on the rods. Sometimes you could talk to them but I didn't very much. I was afraid they might take the sack lunches away.

Still I learned about traveling on the freight trains enough to know that in St. Louis or Little Rock or in railheads like Hoxie even if it was a small town, you could get beat up on or shot for hopping a train, and had to stay hidden as best you could or get ready to run from a yard dick, and you couldn't ever just stand in the boxcar door or sit on top and look at things. Except where I lived nobody cared about that not even the police I guess and we just waved.

Jodell and I were going to hop a freight and ride to the water tank over on the other side of London. Sometimes after school we ran alongside a freight train when it started off but it always got too fast to grab hold of before we got up nerve enough to try. Except once I grabbed hold of the ladder at the first jerk of the wheels. But then I was afraid the train would go all the way to St. Louis without stopping for water and there wouldn't be any way for me to get off and a yard dick would kill me and nobody could trace me through my overalls and my mother and father would never know what happened. When I let go, the train was moving faster than I could run. I skidded through cinders for yards and rolled down the embankment into a patch of weeds.

But if I did get there and came back, I'd be the most important person in all of Woodrow Wilson School. Now the train was going so fast it was hard to read the numbers. But if I did.

———————————

Jimmie Rodgers was a waterboy for the section hands when his daddy was foreman on the Gulf, Mobile & Ohio Railroad, and later he was a brakeman on the New Orleans & Northeastern running between New Orleans and Meridian. He worked on the railroads for fourteen years as a regular.

Working in Utah and Colorado, he got so worn down by the cold and the long hours and the hard sleep that his lungs went bad with one sickness after another until he finally got the T.B. that he died from just nine years after he left the railroads.

Johnny Cash's daddy worked on the railroad that ran by the family shack in Arkansas, close to Kingsland. That was the St. Louis & Southwestern.

The first real movie was *The Great Train Robbery.* The first of the serials was *The Perils of Pauline,* and Pauline is mostly famous for getting tied to the tracks.

I never saw either of those, but I feel as if I did. Everybody does.

The first train I remember for sure in the movies, the first one I can put the name of the movie on, is the first one that Tyrone Power and Henry Fonda robbed in *Jesse James.* Then I remember the one that Mickey Rooney worked on when he was *Young Tom Edison.* About the same time, *Abe Lincoln in Illinois* was Raymond Massey, standing on the platform of the presidential caboose and waving goodbye to his neighbors in Springfield. Then

Ronald Reagan got his legs injured by a train in *King's Row* and a cruel doctor cut them off when he didn't have to.

About seven years after the accident in *King's Row,* I traveled through a part of the South on the presidential campaign train of Henry Wallace, the candidate of the Progressive Party in 1948.

People could walk around on the train, and there was room for a lot more reporters and party workers and just friends than you can take on a plane, and it was possible to stop a few minutes in almost every little town, which was necessary when there wasn't television and which might not be a bad thing to do again.

A few times Wallace came back into the train after giving a speech and had eggs and tomatoes on his clothes. It never seemed to upset him very much. I liked him a lot. There were other people on the train I didn't like at all.

At the same time Harry Truman was on a train, too, stopping at every little town he came to.

Nobody's made much use of the trains to run for President since then.

And it wasn't long before just about everybody followed the politicians into the planes and cars and stopped using the trains to travel on, and freight trains had the tracks almost to themselves.

That happened at the same time we got rid of the whistles and trains started honking. I never thought it was right for a train to honk.

This year my wife Jordan and I got a bedroom on Amtrak—which is bringing people back to the railroads, a kind of national second thought and a good thing—and rode from Kansas City to Chicago to Spokane for a writers' conference. Except for the fact that there should have been more than one dining car and one bar car for three hundred and fifty people on the Chicago-to-Spokane run, which necessitated waiting in line (a hard thing to do on a rolling train) and the fact that the glass on the dome car was so dirty it was impossible to see the Black Hills or the Plains or the Rockies from there—except for these two frustrating facts, the trip was a joy from beginning to end. We discounted the rough track from Chicago to Minneapolis. I've been told it's much worse in the East; this wasn't bad, and west of Minneapolis we didn't spill a drop.

The cars were clean, the food was good and less expensive than in most restaurants, the service was all but obsequious and extremely professional, and after a trip of three days we arrived not ten minutes late.

We were struck by the similarity of train travel and travel by ship. We'd both forgotten how it was. People came to know each other, there were brief romances and there was even a very pretty and charming social director in a mini-skirted uniform who conducted separate bingo games for the children and any adults who cared to play. She was an apparently (I'm sure deceptively) tireless young woman who apparently (I'm sure deceptively) enjoyed every number she called out. She came to our bedroom to announce the schedule of social activities for the day, including an hour of free soft drinks and cookies in the lounge. She was a person, it seemed to me, you liked right off. Jordan called her Miss Amtrak.

There weren't any cars, so far as we could see, made since the 1930's. That was one of the things we liked about it. On all the ceilings were those designs that tell us when we're watching a thirties movie, six lines and a broken circle, like this:

Before we boarded the train, Jordan confessed to fantasies of spies in the next compartment. I smiled at that. I knew that after we had our beds made and were getting to sleep I would hear Dale Robertson running along the roof of the train toward the engine.

Jim McPherson was at the writers' conference and we talked about trains. He'd been a waiter on the same line Jordan and I had just ridden, back before the demise of commercial passenger service, and he had some great stories to tell. So we told our own stories about trains, and then we told stories we'd heard and stories we'd read, and then we talked about doing a book called *Railroad,* the history of trains and stories and poems and essays and songs and pictures, with each of us doing a kind of introduction—Jim's an objective view of culture and technology, especially as it involves the railroad, and mine a subjective story, maybe no more than a series of blackouts, of the trains in one man's life until now.

"Let's do it," Jim said.

"Hell, yes," I said. "Let's do it."

So we did.

M. W.

A RAILROAD TIMETABLE

1804 Oliver Evans built the first American steam locomotive in Philadelphia.

1807 Silas Whitney operated a horse-drawn and gravity wooden tramway on Beacon Hill, Boston.

1815, February 6 John Stevens, of Hoboken, was granted the first railroad charter in America by the New Jersey Legislature. It authorized construction of a rail line between the Delaware and Raritan rivers, near Trenton and New Brunswick.

1825, February The first locomotive to run on rails in America was built by John Stevens and operated experimentally on a half-mile circular track at Hoboken, N.J.

1826, October 7 Gridley Bryant's Granite Railway was opened at Quincy, Mass., to transport granite used in building the Bunker Hill Monument. Horses supplied the motive power for the three-mile-long broad-gauge railroad.

1827, February 28 A charter was granted for the first railroad in Maryland—now the oldest railroad charter in America. The first stone was laid in construction on Independence Day, 1828.

1829, August 8 The locomotive Stourbridge Lion, imported from England, was put on a track at Honesdale, Pa., and operated three miles. Horatio Allen was the engineer.

1830, August 25 Peter Cooper's locomotive Tom Thumb made a trial trip from Baltimore to Ellicott's Mills, Md., and back.

1830, December 25 A railroad at Charleston, S.C., began scheduled passenger service, using the American-built locomotive Best Friend of Charleston. It was the first public carrier by rail in South Carolina and the first railroad in America to use steam power in regular service.

1830 Robert L. Stevens designed the forerunner of the T-rail, used today. The first iron rails of American design were rolled in 1844, and Bessemer steel rails were first rolled at North Chicago Rolling Mills on May 25, 1865.

1831, August 9 The first steam train in New York State ran from Albany to Schenectady, pulled by the locomotive DeWitt Clinton.

1831, November 12 The locomotive John Bull was placed in service at Bordentown, N.J. Isaac Dripps, a Yankee machinist, put the English-built engine together, and subsequently added a "pilot," a four-wheel truck assembly to guide the locomotive over sharp curves.

1831, November The United States mails were carried for the first time by rail—in South Carolina.

1831 A pine-knot fire on an open platform car in South Carolina served as the first locomotive headlight. Between then and the 1850's, candles and whale oil were used in reflector lamps. In 1859 kerosene and gas lamps made their appearance. In 1881 electricity was introduced, and in 1936 the figure-8 oscillating headlight first appeared. The sealed-beam headlight was first placed on locomotives in 1946.

1833, June 6 Andrew Jackson became the first President of the United States to ride on a railroad train—between Ellicott's Mills, Md., and Baltimore.

1835, August 25 The first railroad to Washington, D.C., was opened from Baltimore.

1836, February 5 Henry R. Campbell, of Philadelphia, patented an eight-wheeled engine (4-4-0) which was subsequently termed the American type. His first locomotive was completed May 8, 1837, and, with numerous modifications, remained a popular type until 1895.

1836, April The first car ferry, the Susquehanna, was placed in service on the Susquehanna River, between Havre de Grace and Perryville, Md.

1836, July 13 John Ruggles, U.S. senator from Maine and "father of the U.S. Patent Office," was issued Patent No. 1—first in the numbered series—for a device to increase the power of railway locomotives and to prevent their wheels from sliding.

1836, July 21 Canada's first locomotive, the Dorchester, puffed her way from Laprairie to St. Johns, Que., to open the first Canadian railroad.

1836 The first two locomotives known to have been equipped with whistles were built at Lowell, Mass., under the supervision of George Washington Whistler. The Hicksville was put in service at Jamaica, Long Island, and was reported to make "a shrill, wild unearthly sound something like drawing a saw flat across a bar of iron." The Susquehanna was tried out at Wilmington, Del., traveling at "35 or 40 miles an hour." It was said "to give awful notice of its approach to any point."

1837 First locomotive whistle introduced.

1837 The world's first sleeping car—a remodeled day coach—was operated between Harrisburg and Chambersburg, Pa.

1838, January New York and Washington, D.C., were linked by a chain of railroads, with ferry service across major rivers and stagecoaches between stations in principal cities.

1838, July 7 An act of Congress making every railroad a post route was signed by President Martin Van Buren.

1839, March 4 America's first long-distance railway express service was started by William F. Harnden, former railroad conductor, between Boston and New York.

1848, October 24 Chicago's first locomotive, the Pioneer, was placed on tracks and the first run was made the following day.

1848, December 29 The first direct rail route between Boston and New York was completed.

1850, September 20 President Millard Fillmore signed the first federal railroad land-grant act. The last grant to aid in pioneer railroad development was made in 1871, but land-grant rate reductions on government traffic and mail continued until October 1, 1946, resulting in savings to the federal government of $1,250,000,000 from the time of the first grants.

1850 Oil lamps were introduced on trains for night travel. Gaslight followed in 1860, Pintsch gas in 1883, electricity in 1885 and fluorescent lights in 1938.

1851, July 1 The first refrigerator-type car known to have been built in this country began service when eight tons of butter were transported to Boston from Ogdensburg, N.Y.

1851, August 16 The first international railway link on the North American continent was opened from Laprairie, Que., to Rouses Point, N.Y. By international agreement—first of its kind in the world—rolling stock of foreign ownership was permitted free entry into Canada or the United States, and this arrangement is still in effect.

1851, September 22 The first recorded use of telegraph for train dispatching took place at Turner (now Harriman), N.Y.

1852, December 9 The first locomotive west of the Mississippi River, the Pacific, ran from St. Louis to Cheltenham, a distance of five miles.

1853, January 24 The all-rail route was completed between Eastern cities and Chicago, but several changes of cars were necessary.

Earliest form of block signal was this non-electrical type in 1875.—*New York Public Library Picture Collection*

1853, June A Connecticut railroad equipped a passenger train with flexible connections which provided covered and enclosed passageways (vestibules) between cars.

1854, February 22 A railroad was completed from Chicago to the Mississippi River at Rock Island, opening the first rail route from the Eastern seaboard.

1854 Luxurious, adjustable, reclining-seat cars—"night seat" coaches, as they were called—were placed in service between Philadelphia and Baltimore.

1855, February Susan Morningstar was hired to help clean the Baltimore & Ohio terminal at Baltimore, Md., and thus became the first woman railroad employee.

1855, March The Niagara Suspension Bridge was completed, opening another rail route between the East and West.

1855, September Horse-and-buggy flatcar services, now termed "piggyback" services, became popular transportation for farmers en route to market in Nova Scotia; 1885 marked the inauguration of farmers' truck-wagon trains on Long Island.

1856, February 22 The West Coast's first railroad was opened from Sacramento to Folsom, Calif.

1856, April 21 The first railroad bridge to span the

Mississippi River was opened at Davenport, Iowa. Partially burned on May 6 following collision by the steamer *Effie Afton,* it was rebuilt and reopened on September 8, 1856.

1856, December 2 The first sleeping-car patents were issued to T. T. Woodruff.

1857, April 1 The first Southern rail route between the Atlantic seaboard and the Mississippi River was completed—from Charleston to Memphis.

1857 Meat shipped under refrigeration for the first time—out of Chicago.

1858 Pullman put his first sleeping car into operation.

1859, February 14 Railroads reached the Missouri River at St. Joseph.

1859, September 1 The first Pullman sleeping car left Bloomington, Ill., on an overnight trip to Chicago. The first Pullman conductor was Jonathan L. Barnes.

1862, March 31 The Oregon Pony, the first locomotive in the Pacific Northwest, arrived at Portland, Oreg.

1862, April 12 A race and battle took place between Union soldiers, on the locomotive General, and Confederates, on the locomotive Texas—from Big Shanty to Ringgold, between Atlanta and Chattanooga.

1862, July 1 President Lincoln signed an act authorizing construction of a line of railroads from the Missouri River to the Pacific Coast.

1862, July 28 An experimental post-office car for sorting mail en route was placed in service between Hannibal and St. Joseph, Mo.

1863 The Brotherhood of the Footboard, the first viable railroad labor union, was organized.

1863 The first dining cars were introduced, running between Philadelphia and Baltimore.

1864, August 28 The first permanent railway post-office car for picking up, sorting and distributing mail en route was placed in operation on a run from Chicago to Clinton, Iowa.

1865, November 1 A tank car especially built for transporting oil took on its initial load at Titusville, Pa.

1865 The block signal system, through telegraphic communication, was introduced by Ashbel Welch.

1866, April 20 The first code of rules to govern the interchange of freight cars was adopted at a meeting of six freight lines held in Buffalo.

1866 Automatic block signals were introduced.

1867, December 13 A railroad pushing eastward from Sacramento entered Nevada, near Crystal Peak.

1868, April 21 Eli H. Janney obtained the first patent for an automatic coupler. A second patent was issued April 29, 1873, for the basic car-coupler design generally in use today. Standard, interchangeable, automatic car couplers were introduced in 1887. Following extensive experiments, further improvements were made and standardized in subsequent years.

1868 The first Pullman-built dining car, the Delmonico, was placed in service.

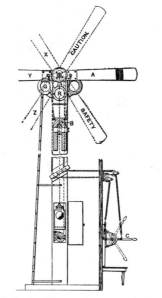

Mosier's Three Position Semaphore Signal.—*New York Public Library Picture Collection*

1869, January 23 George Westinghouse applied for an air-brake patent.

1869, February A railroad building westward from Omaha entered Utah Territory, at Wahsatch.

1869, May 10 The Golden Spike ceremony at Promontory, Utah, signalized completion of the first transcontinental rail route.

1869, July 4 The first bridge to span the Missouri River was opened at Kansas City, thus establishing a through route from Chicago.

1870 First coast-to-coast run (Boston to San Francisco).

1871, August 16 The first narrow-gauge railroad was opened a few miles out of Denver, Colo., and was completed to Colorado Springs on October 27,

1871. The locomotive Montezuma, which was used, was the first narrow-gauge passenger engine built or operated in this country.

1875 Pullman put his first parlor car into operation.

1877, May 21 Tests at Altoona, Pa., marked the first use of telephone communication for railroad purposes.

1877, July First national strike, against Pennsylvania and B & O lines.

1880 Alonzo C. Mather designed the first humane cattle car.

1881, March 8 The first rail route was completed to Southern California via New Mexico and Arizona.

1881 The first steam-heating system was installed in passenger trains, replacing stoves and hot-water heaters.

1883, September 8 Entrance of the first rail route from the Great Lakes into Washington Territory was celebrated. Many American and foreign notables attended the spike-driving ceremony. The line was extended to Puget Sound via the Cascade Mountains on July 1, 1887.

1883, November 18 Standard time, sponsored by the railroads, was adopted throughout the United States.

1885, November 7 The last spike was driven in the first Canadian transcontinental line at Craigellachie, B.C., and the first "special" train reached Port Moody from Montreal the next morning. The line was fully opened to Vancouver, B.C., May 23, 1887.

1885 Master Car-Builders approved the use of the Janney automatic coupler.

1886 The standardization of gauge (4 ft. 8½ in.) of railroads in the South was completed, enabling an interchange of cars throughout the country for the first time.

1887, February 4 The Interstate Commerce Act, creating the Interstate Commerce Commission, was signed by President Grover Cleveland.

1887, April 14 The General Time Convention, a predecessor of the Association of American Railroads, adopted the first standard code of train rules.

1887, June 17-18 Successful test runs were made of a passenger train hauled by an oil-burning locomotive. It ran from Altoona, Pa., to Pittsburgh and back.

1887, December A direct rail route linking Seattle and Portland with San Francisco, Los Angeles and San Diego was completed.

1887 Extensive air-brake tests conducted during 1886–87 on fifty-car freight trains at Burlington, Iowa, led to the adoption of an automatic, quick-action, triple-valve brake for freight service.

1887 The first trains in America to be fully equipped with electric lights ran between New York and Chicago, Boston and New York, New York and Florida and from Springfield to Northampton, Mass.

1893, May 10 Locomotive No. 999 made the world's first 100-mile-an-hour run at Batavia, N.Y.

1893 Air brakes and automatic couplers required by law.

1894, May 11 Great railroad strike began with Pullman workers.

1894, June 12 First national convention of American Railway Union.

1894, July 17 Eugene V. Debs imprisoned. Strike ended two days later.

1895 The first steam railroad conversion to electrification in the United States was completed on three railroads operating in Massachusetts, New Jersey and Maryland.

1901 Mechanical coal stokers for locomotives were introduced.

1904 All-steel passenger cars were placed in service.

1905, June 12 The fastest train speed officially recorded on an American railroad—127.6 miles per hour—was made on a 3-mile run near Ada, Ohio.

1914 First tests were begun looking toward the use of radio in railroad communications.

1917, March The American Short Line Railroad Association was organized.

1917, December 28 The federal government took control of railroads in the United States as a wartime emergency measure, with fiscal control becoming effective January 1, 1918. They were returned to their owners on March 1, 1920.

1925, October 20 The first diesel locomotive (a switcher) was put in service.

1927, July 25 A coordinated system of centralized traffic control—installed on a 40-mile route at Berwick, Ohio—was placed in operation. "CTC" has since been installed on more than 40,000 miles of track.

1928, December 7 The Railway Express Agency was organized to handle nationwide express business. Its name was changed to REA Express in 1960.

1929, January 12 The Cascade Tunnel—7.79 miles in length and longest in the Western Hemisphere—was opened in the State of Washington.

1929, September 9 The first air-conditioned Pullman car was operated between Chicago and Los Angeles.

1931, May 24 The world's first completely air-conditioned passenger train was placed in service between Washington and New York.

1934, February 12 The first lightweight streamliner, equipped with distillate-electric motive power, was delivered. After an extensive exhibition tour, the train was placed in scheduled service between Salina, Kans., and Kansas City, Mo., on January 31, 1935.

1934, May 26 The first diesel-powered streamlined train was completed April 9, 1934, and ran the 1,015 miles between Denver and Chicago nonstop at an average speed of 77.6 miles an hour.

1934, October 12 The Association of American Railroads was formed by consolidation of the American Railway Association and other organizations, some of which dated back to 1876.

1934, November 11 The first lightweight streamlined passenger train to use diesel power started operating between Lincoln, Nebr., and Kansas City, Mo.

1937, March A two-way train telephone communication system was inaugurated between Albion, Pa., and North Bessemer Yard, Pittsburgh.

1937, July 1 The Federal Railroad Retirement Act went into effect for all railroads, replacing voluntary retirement and disability benefits on some eighty major railroads.

1941 The first diesel road freight locomotives were placed in regular service.

1945, May 17 The Federal Communications Commission allocated radio channels for exclusive railroad use, and the first construction permit was granted on February 27, 1946.

1945, July 23 The first modern domed observation car was introduced on the run between Chicago and Minneapolis.

1945, September 2 V-J Day ended World War II. During 45 months of war, the railroads had moved 90 percent of all Army and Navy freight and more than 97 percent of all military personnel in organized groups within the United States, including the operation of 113,891 special troop trains.

1948, November 15 Track tests began on the first gas-turbine-electric locomotive to be built and operated in the United States. The first unit went into regular pool service January 1, 1952.

1952, May Diesel ownership, as expressed in

power units, exceeded ownership of steam locomotives for the first time (19,082 diesel units to 18,489 steam locomotives).

1955, December 1 Remote control of a multiple-unit car was demonstrated between New Rochelle and Rye, N.Y., from a control panel located at Larchmont, N.Y. The car's movements were protected at all times by standard automatic train-control equipment.

1956, March The first large-scale electronic data-processing computer was introduced into railroad operations, after years of testing and experimentation with varied types of automatic office equipment. Stockholder dividend checks were processed first, and on March 12, 1957, company payroll checks were printed.

1960, February Unit train operations were inaugurated in daily coal-mine-to-power-plant runs.

1962, July 3 The nation's first silicon rectifier locomotive, one of six, was delivered to an Eastern railroad.

1962, October 26 Railroad train information was first transmitted instantaneously from St. Louis, Mo., to Dallas, Texas, via Telstar. Wallace Coleman thus became the first railroader to use satellite communication system.

1965, September 30 President Johnson signed legislation authorizing a joint railroad-government high-speed program along the Northeast Corridor from Washington to New York City and on to Boston.

1967, April 1 The U.S. Department of Transportation came into being. Transferred to it were eleven offices from other federal agencies.

1967, October Railroads announced plans for an Automatic Car Identification (ACI) system to make possible prompt location of freight cars. A 1970 start-up was proposed in conjunction with TeleRail Automated Information Network (TRAIN), with the central computer to be located at the Association of American Railroads' headquarters in Washington.

1969, January 15 High-speed Metroliner rail service was inaugurated between Washington and New York.

1969, April 8 High-speed Turbo-train service began between New York and Boston.

1971, May 1 Establishment of the National Railroad Passenger Corporation (Amtrack).

1974, September Amtrak and Greyhound Bus Lines reached agreement allowing either to write interconnecting train-bus tickets.

1974, Amtrack carried 18.5 million passengers, continuing a steady increase in the use of the rails for travel since the establishment of Amtrack.

PAYDAY HUSSEY'S CAMP BB-RRR

THE EARLY DAYS
1763-1860

Courtesy Baltimore & Ohio Railroad

The vibrations will bring about nervous diseases. . . .

— *Lyons Academy of Medicine*

THE DAWN OF A NEW IDEA

Rupert Sargent Holland

Men probably laughed at Roger Bacon, who said about 1216 that carriages would some day move without horses, and they certainly laughed at Solomon de Caus, a Frenchman, who was confined in an asylum in Paris on account of his mad notions, among which was the proposition that steam might be employed for the propulsion of carriages on land and ships at sea. The English Marquis of Worcester visited De Caus in 1641, heard some of his novel ideas concerning the use of the steam of boiling water, read a book on the subject he had written, and went home and built a steam-engine. Of this nobleman Macaulay wrote: "The Marquis had observed the expansive power of moisture rarified by heat. After many experiments, he had succeeded in constructing a rude steam-engine, which he called a fire-waterwork, and which he pronounced to be an admirable and most forcible instrument of propulsion."

The Marquis, however, like Solomon de Caus, and many other inventors and explorers, was suspected of being mad and his fire-waterwork was regarded merely as a toy. Next Savery, a Cornish miner and engineer, built an engine for the purpose of raising water by the aid of fire and proposed the use of steam for propelling carriages on roads. He took no steps to carry out this suggestion in practical form, but by the middle of the eighteenth century the theory that had been laughed at in earlier days was attracting the attention of many experimental minds. Among those now interested was James Watt, to whom the idea was introduced by Dr. Robinson, a student at Glasgow, in 1759. "He threw out," said Watt, "the idea of applying the power of the steam-engine to the moving of wheel-carriages, and to other purposes; but the scheme was not matured, and was soon abandoned, on his going abroad."

Watt made use of this idea to the extent of describing an engine in which the expansive force of steam was utilized as the motive power in the specification of his patent of 1769 and also in that of 1784. Others were busy with the subject; a friend wrote to Watt that "one Moore, a linendraper of London, had taken out a patent for moving wheel-carriages by steam"; the linendraper, however, did not put his invention in practice, and Watt, although he described such a steam-driven vehicle, was too busy perfecting his condensing engine to build his proposed locomotive.

The first actual model of a steam-carriage, of which there is a record, was made by Cugnot, a Frenchman, who demonstrated his model to the Marshal de Saxe in 1763. With funds supplied by the French king he constructed an engine, but when it was set in motion it promptly proceeded to knock down a wall which was in its way. Regarded, therefore, as too dangerous a machine for ordinary purposes, Cugnot's engine was stored as a curiosity in the Arsenal Museum at Paris. An American, Oliver Evans, invented a steam-carriage in 1772 and later obtained from the State of Maryland the exclusive right to make and use such a vehicle, but did not follow up his invention. William Symington in 1786 exhibited the working model of a steam-carriage he had constructed to some professors of Edinburgh. The Scotch roads were so nearly impassable, however, that Symington gave over his steam-carriage and turned his attention to perfecting a steamboat.

William Murdoch, an assistant of Watt, built the first English model of a steam-carriage in 1784, constructed on the high-pressure principle and with three wheels. The boiler was heated by a spirit-lamp, and the entire machine was little more than a foot in height. One night, after returning from work at the mine in Redruth, Cornwall, Murdoch decided to try out his little locomotive and took it to the walk leading to a country church on the outskirts of town. The walk was narrow and bounded by high hedges. The inventor lighted his lamp, the water began to boil, and off went the engine, followed by Murdoch. The night was dark. The locomotive gained speed, and then were heard shouts from the road ahead. Hurrying his steps, Murdoch found that the clergyman of the parish, walking towards town, had encountered the hissing little demon, which he had taken to be a manifestation of Satan.

While various inventors were thus busied, the labor of working the coal mines of England was much simplified by the adoption of rail- and tram-roads, worked by horses. Watt's invention of the steam-engine had given a great impetus to manufacturing and trade of all kinds and soon it was proposed to extend the use of railroads from the collieries to the transportation of merchandise from town to town, especially in those districts where there were no canals available. In 1801 Dr. James Anderson, of Edinburgh, urged the general adoption of railways, worked by horse-power, on turnpike roads. "Diminish carriage expense but one farthing," said he, "and you widen the circle of intercourse; you form, as it were, a new creation, not only of stones and earth, and trees and plants, but of men also, and, what is more, of industry, happiness, and joy." The next year Mr. Edgeworth suggested a plan for the carriage of passengers. "Stage-coaches," he declared, "might be made to go at six miles an hour, and post-chaises and gentlemen's travelling carriages at eight,—both with one horse; and small stationary steam-engines, placed from distance to distance, might be made, by means of circulating chains, to draw the carriages, with a great diminution of horse-labour and expense."

Then Richard Trevethick, a captain in a Cornish tin-mine and a pupil of William Murdoch, determined to build a steam-carriage to use on country roads. He took out a patent in 1802. The carriage he constructed looked like the ordinary four-wheeled stagecoach. It had one horizontal cylinder, which, with the boiler and the furnace-box, was placed in the rear of the hind axle; the motion of the piston was transmitted to a separate crank-axle, from which the axle of the driving-wheel derived its motion. This was the first successful high-pressure engine built on the principle of moving a piston by the elasticity of steam against the pressure only of the atmosphere.

Trevethick's steam-carriage excited considerable interest in Cornwall, but as that district was so remote from the commercial world the inventor and his cousin, Andrew Vivian, decided to take it to London to exhibit to business men. They set out with the locomotive for Plymouth, from which port it was to be conveyed to the metropolis by ship. As the two drove along the road their carriage battered down the rails of a gentleman's garden, but went merrily on. Then Vivian sighted a closed toll-gate on the highway ahead and called to Trevethick, who was seated behind, to slacken

The Best Friend of Charleston pulled the first train for the South Carolina Canal & Rail Road Company when it began the first scheduled steam railroad service in the United States, Christmas Day 1830.—*Southern Railway Company photo*

1. A wooden model of the 1812 English rack rail locomotive. The cogwheel geared into the rack outside of the running rail. Built by John Blenkinsop, the five-ton locomotive operated between Leeds and the Middleton Colliery, a distance of 3½ miles.—*Courtesy of Baltimore & Ohio Railroad*

2. A wooden model of the 1812 manual power engine built by William Hedley of the Wylam Colliery in England. The engine proved that sufficient friction existed between wheels and rails to pull a coal train.—*Courtesy of Baltimore & Ohio Railroad*

3. One of the first locomotives with power transmission by a connecting rod outside the wheels.—*Courtesy of Baltimore & Ohio Railroad*

4. The first locomotive on the first common carrier railroad (England's Stockton & Darlington Railway) in 1825. According to old accounts, the train consisted of "six waggons loaded with coals, passengers on top of them; one waggon of surveyors and engineers; one coach occupied by directors and proprietors; six waggons filled with strangers; fourteen waggons packed with workmen and others."—*Association of American Railroads photo*

speed. The latter at once shut off steam, but the momentum of the carriage was so great that it went some distance and stopped just at the gate, which was opened like lightning by the toll-keeper.

"What have us got to pay here?" asked Vivian.

"Na—na—na—na!" stammered the gateman, trembling in every limb, and his teeth chattering as if he had the ague.

"What have us got to pay, I say?" repeated Vivian.

"Na—noth—nothing to pay! My de—dear Mr. Devil, do drive on as fast as you can! Nothing to pay!"

The locomotive arrived safely in London, was exhibited publicly, and pulled behind it a wheel-carriage filled with passengers. Crowds flocked to see it, but, actuated by some strange impulse, Trevethick gave over the exhibition and took his engine away. It had attracted much attention, however, and Sir Humphrey Davy, the inventor of the safety-lamp for use in mines, wrote to a friend: "I shall hope soon to hear that the roads of England are the haunts of Captain Trevethick's dragons—a characteristic name."

Such was the state of the roads that it was regarded as impractical to run a steam-carriage on them, and Trevethick gave up the notion of putting his invention to general use.

Mines and cotton-mills were now more busy than ever and the increase of trade throughout England called for better means of transport than by horse-power. The steam-engine appeared to be the answer, and the problem of the moment was to discover a more effectual adhesion between the wheels and the rails. Mr. Blenkinsop, of Leeds, in 1811 took out a patent for a racked- or tooth-rail to be laid at one side of the road, into which the toothed-wheel of the locomotive should work as pinions do in a rack. The boiler of his engine was supported by a carriage with four wheels without teeth, and rested directly on the axles. These wheels were independent of the working parts of the engine and merely supported its weight on the rails, the progress being made by means of the cogged wheel working in the cogged-rail. The engine had a double cylinder, the invention of Matthew Murray, a mechanical engineer of Leeds. The connecting-rods gave the motion to two pinions by cranks at right angles to each other; these pinions communicated the motion to the wheel that worked in the toothed-rail.

Blenkinsop's engines were put into use on the railway from the Middleton collieries to Leeds, a distance of about three miles and a half. They succeeded in drawing as many as thirty coal-wagons at a speed of about three miles and a quarter an hour. They were employed for many years in hauling coal and constituted the first regular use of locomotive power for commercial purposes.

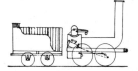

Other plans were devised to solve the problem of adhesion between the wheel and the rail. The Messrs. Chapman, of Newcastle, invented a locomotive that worked along the road by means of a chain that was stretched from one end of it to the other. This chain was passed around a grooved barrel-wheel under the engine, and when the wheel turned the locomotive pulled itself along the railway. This method proved very clumsy and the mechanism was so expensive and so difficult to keep in repair that the invention was soon discarded. William Brunton, of the Butterly Works, in Derbyshire, patented in 1813 his Mechanical Traveller, a locomotive provided with legs and feet, that worked alternately at the rear of the engine like the limbs of a horse. In one of its trial runs the engine of this strange device unfortunately exploded and killed several bystanders, and the locomotive was sent to the scrap-heap, although other steam-carriages with legs were subsequently built and some of these were used outside of London, where they climbed steep hills with surprising ease. All over the country odd-looking steam monsters were now puffing and prancing, as many men tried to work out the problem of locomotive traction upon railways.

A mine owner in the North of England, Mr. Blackett, of Wylam, made many experiments. The Wylam wagon-way was constructed of wooden rails laid between the colliery at Wylam and the village of Lemington, four miles down the Tyne. At Lemington the coal was loaded in barges and floated down the river past Newcastle and thence shipped to the London market. Each coal wagon from the mine was drawn by one horse, with a man in charge. This method of transport was so slow that only two trips were made by each man and horse in one day and three on the day following. In an effort to improve this condition Blackett took up the wooden road in 1808 and built a "plateway" of cast-iron, a single

line with sidings. This new road proved so much smoother that a horse was able to draw two wagons over it instead of one. Then Blackett decided to try locomotive power and altered the road so that he might use the rack-rail and toothed driving-wheel worked out by Blenkinsop. He had an engine built according to Trevethick's patent, a very awkward affair which, when set on the rails, would not move an inch. Undiscouraged, he constructed another, which proved more successful and was found capable of drawing eight or nine loaded coal wagons from the mine to Lemington. Its weight, however, was so great that the cast-iron plates on which it ran were constantly breaking. In addition it frequently got out of order, so that horses had to follow it to pull the wagons when the engine ceased its efforts, and it required so much attention in the way of repairs that the workmen declared it "a perfect plague."

One dark evening "Black Billy," as the locomotive was named, was puffing along the High Street Road on its way up from New-

burn. A stranger, who had never heard of the engine, was walking on the road and suddenly encountered the iron monster, working its piston up and down, snorting out loud blasts of steam and puffing fire and smoke. Frightened almost out of his senses, the stranger jumped a hedge, fled across the fields, and cried to the first person he met that he had just seen a "terrible deevil on the High Street Road." The story went around, and many were the jeers cast at Blackett on account of this "deevil" of his that scared wayfarers and set fire to trees and fields.

Notwithstanding jeers and opposition Blackett continued his experiments, studying now the proportion which the power of the engine should bear to the weight, and ultimately demonstrated that the weight of the engine would of itself produce sufficient adhesion to the rails to enable it to draw the requisite number of wagons on a smooth tram-road. This put an end to the fallacy on that point that had previously been such an obstacle to the use of steam-carriages, and proved that rack-rails, toothed-wheels, chains and legs were all unnecessary for the successful traction of loaded wagons on a road that was moderately level.

The steam that blew into the air at high pressure from the piston while the locomotive was moving considerably annoyed horses on the Wylam road, which was a public highway, and one of the neighbors threatened to take steps to prevent the nuisance. To diminish this objection to his plan Blackett gave orders that whenever any horse, or vehicle drawn by horses, came into view, the engine was to be stopped and the blast of steam discontinued until the animals were out of sight. This course of procedure caused much inconvenience to those who ran the locomotive, and so this scheme was adopted: a reservoir was provided directly behind the chimney, into which the waste steam was thrown after it had been used in the cylinder; from this reservoir the steam could gradually escape into the air without noise. This plan was devised expressly for the object of preventing any blast in the chimney, but the great value of this innovation was not appreciated until George Stephenson built his locomotive and established the steam railway in England.

JOHN STEVENS

DOCUMENTS TENDING TO PROVE
THE SUPERIOR ADVANTAGES
OF RAIL-WAYS AND STEAM-CARRIAGES
OVER CANAL NAVIGATION

1812

The following documents, on a subject calculated, I should suppose, to attract public attention, are committed to the press from an estimation of their importance, and from a full conviction of the practicability of the proposed improvement. On a subject of such deep interest to the community at large, I presume no apology will be necessary for the liberty I now take of laying before the public private communications.

Had the subject matter of this publication been exhibited to public view in the shape of an entire and connected essay, written expressly for the purpose, numerous repetitions and inaccuracies, both in style and matter, would not have occurred. But, I am inclined to believe, that the desultory manner in which it is now handled, and the unavoidable repetitions necessarily resulting therefrom, will render it more generally impressive.

Although my proposal has failed to gain the approbation of the Commissioners for the improvement of inland navigation in the State of New-York, yet I feel by no means discouraged respecting the final success of the project. The very objections their Committee have brought forward serve only to increase, if possible, my confidence in the superiority of the proposed rail-ways to canals.

So many and so important are the advantages which these States would derive from the general adoption of the proposed rail-ways, that they ought, in my humble opinion, to become an object of primary attention to the national government. The insignificant sum of two or three thousand dollars would be adequate to give the project a fair trial. On the success of this experiment a plan should be digested, "a general system of internal communication and conveyance" adopted, and the necessary surveys made for the extension of these ways in all directions, so as to embrace and unite every section of this extensive empire. It might then indeed be truly said, that these States would constitute one family, intimately connected, and held together in indissoluble bonds of union.

Should the national government be induced to make an appropriation to the amount above stated, an experiment could soon be made, either in the vicinity of this city, or at Washington, as may be deemed most expedient.

But the attention of the general government is urged more imperatively to this object from the consideration of its great national importance in a fiscal point of view. If any reliance can be placed on the calculations I have made, the revenue which this mode of transportation, when brought into general use, would be capable of producing, would far exceed the aggregate amount of duties on foreign importations. However extravagant this position may at first sight appear, I contend it is capable of the strictest demonstration. It is an indisputable fact, that the aggregate amount of internal commerce is vastly greater than that of external commerce. But one half of the latter, viz. exports, are, by the constitution, exempted from the payment of duties; the other half, foreign imports only, are subject to the payment of duties.

The far greater part of domestic commerce consists of bulky articles, many of which *now* pay fifty per cent on transportation to market. By the introduction of the proposed rail-ways,

Day scene at a railroad junction, departing trains, 1879.—*Library of Congress*

Railroad Saloon, September 19, 1868.—*New York Public Library Collection*

nine-tenths at least of this enormous tax would in many instances be saved, and the expense of transportation reduced from fifty to five per cent. A toll of five per cent. would raise it to ten per cent. But still the farmer, remotely situated, would save four-fifths of his present expense in the transportation of his produce to market. An average toll, then, of five per cent. would constitute a very moderate impost. But the product of such an impost would, at no distant period, be immense. That it would far exceed any amount which could possibly be derived from duties on foreign imposts, cannot admit of a doubt.

At a period like the present, when the ordinary sources of revenue no longer continue to pour into the treasury of the United States their tributary streams, and when too we are called upon to make "arrangements and exertions for the general security;" at such a period the merits of a system promising, not merely to facilitate most astonishingly "internal communication and conveyance," but to furnish new and abundant sources of revenue, ought surely to command the attention of the general government, and cannot fail to "be seen in the strongest lights."

The extension and completion of the main arteries of such a system of communication would by no means be a work of time. It would be exempted totally from the difficulties, embarrassments, casualties, interruptions, and delays incident to the formation of canals. Requiring no supply of water—no precision and accuracy in levelling, the work could be commenced and carried on in various detached parts—its progress would be rapid, and its completion could be ascertained with certainty. Innumerable ramifications would from time to time be extended in every direction. Thus would the sources of private and public wealth, going hand in hand, increase with a rapidity beyond all parallel. For every shilling contributed towards the revenue, a dollar at least would be put into the hands of individuals.

But there remains another important point of view in which this improvement demands the attention of the general government. The celerity of communication it would afford with the distant sections of our wide extended empire, is a consideration of the utmost moment. To the rapidity of the motion of a steam-carriage on these rail-ways, no definite limit can be set. The flying Proas, as they are called by voyagers, belonging to the natives of the Islands in the Pacific Ocean, are said at times to sail at the rate of more than twenty miles an hour. But as the resistance of the water to the progress of a vessel increases as the squares of her velocity, it is obvious that the power required to propel her must also be increased in the same ratio. Not so with a steam-carriage— as it moves in a fluid 800 times more rare than water, the resistance will be proportionably diminished. Indeed the principal resistance to its motion arises from friction, which does not even increase in a direct ratio with the velocity of the carriage. If, then, a Proa can be driven by the wind (the propulsive power of which is constantly diminishing as the velocity of the Proa increases) through so dense a fluid as water, at the rate of twenty miles an hour, I can see nothing to hinder a steam-carriage from moving on these ways with a velocity of one hundred miles an hour.*

I will now just observe, that should it be considered an object of sufficient importance, sails might be used whenever the wind was favourable. Van Bram gives a curious account of the peasantry in the country round Pekin availing themselves of sails, when the wind favoured them, for propelling the wheel-barrows in which their products are carried to market.

In a military point of view, the advantages resulting from the establishment of these rail-ways and steam-carriages, would be incalculable. It would at once render our frontiers on every side invulnerable. Armies could be conveyed in twenty-four hours, a greater distance than it would now take them weeks or perhaps months to march.

---

* This astonishing velocity is considered here as merely possible. It is probable that it may not in practice be convenient to exceed twenty or thirty miles per hour. Actual experiments, however, can alone determine this matter, and I should not be surprised at seeing steam-carriages propelled at the rate of forty or fifty miles per hour.

Thus then this improvement would afford us prompt and effectual means, not only of guarding against the attacks of foreign enemies, but of expeditiously quelling internal commotions; and thus securing and preserving for ever domestic tranquility.

Whatever constitutional doubts may be entertained respecting the power of Congress to cut and form canals, there can be none about the power to lay out and make roads.

I shall now close this topic with an extract of a Message from President Madison to the Senate and House of Representatives of the United States.

"The utility of Canal navigation is universally admitted, and it is not less certain, that scarcely any country offers more extensive opportunities for that branch of improvements than the United States; and none, perhaps, inducements equally persuasive, to make the

35

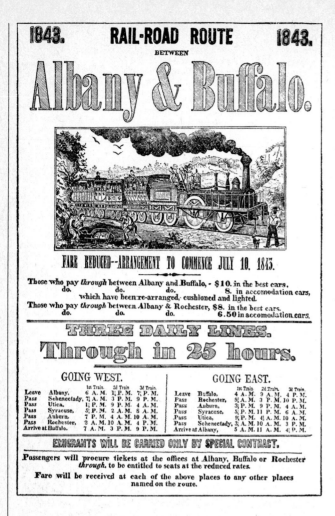

most of them. The particular undertaking contemplated by the State of New-York, which marks an honourable spirit of enterprise, and comprises objects of national, as well as more limited importance, will recall the attention of Congress to the signal advantages to be derived to the United States, from a general system of internal communication and conveyance; and suggest to their consideration whatever steps may be proper on their part, towards its introduction and accomplishment. As some of those advantages have an intimate connection with arrangements and exertions for the general security, it is a period calling for these, that the merits of such a system will be seen in the strongest lights.

"JAMES MADISON.
"Washington, Dec. 2, 1811."

From local circumstances, these rail-ways are calculated to become pre-eminently beneficial to the southern States. The great predominance of sand, and the deficiency of gravel or stone, precludes the practicability of making good turnpike roads; but the level surface, and great abundance of pine timber throughout this district of country, would not only render the construction of these rail-ways very cheap, but peculiarly advantageous. By preserving nearly a horizontal level, the power requisite for the transportation of heavy bodies would be reduced astonishingly. The cheapness of fuel would reduce too the expense of supporting this power to almost nothing. Articles would be transported one hundred miles on these ways, at less expense than they could now be carried on mile on a deep sandy road. This projected improvement is surely then an object worthy of the most serious attention of the inhabitants of the southern States. It would at once more than double the value of their products. It appears to me calculated to hold out the most flattering prospects of gain to such enterprising individuals or companies as might be induced to embark a capital in this object.

But, I consider it, in every point of view, so exclusively an object of national concern, that I shall give no encouragement to private speculations, until it is ascertained that Congress will not be disposed to pay any attention to it.

Should it, however, be destined to ramain unnoticed by the general government, I must confess I shall feel much regret, not so much from personal as from public considerations. I am anxious and ambitious that my native country should have the honour of being the first to introduce an improvement of such immense importance to society at large, and should feel the utmost reluctance at being compelled to resort to foreigners in the first instance. As no doubt exists in my mind, but that the value of the improvement would be duly appreciated, and carried into immediate effect by transatlantic governments, I have been the more urgent in pressing the subject on the attention of Congress. Whatever then may be its fate, should this appeal by considered obtrusive and unimportant, or from whatever other cause or motive should it be suffered to remain unheeded, I still have the consolation of having performed what I conceive to be a public duty.

JOHN STEVENS.
New-York, May 15, 1812.

THE RAILWAY TRAIN

Emily Dickinson

I like to see it lap the miles,
And lick the valleys up,
And stop to feed itself at tanks;
And then, prodigious, step

Around a pile of mountains,
And, supercilious, peer
In shanties by the sides of roads;
And then a quarry pare

To fit its sides, and crawl between,
Complaining all the while
In horrid, hooting stanza;
Then chase itself down hill

And neigh like Boanerges;
Then, punctual as a star,
Stop—docile and omnipotent—
At its own stable door.

Lookout Mountain, Tennessee. And the Chattanooga Railroad, 1866.—*Library of Congress*

SIDETRACK INTERIORS

A dome car on Amtrak's San Francisco Zephyr.—*Photo courtesy of Amtrak*

Southern Railway's tavern-observation car on The Southerner, in the forties.—*Photo by Southern Railway System*

One of the unspoken principles of environmental design is the Seesaw Law, which says that any area meant to hold human beings will express a sum of elegance and efficiency equal to twice one-half the potential for either, which is to say that a railroad lounge car may be purely elegant and purely efficient at the same time. The law is unrepealable, and some wish it had never been put on the books. Others think that if we had to make a choice, we ought to have made it the other way—elegance or efficiency. If there were a choice, which there isn't, it would probably depend on the length of the trip. Railroad cars evolve, like everything else, by principles more complicated than seesaws.

The interior of a Pullman Parlor Car. Circa 1876.—*Courtesy of the New York Public Library*

The bar end of Mo-Pac's "Solarium."—*Missouri Pacific Railroad photo*

The Smoking Saloon of a Pullman Parlor Car. Circa 1876.—*Courtesy of the New York Public Library*

A Louisville & Nashville passenger car before the turn of the century.—*Courtesy of Louisville & Nashville Railroad*

PAY DAY HUSSEY'S CAMP B.R. RR

THE UNDERGROUND RAILROAD AND THE CIVIL WAR
1850-1865

This Side Up With Care

— words on the box in which a slave shipped himself to freedom

The Underground Railroad, that network of escape routes running from the slave states to Canada, was more than a metaphor; its claim on these pages is much stronger than that. Many of the slaves who made their way to freedom actually did travel, hidden as freight, over the commercial railroad lines. Henry Brown is the most famous of these uncounted men and women who endured the small boxes in silence and terror. He was a slave in Virginia in 1848 when he made himself a wooden crate 3 feet 1 inch by 2 feet by 2 feet 6 inches and managed to have himself shipped in it from Richmond to Philadelphia by the Adams Express Company. The exploit was celebrated in the following song, while "Box" Brown traveled about the North telling his story to large audiences.

Brown laid down the shovel and the hoe,
Down in the box he did go;
No more Slave work for Henry Box Brown,
In the box by express he did go.

THE STORY OF THE UNDERGROUND RAILROAD

One of the most pervasive myths in American life is the myth of the machine. It is employed in defining individual personalities, interpersonal relationships and corporate structures. The basic document of American society, the United States Constitution, has been praised traditionally for the efficiency with which it regulates relations between the executive, legislative and judiciary branches of the federal government. We speak of "the machinery of the Constitution" with the same admiration used to describe a well-loved artifact like a 1929 Ford. The Constitution *is* capable of operating almost indefinitely, with the proper care and maintenance, like a piece of metal machinery. And like a machine, the Constitution must be repaired from time to time, either through amendment or through judicial reinterpretation of its sections, articles and clauses—its nuts and bolts. But unlike a machine, the Constitution can undergo extensive repairs without a complete overhaul of its basic design. It is this capacity to change with the times without abandoning its basic design which makes the United States Constitution more human than machinelike in its operations. It can be a humanizing force as much as it can be a mechanical one. It is protean rather than permanently formed; it is open to improvisation, despite its structure. Each amendment, for example, reduces to short, declaratory sentences the wisdom learned from a generation or more of human activity, human interaction, human tragedy. This wisdom has expressed itself in the manner of choosing Vice-Presidents, in the repeal of prohibition legislation, in the extension of the franchise to women, and especially in the granting of freedom, legal protection and enfranchisement to the ancestors of present-day black Americans.

The earliest attempt at humanizing the processes of the Constitution was rooted in the metaphorical relationship existing between men and machines. This was the effort of many thousands of progressive Americans, called abolitionists, to address the dehumanizing effects of chattel slavery. They represented a moral consciousness which is the heritage of all who value the Constitution. The issue as they saw it was exceedingly simple and exceedingly complex: Could a nation whose sacred documents declared universal freedom reconcile those ideals with the existence of chattel slavery based on color? They answered "No," and began a movement which resulted in the extension of constitutional guarantees to the nation's slaves. They were the engineers of that mid-nineteenth-century moral force which history has called the Underground Railroad.

If the chief contribution of the nineteenth-century American railroad was the distribution of people and goods, then the chief contribution of its moral counterpart was a redistribution of the concept of freedom. The beginnings of this movement are obscure. We know that as early as 1688, in the *Germantown Protest,* Pennsylvania Quakers expressed their moral opposition to the existence of slavery. We also know that during that same period the American jurist Samuel Sewall, also a Quaker, condemned the traffic in men in his famous *The Selling of Joseph.* We know that as early as the 1820's there were many Northerners, both white and black, who were disturbed by the correlation between color and indefinite servitude that was becoming a permanent institution in Southern life. The first few miles of track might have been laid by a recognition of the embarrassing contradiction between professions of democratic/Christian ideals and the existence of chattel slavery. The tracks were extended, once the moral cost of this contradiction was assessed, by people of good will in the North; but the Quakers were the engine behind which such people rallied. Perhaps another section of the track was laid by the recognition that it was not enough to not own slaves; one must also help those who had escaped the institution. And still another section fell into place when it was understood that extending help to fugitive slaves was inadequate; if one believed truly in democratic/Christian ideals, one must actively encourage slaves to escape on their own. Still another section of track came into existence through the recognition that after slaves had been helped and encouraged to escape the Southern institution, provision must be made for their safety from slave catchers in the employ of their former masters, and that they must be offered an opportunity to begin new lives in the North, the Midwest and Canada.

The Underground Railroad began full operation in 1850, following passage of the Fugitive Slave Law by the United States Congress. Here was a fine piece of legislative machinery, one with the full weight of the Constitution behind it, compelling state officials and citizens alike to cooperate with slave catchers in returning fugitive slaves to their masters. Now there were two forces in operation on a single set of tracks. The inevitable collision of the forces of law and the forces of conscience posed agonizing dilemmas for all. Either the law or the moral force had to be overrun. The weight of constitutional authority was behind the Fugitive Slave Law; so ruled the United States Supreme Court, Justice Roger B. Taney writing, in *Dred Scott* v. *Sanford,* 1857. A slave was property and, as such, had no rights against his master's claims under the law. The response of the abolitionists to both the law and the decision was expressed in the popular anti-slavery song written by the Hutchinsons: "Get Off the Track." Hereafter there was entrenched and bitter opposition to the law, in the North, in the Border States, and in the Midwest. The battle between the two sides prefigured the issue, at least as Abraham Lincoln saw it, to be outlined in blood a few years later. Both were wars fought in part to save the nation's highest dream of itself.

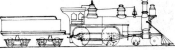

Every schoolchild knows by now the names of the chief engineers of the road: Frederick Douglass, William Lloyd Garrison, Thaddeus Stephens, Harriet Tubman. Most people are familiar with the extra fuel provided by Harriet Beecher Stowe's *Uncle Tom's Cabin.* American historians have rediscovered the slave narratives—the hundreds, perhaps thousands, of epic adventures recounted by fugitive slaves to audiences in the North. But unfamiliar to most people are the simple but highly principled letters and statements made by the many men and women who worked tirelessly during the 1850's and 1860's as agents, stationmasters and conductors along a vast network of human sympathy extending from the Southern states to the Border States and Ohio, from New England to Canada. Theirs are names not likely to be found in most scholarly accounts of the Railroad's operations. They were members of the Society of Friends in Philadelphia, members of the Vigilance Committees of New Bedford, Boston, Delaware City, Delaware. The names are sometimes unfamiliar: Sheridan Ford, E. F.

Pennypacker, Levi Coffin, Joseph C. Bustill, G. S. Nelson, W. M. Penn, Miss Theodocia Gilbert, Dr. J. C. Griscom, Dr. H. T. Childs, Mrs. H. S. Duterte, E. M. Davis, J. M. McKim, Professor C. D. Cleveland, Lewis Thompson, William Still, James Mott, Lucretia Mott, Passmore Williamson, Thomas Williamson, Edward Hopper, Rev. Hiram Wilson, Thomas Garrett, Samuel Rhodes, Rev. Thomas H. Kennard, Peter Lewis, Charles Gibson, William S. Pierce, William B. Berney, Sarah Pugh—and thousands of others beyond the reach now of recoverable history.

One white man named Seth Concklin, in 1851, went into Mississippi from Philadelphia to bring out a Negro family. He was captured with them en route to the Canadian border:

> RUNAWAY NEGROES CAUGHT—At Vincennes, Indiana, on Saturday last, a white man and four negroes were arrested. The negroes belong to B. McKiernon, of South Florence, Alabama, and the man who was running them off called himself John H. Miller. The prisoner was taken charge by the Marshall of Evansville.
>
> April 9, 1851

But news about "Miller" had already been forwarded to the Executive Committee of the Pennsylvania Anti-Slavery Society by a friend in Evansville:

> A report found its way into the papers to the effect that "Miller," the white man arrested in connection with the capture of the family, was found drowned, with his hands and feet in chains and his skull fractured. It proved, as his friends feared, to be Seth Concklin. And in irons, upon the river bank, there is no doubt he was buried . . . If curious to know your correspondent, I may say I was formerly Editor of the "New Concord Free Press," Ohio. I only add that every case of this kind only tends to make me abhor my (no!) *this* country more and more. It is the Devil's Government, and God will destroy it.
>
> Yours for the slave, N. R. Johnson

There were many Seth Concklins and N. R. Johnsons along the route of the Underground Railroad.

J. A. M.

ADVERTISEMENTS FOR ESCAPED SLAVES

$150 REWARD—Ran away from the subscriber, living near Upper Marlboro', Prince George's county, Md., on the 11th day of September, 1858, a negro man, "Nace," who calls himself "Nace Shaw;" is forty-five years of age, about five feet 8 or 9 inches high, of a copper color, full suit of hair, except a bald place upon the top of his head. He has a mother living in Washington city, on South B street, No. 212 Island.

I will pay the above reward no matter where taken, if secured in jail so that I get him again.
SARAH ANN TALBURTT.

RAN AWAY—On Saturday night, 20th inst., from the subscriber, living near Mount Airy P.O., Carroll county, two Negro men, PERRY and CHARLES. Perry is quite dark, full face; is about 5 feet 8 or 9 inches high; has a scar on one of his hands, and one on his legs, caused by a cut from a scythe; 25 years old. Charles is of a copper color, about 5 feet 9 or 10 inches high; round shouldered, with small whiskers; has one crooked finger that he cannot straighten, and a scar on his right leg, caused by the cut of a scythe;

22 years old. I will give two hundred and fifty dollars each, if taken in the State and returned to me, or secured in some jail so that I can get them again, or a $1,000 for the two, or $500 each, if taken out of the State, and secured in some jail in this State so that I can get them again.
ROBERT DADE.

One Hundred Dollars Reward.—Ran away from the subscriber, living in Rockville, Montgomery county, Md., on Saturday, 31st of May last,
NEGRO MAN, ALFRED,
about twenty-two years of age; five feet seven inches high; dark copper color, and rather good looking.

He had on when he left a dark blue and green plaid frock coat, of cloth, and lighter colored plaid pantaloons.

I will give the above reward if taken out of the county, and in any of the States, or fifty dollars if taken in the county or the District of Columbia, and secured so that I get him again.
John W. Anderson.

LETTERS TO WILLIAM STILL, CONDUCTOR ON THE UNDERGROUND RAILROAD

LETTER FROM S. H. GAY, ESQ., EX-EDITOR OF THE ANTI-SLAVERY STANDARD AND NEW YORK TRIBUNE.

FRIEND STILL:—The two women, Laura and Lizzy, arrived this morning. I shall forward them to Syracuse this afternoon.

The two men came safely yesterday, but went to Gibbs'. He has friends on board the boat who are on the lookout for fugitives, and send them, when found, to his house. Those whom you wish to be particularly under my charge, must have careful directions to this office.

There is now no other sure place, but the office, or Gibbs', that I could advise you to send such persons. Those to me, therefore, must come in office hours. In a few days, however, Napoleon will have a room down town and at odd times they can be sent there. I am not willing to put any more with the family where I have hitherto sometimes sent them.

When it is possible I wish you would advise me two days before a shipment of your intention, as Napoleon is not always on hand to look out for them at short notice. In special cases you might advise me by Telegraph, thus: "One M. (or one F.) this morning. W. S." By which I shall understand that one Male, or one Female, as the case may be, has left Phila. by the 6 o'clock train—one or more, also, as the case may be.

Aug. 17th, 1855.　　　Truly Yours, S. H. GAY.

TOPSHAM, VT., December 26th, 1855.

WM. STILL, MY DEAR FRIEND:—I wrote to you some two or three weeks ago, enclosing the letter to the care of a friend in Philadelphia, whom I wished to introduce to you. I have had no answer to that letter, and I am afraid you have not received it, or that you have written me, and I have not received yours. In that letter I wished to receive information respecting the best way to expend money for the aid of fugitives. Lest you may not have received it, I write you again though briefly. . . .

Mrs. Stowe makes Dred utter many a truth. Would that God would write it indelibly on the heart of the nation. But the people will not hear, and the cup of iniquity will soon fill to overflowing; and whose ears will not be made to tingle when the God of Sabaoth awakes to plead the cause of the dumb?

Yours, very sincerely,　　　N. R. JOHNSTON.

P.S. When I was in New York last Fall, October, I was in the Anti-Slavery office one day, when a friend in the office showed me a dispatch just received from Philadelphia, signed W. S., which gave notice of "six parcels" coming by the train, etc. And before I left the office the "parcels" came in, each on two legs. Strange parcels, that would run away on legs.

My heart leaped for joy at seeing these rescued ones. O that God would arise and break the yoke of oppression! Let us labor on and ever, until our work is done, until all are free.

Since the late Republican farce has closed I hope to get some more subscribers for the Standard. Honest men's eyes will be opened after a while, and the standard of right and expediency be elevated. Let us "hope on and ever."

Yours, for the right,　　　N. R. J.

LETTER FROM JOHN H. HILL, A FUGITIVE, APPEALING IN BEHALF OF A POOR SLAVE IN PETERSBURG, VA.

HAMILTON, Sept. 15th, 1856.

DEAR FRIEND STILL:—I write to inform you that Miss Mary Wever arrived safe in this city. You may imagine the happiness manifested on the part of the two lovers, Mr. H. and Miss W. I think they will be married as soon as they can get ready. I presume Mrs. Hill will commence to make up the articles to-morrow. Kind Sir, as all of us is concerned about the welfare of our enslaved brethren at the South, particularly our friends, we appeal to your sympathy to do whatever is in your power to save poor Willis Johnson from the hands of his cruel master. It is not for me to tell you of his case, because Miss Wever has related the matter fully to you. All I wish to say is this, I wish you to write to my uncle, at Petersburg, by our friend, the Capt. Tell my uncle to go to Richmond and ask my mother whereabouts this man is. The best for him is to make his way to Petersburg; that is, if you can get the Capt. to bring him. He have not much money. But I hope the friends of humanity will not withhold their aid on the account of money. However we will raise all the money that is wanting to pay for his safe delivery. You will please communicate this to the friends as soon as possible.

Yours truly,　　　JOHN H. HILL.

THE ANDREWS RAID

William Pittinger, a soldier from Ohio, took part in the "secret and very dangerous" mission which came to be known as the Andrews Raid, and a hundred years later to be filmed as *The Great Locomotive Chase*. It was April 8, 1862, the day following the battle of Shiloh. General Mitchel has just taken Huntsville, Alabama, and sent a detachment west over the Memphis & Charleston Railroad to open communications with the Union Army at Shiloh (Pittsburg Landing), and moved the rest of his army by rail to within 30 miles of Chattanooga. Pittinger tells what happened then:

The soldiers for this expedition, of whom the writer was one, were selected from the three Ohio regiments belonging to General J. W. Sill's brigade, being simply told that they were wanted for secret and very dangerous service. So far as known, not a man chosen declined the perilous honor. Our uniforms were exchanged for ordinary Southern dress, and all arms, except revolvers, were left in camp. On the 7th of April, by the roadside about a mile east of Shelbyville, in the late twilight, we met our leader. Taking us a little way from the road, he quietly placed before us the outlines of the romantic and adventurous plan, which was: to break into small detachments of three or four, journey eastward into the mountains, and then work southward, traveling by rail after we were well within the Confederate lines, and finally meet Andrews at Marietta, Georgia, more than 200 miles away, the evening of the third day after the start. When questioned, we were to profess ourselves Kentuckians going to join the Southern army.

On the journey we were a good deal annoyed by the swollen streams and the muddy roads consequent on three days of almost ceaseless rain. Andrews was led to believe that Mitchel's column would be inevitably delayed; and as we were expected to destroy the bridges the very day that Huntsville was entered, he took the responsibility of sending word to our different groups that our attempt would be postponed one day—from Friday to Saturday, April 12th. This was a natural but a most lamentable error of judgment.

One of the men was belated and did not join us at all. Two others were very soon captured by the enemy; and though their true character was not detected, they were forced into the Southern army, and two, who reached Marietta, failed to report at the rendezvous. Thus, when we assembled, very early in the morning, in Andrews' room at the Marietta Hotel for final consultation before the blow was struck, we were but twenty. . . .

But Andrews declared his purpose to succeed or die, offering to each man, however, the privilege of withdrawing from the attempt—an offer no one was in the least disposed to accept. Final instructions were then given, and we hurried to the ticket office in time for the northward-bound mail train, and purchased tickets for different stations along the line in the direction of Chattanooga.

Our ride as passengers was but eight miles. We swept swiftly around the base of Kenesaw Mountain, and soon saw the tents of the forces camped at Big Shanty (now Kenesaw Station) gleam white in the morning mist. Here we were to stop for breakfast and attempt the seizure of the train. The morning was raw and gloomy, and a rain, which fell all day, had already begun. It was a painfully thrilling moment! We were but twenty, with an army about us and a long and difficult road before us crowded with enemies. In an instant we were to throw off the disguise which had been our only protection, and trust our leader's genius and our own efforts for safety and success. . . .

When we stopped, the conductor, engineer, and many of the passengers hurried to breakfast, leaving the train unguarded. Now was the moment of action! Ascertaining that there was nothing to prevent a rapid start, Andrews, our two engineers, Brown and Knight, and the fireman hurried forward, uncoupling a section of the train consisting of three empty baggage or box cars, the locomotive and tender. The engineer and fireman sprang into the cab of the engine, while Andrews, with hand on the rail and foot on the step, waited to see that the remainder of the band had gained entrance into the rear box car. This seemed difficult and slow, though it really consumed but a few seconds, for the car stood on a considerable bank, and the first who came were pitched in by their comrades, while these, in turn, dragged in the others, and the door was instantly closed. A sentinel, with musket in hand, stood not a dozen feet from the engine watching the whole proceeding, but before he or any of the soldiers and guards around could make up their minds to interfere, all was done, and Andrews, with a nod to his engineer, stepped on board. The valve was pulled wide open, and for a moment the wheels of the "General" slipped around ineffectively; then, with a bound that jerked the soldiers in the box car from their feet, the little train darted away, leaving the camp and station in the wildest uproar of confusion. The first step of the enterprise was triumphantly accomplished.

According to the time-table, of which Andrews had secured a copy, there were two trains to be met. These presented no serious hindrance to our attaining high speed, for we could tell just where to expect them. There was also a local freight not down on the time-table, but which could not be far distant. Any danger of collision with it could be avoided by running according to the schedule of the captured train until it was passed; then, at the highest possible speed, we would run to the Oostenaula and Chickamauga bridges, lay them in ashes, and pass on through Chattanooga to Mitchel, at Huntsville, or wherever eastward of that point he might be found, arriving long before the close of the day. It was a brilliant prospect, and, so far as human estimates can determine, it would have been realized had the day been Friday instead of Saturday. On Friday every train had been on time, the day dry, and the road in perfect order. Now the road was in disorder, every train far behind time, and two "extras" were approaching us. But of these unfavorable conditions we knew nothing, and pressed confidently forward.

We stopped frequently, at one point tore up the track, cut telegraph wires, and loaded on crossties to be used in bridge burning. . . .

At Etowah Station we found the "Yonah," an old locomotive owned by an iron company, standing with steam up; but not wishing to alarm the enemy till the local freight had been safely met, we left it unharmed. Kingston,

thirty miles from the starting-point, was safely reached. A train from Rome, Ga., on a branch road, had just arrived and was waiting for the morning mail—our train. We learned that the local freight would soon come also, and taking the side track, waited for it. When it arrived, however, Andrews saw to his surprise and chagrin that it bore a red flag, indicating another train not far behind. Stepping to the conductor, he boldly asked, "What does it mean that the road is blocked in this manner when I have orders to take this powder to Beauregard without a minute's delay?" The answer was interesting but not reassuring: "Mitchel has captured Huntsville and is said to be coming to Chattanooga, and we are getting everything out of there." He was asked by Andrews to pull his train a long way down the track out of the way, and promptly obeyed.

It seemed an exceedingly long time before the expected "extra" arrived; and when it did come it bore another red flag! The reason given was that the "local," being too great for

A Civil War contribution to the uses of railroads in wartime was the development of railborne mortars like this one employed by the Union in the Virginia campaigns.—*Courtesy of Southern Railway System*

one engine, had been made up in two sections, and the second section would doubtless be along in a short time. This was terribly vexatious; yet there seemed nothing to do but wait. To start out between the sections of an extra train would be to court destruction. There were already three trains around us, and their many passengers, and others, were growing very curious about the mysterious train which had arrived on the time of the morning mail, manned by strangers. For an hour and five minutes from the time of arrival at Kingston, we remained in the most critical position. The sixteen of us who were shut up tightly in a box car, personating Beauregard's ammunition—hearing sounds outside, but unable to distin-

could run! Finding a hand-car they mounted it and pushed forward till they neared Etowah, where they ran on the break we had made in the road and were precipitated down the embankment into the ditch. Continuing with more caution, they reached Etowah and found the "Yonah," which was at once pressed into

The Richmond, Virginia, railyards in ruins, 1865.—*Courtesy of Southern Railway System*

guish words—had perhaps the most trying position. Andrews sent us, by one of the engineers, a cautious warning to be ready to fight in case the uneasiness of the crowd around led them to make any investigations, while he himself kept near the station to prevent the sending off of any alarming telegram. So intolerable was our suspense that the order for a deadly conflict would have been felt as a relief. But the assurance of Andrews quieted the crowd until the whistle of the expected train from the north was heard; then, as it glided up to the depot, past the end of our side track, we were off without more words.

But unexpected danger had arisen behind us. Out of the panic at Big Shanty two men emerged, determined, if possible, to foil the unknown captors of their train. There was no telegraph station, and no locomotive at hand with which to follow; but the conductor of the train, W. A. Fuller, and Anthony Murphy, foreman of the Atlanta railway machine shops, who happened to be on board of Fuller's train, started on foot after us as hard as they

service, loaded with soldiers who were at hand, and hurried with flying wheels towards Kingston. Fuller prepared to fight at that point, for he knew of the tangle of extra trains, and of the lateness of the regular trains, and did not think we would be able to pass. We had been gone only four minutes when he arrived and found himself stopped by three long, heavy trains of cars headed in the wrong direction. To move them out of the way so as to pass would cause a delay he was little inclined to afford—would indeed have almost certainly given us the victory. So, abandoning his engine, he, with Murphy, ran across to the Rome train, and, uncoupling the engine and one car, pushed forward with about forty armed men. As the Rome branch connected with the main road above the depot, he encountered no hindrance, and it was now a fair race. We were not many minutes ahead.

Four miles from Kingston we again stopped and cut the telegraph. While trying to take up a rail at this point, we were greatly startled. One of the rails was loosened and eight of us were pulling at it, when distant, but distinct, we heard the whistle of a pursuing engine! With a frantic pull we broke the rail and all tumbled over the embankment with the effort. We moved on, and at Adairsville we found a mixed train (freight and passenger) waiting, but there was an express on the road that had not yet arrived. We could afford no more delay, and set out for the next station, Calhoun, at terrible speed, hoping to reach that point before the express, which was behind time, should arrive. The nine miles which we had to travel were left behind in less than the same number of minutes! The express was just pulling out, but, hearing our whistle, backed before us until we were able to take the side track; it stopped, however, in such a manner as completely to close up the other end of the switch. The two trains, side by side, almost touched each other, and our precipitate arrival caused natural suspicion. Many searching questions were asked which had to be answered before we could get the opportunity of proceeding. We, in the box car, could hear the altercation and were almost sure that a fight would be necessary before the conductor would consent to "pull up" in order to let us out. Here, again, our position was most critical, for the pursuers were rapidly approaching.

Fuller and Murphy saw the obstruction of the broken rail, in time to prevent [a] wreck, by reversing their engine; but the hindrance was for the present insuperable. Leaving all their men behind, they started for a second foot-race. Before they had gone far they met the train we had passed at Adairsville and turned it back after us. At Adairsville they dropped the cars, and, with locomotive and tender loaded with armed men, they drove forward at the highest speed possible. They knew that we were not many minutes ahead, and trusted to overhaul us before the express train could be safely passed.

But Andrews had told the powder story again, with all his skill, and had added a direct request in peremptory form to have the way opened before him, which the Confederate conductor did not see fit to resist; and just before the pursuers arrived at Calhoun we were again under way. Stopping once more to cut wires and tear up the track, we felt a thrill of exhilaration to which we had long been strangers. The track was now clear before us to Chattanooga; and even west of that city we had good reason to believe that we would find no other train in the way till we had reached Mitchel's lines. If one rail could now be lifted we would be in a few minutes at Oostenaula bridge, and, that burned, the rest of the task would be little more than simple manual labor, with the enemy absolutely powerless. We worked with a will.

But in a moment the tables were turned! Not far behind we heard the scream of a locomotive bearing down upon us at lightning speed! The men on board were in plain sight and well armed! Two minutes—perhaps one—would have removed the rail at which we were toiling; then the game would have been in our own hands, for there was no other locomotive beyond that could be turned back after us. But the most desperate efforts were in vain. The rail was simply bent, and we hurried to our engine and darted away, while remorselessly after us thundered the enemy.

Now the contestants were in clear view, and a most exciting race followed. Wishing to gain a little time for the burning of the Oostenaula bridge, we dropped one car, and shortly after, another; but they were "picked up" and pushed ahead to Resaca station. We were obliged to run over the high trestles and covered bridge at the point without a pause. This was the first failure in the work assigned us.

The Confederates could not overtake and stop us on the road, but their aim was to keep close behind so that we might not be able to damage the road or take in wood or water. In the former they succeeded, but not the latter. Both engines were put at the highest rate of speed. We were obliged to cut the wire after every station passed, in order that an alarm might not be sent ahead, and we constantly strove to throw our pursuer off the track or to obstruct the road permanently in some way so that we might be able to burn the Chickamauga bridges, still ahead. The chances seemed good that Fuller and Murphy would be wrecked. We broke out the end of our last box car and dropped cross-ties on the track as we

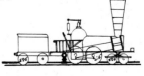

ran, thus checking their progress and getting far enough ahead to take in wood and water at two separate stations. Several times we almost lifted a rail, but each time the coming of the Confederates, within rifle range, compelled us to desist and speed on. Our worst hindrance was the rain. The previous day (Friday) had been clear, with a high wind, and on such a day fire would have been easily and tremendously effective. But today a bridge could be burned only with abundance of fuel and careful nursing.

Thus we sped on, mile after mile, in this fearful chase, around curves and past stations in seemingly endless perspective. . . .

•We made no attempt to damage the long tunnel north of Dalton, as our enemies had greatly dreaded. The last hope of the raid was now staked upon an effort of a different kind. A few more obstructions were dropped on the track and our speed was increased so that we soon forged a considerable distance ahead. The side and end boards of the last car were torn into shreds, all available fuel was piled upon it, and blazing brands were brought back from the engine. By the time we approached a long covered bridge the fire in the car was fairly started. We uncoupled it in the middle of the bridge, and with painful suspense awaited the issue. Oh, for a few minutes till the work of conflagration was fairly begun! There was still steam-pressure enough in our boiler to carry us to the next wood-yard, where we could have replenished our fuel, by force if necessary, so as to run us as near to Chattanooga as was deemed prudent. We did not know of the telegraph message which the pursuers had sent ahead. But, alas! the minutes were not given. Before the bridge was extensively fired the enemy was upon us. They pushed right into the smoke and drove the burning car before them to the next side-track.

With no car left, and no fuel, the last scrap having been thrown into the engine or upon the burning car, and with no obstruction to drop on the track, our situation was indeed desperate.

But it might still be possible to save ourselves if we left the train in a body and took a direct course toward the Union lines. Confederate pursuers with whom I have since conversed have agreed on two points—that we could have escaped in the manner here pointed out; and that an attack on the pursuing train would likely have been successful. But Andrews thought otherwise, at least in relation to the former plan, and ordered us to jump from the locomotive, and, dispersing in the woods, each endeavored to save himself.

The question is often asked, "Why did you not reverse your engine and thus wreck the one following?" Wanton injury was no part of our plan, and we could not afford to throw away our engine till the last extremity. When the raiders were jumping off, however, the engine was reversed and driven back, but by that time the steam was so nearly exhausted that the Confederate engine had no difficulty in reversing and receiving the shock without injury. Both were soon at a stand-still, and the Confederates, reinforced by a party from a train which soon arrived on the scene—the express passenger, which had been turned back at Calhoun—continued the chase on foot.

It is easy now to understand why Mitchel paused thirty miles west of Chattanooga. The Andrews raiders had been forced to stop eighteen miles south of the same town, and no flying train met Mitchel with tidings that all the railroad communications of Chattanooga were destroyed, and that the town was in a panic and undefended.

A few words will give the sequel to this remarkable enterprise. The hunt for the fugitive raiders was prompt, energetic, and successful. Several were captured the same day, and all but two within a week. Even these two were overtaken and brought back, when they supposed that they were virtually out of danger. Two who had reached Marietta but had failed to board the train . . . were identified and added to the band of prisoners.

Now follows the saddest part of the story. Being in citizens' dress within an enemy's lines, the whole party were held as spies. A court-martial was convened, and the leader and seven out of the remaining twenty-one were condemned and executed. The others were never brought to trial, probably because of the advance of Union forces and the consequent confusion into which the affairs of the Departments of East Tennessee and Georgia were thrown. Of the remaining fourteen, eight succeeded, by a bold effort—attacking their guard in broad daylight—in making their escape from Atlanta, Ga., and ultimately in reaching the North. The other six, who shared in this effort, but were recaptured, remained prisoners until the latter part of March, 1863, when they were exchanged through a special arrangement made by Secretary Stanton. All the survivors of this expedition received medals and promotion. The pursuers also received expressions of gratitude from their fellow Confederates, notably from the Governor and Legislature of Georgia.

THE DRINKING GOURD

"The Drinking Gourd" is one of the Negro slave songs with more meaning than the overseers caught. It contains explicit directions to the place where the old white man with a wooden leg waits to lead escaping slaves to the first station of the Underground Railroad. "The drinking gourd" is the big dipper, with its handle pointing north.

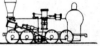

When the sun comes back and the first quail calls,
Follow the drinking gourd,
For the old man is waiting for to carry you to freedom
If you follow the drinking gourd.

Refrain: Follow the drinking gourd,
      Follow the drinking gourd,
      For the old man is waiting for to carry you to freedom
      If you follow the drinking gourd.

The river bank will make a very good road,
The dead trees show you the way,
Left foot, peg foot travelling on,
Following the drinking gourd.

The river ends between two hills,
Follow the drinking gourd.
There's another river on the other side,
Follow the drinking gourd.

Where the great big river meets the little river,
Follow the drinking gourd.
The old man is a-waiting for to carry you to freedom,
If you follow the drinking gourd.

SIDETRACK THE DEPOTS

The Poplar Bluff, Missouri depot, built about 1910. Note the tire tracks on the unpaved road.—*Courtesy of St. Louis-San Francisco Railway Co.*

A., T. and S. Fe Depot, Topeka, Ks., 1880. J R Riddle Phot

—*Photo courtesy of Santa Fe Railway*

Depots didn't come into existence with the railroad. Stagecoaches stopped at wayside stations where passengers could rest and get something to eat. In the East, as in Europe, the travelers' inns offered a place to sleep for the night, and sometimes entertainment. Even in Chaucer's day, a traveler could find wayside rest and hospitality.

Changes in the means of locomotion meant little to the keepers of way stations. There was very little about a railroad depot that would make a stagecoach passenger feel that he'd got off at the wrong stop. There were only the sounds of the engines and, in the depots remembered best, the telegrapher's key that talked to trains and stations up and down the track in that mesmerizing *click-click* that meant something important was being said.

Southern R. R. Station, Macon, Ga.

Southern Railroad Station in Macon, Georgia. No date is given, but the bus at the right of the picture and the attire of the woman place it shortly before World War I. The building dates from the 1880's.—*Courtesy of Southern Railway System*

Atlanta, Georgia. The architectural style was popular in the 1850's and again in the 1920's, when this building was constructed.—*Courtesy of Southern Railway System*

Amtrak's Blue Ridge at Harper's Ferry, West Virginia.— *Photo courtesy of Amtrak*

Asheville, North Carolina—1890.—*Courtesy of Southern Railway System*

The Little Rock, Arkansas, Union Station, built in 1906.— *Courtesy of Missouri Pacific Railroad.*

PAYDAY HUSSEY'S CAMP B.B.&B. R.R.

THE MOVE WEST
1865-1900

**There is more poetry in the rush of a single
railroad train across the continent than in
all the gory story of burning Troy . . .**

— Joaquin Miller

CRAZY JUDAH

Theodore Dehone Judah was a brilliant twenty-eight-year-old engineer filled with strong opinions and impatience when he left New England and took himself West in 1859. He had been engaged to build the first railroad in California, from Sacramento to Folsom, and he did that quickly and well, but his imagination was caught almost at once by the idea of a rail line that would run from the Pacific to the Atlantic, joining the nation together.

Although there were many who thought he was crazy and said so, he took ads in papers and gave speeches until he roused the interest surveyed the first part of the route at his own expense. In a moment of exultation, bending over a store counter in Dutch Flat, he wrote "The Articles of Association of The Central Pacific Railroad of California."

He continued to harp on his plan to anyone who would listen, and found four men who did listen, but for the wrong reason—one he deliberately gave them. Charley Crocker (a dry-goods merchant), Leland Stanford (a wholesale grocer) and two partners in a hardware store (Mark Hopkins and Collis P. Huntington) backed Judah with enough capital to incorporate, on the assumption that the road was to be

This track gang and a friend posed for a picture somewhere on the LaCrosse Division of the old Burlington line.—*Photo courtesy of Burlington Northern*

and support of enough men to justify a trip in 1859 to Washington to sell the idea to Congress. Unfortunately, as Judah was trying to tie the nation together, it was about to fall apart, and the attention of Congress was on the rising conflict between the North and South.

Judah returned to California more determined than ever to see his plan through and simply a quick-profit venture to carry passengers and freight between Sacramento and the silver boom towns of Nevada. Judah carefully planted that assumption as bait for profiteers whom he never expected to share his vision.

Judah set to work on the line immediately, carrying the tracks into the Sierras as fast as the spring thaw would allow him to move, and worked until he had to yield the mountains over to the coming winter. Then he went back to Washington to lobby for the Pacific Railroad bill. President Lincoln signed the bill on July 1, 1862, calling for the Union Pacific—incorporated by the same bill—and the Central Pacific to build toward one another, to meet at or near the California border, and to lay a telegraph line as they went. Included in the bill were loans to the companies of up to $48,000 per mile of track laid, and grants of 10 miles of land alongside the tracks.

The fact that no government money was to be made available until 40 miles of track had been laid meant to Judah's four partners that this section should be laid as quickly and cheaply as possible. Judah—just back from Washington, filled now with a sense of victory and feeling that his dream was about to be realized—insisted that every mile of track be laid with care, to be safe and to last. He had his mind on the meeting of the rails at the state line; his partners had their minds on the silver cities in Nevada, the passenger traffic and especially the freight. They remembered the gold rush of '49, and knew that booms don't

last. They meant to grab what there was to be had and move on to other investments. Judah said no, and tried to persuade the four to his vision, but in the end saw that there was no way to turn their minds from profit. They bought him out, and he headed again for Washington—probably to raise money to buy the line back from his ex-partners—but he contracted yellow fever on his trip around the Horn, and died of it a few days after landing in New York, at the age of thirty-seven.

The intercontinental railroad was laid, finally, and Crocker, Stanford, Hopkins and Huntington grew famous, rich and, of course, powerful. Judah was forgotten until 1923, when the workers on his railroad—now the Southern Pacific—pooled their money to raise a monument to him in Sacramento. Except for the few who stop to look at the monument, he is still almost forgotten.

M. W.

THE ENGINEERS WHO RODE AHEAD OF THE RAILS

The engineers who rode ahead of the rails on horseback with canteens and rifles and blankets were tough men and no mean mathematicians.

From triangle BVM,

$$m = f \cosin F, \quad \text{and} \quad n = f \sin F. \qquad (a)$$

In formula (207) h = actual heel distance − thickness of switch-rail point.

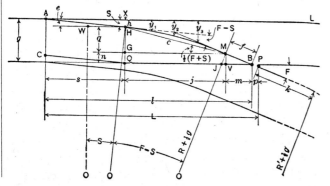

In triangle MGH, $q = g - h - n$, and

$$HM = c = q \operatorname{cosec} \tfrac{1}{2}(F + S) = \frac{q}{\sin \tfrac{1}{2}(F + S)}. \qquad (b)$$

Also,

$$GM = j = q \operatorname{cotan} \tfrac{1}{2}(F + S) = \frac{q}{\tan \tfrac{1}{2}(F + S)}. \qquad (c)$$

From triangle HMO,

$$R + \tfrac{1}{2}g = \frac{c}{2 \sin \tfrac{1}{2}(F - S)} = \tfrac{1}{2}c \operatorname{cosec} \tfrac{1}{2}(F - S). \quad (208)$$

At the frog-point,

$$p = \frac{\tfrac{1}{2}w'}{\sin \tfrac{1}{2}F} = \tfrac{1}{2}w' \operatorname{cosec} \tfrac{1}{2}F. \qquad (d)$$

From the figure,

$$l = s + j + m, \quad \text{and} \quad L = s + j + m + p. \quad (209)$$

In the formulas for c and q, g and h must be reduced by the thickness of switch-rail point before solving.

57

THE HELL-BOUND TRAIN

A Tex - as cow-boy on a bar - room floor Had drank ___ so much he could hold no ___ more.

A Texas cowboy on a barroom floor
Had drank so much he could hold no more.

He fell asleep with a troubled brain
To dream he rode on the Hell-bound train.

The engine with murderous blood was damp
And the headlight was a big brimstone lamp.

The imps for fuel were shoveling bones
And the furnace rang with a thousand groans.

The boiler was filled full of lager beer
And the Devil himself was the engineer.

The passengers they were a mixed-up crew,
Church member, atheist, Gentile, and Jew.

There were rich men in broadcloth and poor in
rags,
Handsome girls and wrinkled hags.

With red men, yellow men, black, and white,
All chained togther, a fearful sight.

The train rushed on at an awful pace,
The sulphurous fumes scorched their hands and
face.

Faster and faster the engine flew,
And wilder and wilder the country grew.

Brighter and brighter the lightning flashed,
And louder and louder the thunder crashed.

Hotter and hotter the air became
Till the clothes were burned from each shrinking
frame.

Then out of the distance there rose a yell:
"Ha, ha," said the Devil, "the next stop is Hell."

Then oh, how the passengers shrieked with pain
And begged the Devil to stop the train.

But he capered about and danced with glee
And he laughed and mocked at their misery.

"My friends, you have paid for your seats on this
road,
The train goes through with a complete load.

"You've bullied the weak, you've cheated the
poor,
The starving brother turned from your door.

"You've laid up gold till your purses bust
And given free play to your beastly lusts.

"The laborer always expects his hire,
So I'll land you safe in a lake of fire.

"Your flesh will scorch in the flames that roar,
My imps torment you forevermore."

Then the cowboy awoke with an anguished cry,
His clothes were wet and his hair stood high.

He prayed as he'd never prayed before
To be saved from Hell's front door.

His prayers and pleadings were not in vain,
For he never rode on the Hell-bound train.

Construction crews sometimes lived in traveling bunkhouses. This crew is accompanied on a St. Paul, Minneapolis and Manitoba construction train by federal troops.—*Photo courtesy of Burlington Northern*

MULE SKINNER BLUES

Well, I like to work, I'm rolling all the time;
Yes, I like to work, I'm rolling all the time;
I can carve my initials right on a mule's behind.

Well, it's hey, little water boy, bring your water
'round,
And it's hey, little water boy, bring your water
'round;
If you don't like your job, set that water bucket
down.

I'm a-workin' on that new road at a dollar and a
dime a day,
Workin' on that new road—dollar and a dime a
day;

I got three women waitin' on a Saturday night
just to draw my pay.

Good morning, Captain—Good morning, Shine;
That there mule skinner didn't know that mule
was mine.

Workin' on the railroad, makin' a dollar and a
quarter a day;
Gals in town on Saturday night, they spend my
little pay.

Workin' on the railroad—dollar and a dime a day;
Give my woman the dollar and throw the dime
away.

THE UNKNOWN BANDITS: EVANS AND SONTAG

Of all the outlaws and desperadoes whose legends have contributed to the color of the American West, perhaps none have been more neglected than Christopher Evans and John Sontag. Like the James Gang and the Daltons, they were associated with train robberies; but unlike the James and Dalton legends, few stories of their exploits have survived.

Evans and Sontag were accused of executing five successful train robberies, and killing several men, between 1889 and 1891 in the San Joaquin Valley of northern California. They were never convicted of any robbery, but for a period of about two years the two men held the attention of a posse numbering in the thousands, as well as Wells, Fargo Company, the Southern Pacific Railroad, the residents of San Francisco and some of the ablest writers on William Randolph Hearst's San Francisco *Examiner,* including Ambrose Bierce and Joaquin Miller. They were at the center of one of the greatest and most colorful manhunts in California history, and when it was over they claimed a following of sympathizers throughout the state.

Like most other people in California, Evans and Sontag were migrants from other areas of the country. Christopher Evans was born in 1847, near Ottawa, Canada, of Irish-German descent. At sixteen, in 1863, he crossed the American border and enlisted in the Union Army. After the Civil War he joined the United States cavalry and served as a scout under General George Armstrong Custer in actions against the Sioux in Minnesota and Dakota. After ten years as a scout, and shortly before Custer's last command at the Little Big Horn, Evans quit the cavalry and followed the Union Pacific tracks westward to California. He married, worked at a variety of jobs and settled on a small ranch at Visalia, in the San Joaquin Valley. Evans was a small, wiry man with brown-red hair and intense gray-green eyes. He was a man of action as well as a man of thought: he could shoot from the hip and quote from memory long passages from Sir Walter Scott, Swinburne, Tennyson and Shakespeare. He loved poetry and nature and the Sierra Nevadas.

John Sontag came to California from Minnesota. He was born John Contant, of Dutch-German background, in either Missouri or Connecticut. He, too, followed the Union Pacific tracks westward, finding employment in Fresno as a brakeman for the Southern Pacific. Sontag was small of frame, with dark-blue eyes and deep-black hair and beard. He was said to be very handsome, although in poor health because of a missing lung damaged while working in the Fresno yards. The lung had been removed at the Southern Pacific hospital at Sacramento; Sontag, it is said, was embittered by both the inadequate medical treatment he had received and the company's lack of concern for his welfare— Southern Pacific refused to give him an easier job after his injury. Sontag quit the Southern Pacific and moved to Visalia, where he met and was hired by Christopher Evans. The two men became close companions, and Sontag, twenty-five, developed an affection for Evans' older daughter, Eve.

Few poor people in California held a good opinion of the Southern Pacific Railroad, and not just because it held a monopoly on most

Chris Evans.—*Photo courtesy of Danforth Library, Berkeley*

The two lines racing to meet at Promonotory Point set up similar and highly systematized plans of construction. The surveyors were followed a hundred miles back by the graders, and a hundred miles farther back were the track layers. The military discipline became more than a matter of form when Indian attacks had to be fought off by half the workers while the other half worked.

Cheyenne and Laramie are two of several towns that began as temporary terminal points. These sites at track's end were notorious as "Hell on Wheels" where the men tried to forget weeks of hard labor and strict discipline.—*Union Pacific Railroad Museum Collection*

transportation in the state. the people who poured into California in the years following the Civil War were mostly Southerners, many from the mountains of Tennessee. They openly resented Charles Crocker, Leland Stanford, Mark Hopkins and Collis P. Huntington, "the Big Four" of the Southern Pacific, who, besides being Yankees, had great influence in state and national politics. Concurrent with this sectional bitterness was the resentment of many settlers and farmers in the San Joaquin Valley toward the discriminatory rates for short hauls charged by the Southern Pacific. The railroad increased its rates just before harvest time and lowered them again just after the harvest had been shipped out, thus justifying, at least on paper, its claim to the Railroad Commission that the average rate for yearly service to farmers in the Valley was low. Besides this, the Southern Pacific required that all freight shipped in from the East be billed to San Francisco or other large cities and not to the smaller towns. This practice required struggling farmers to pay for the unloading of their goods, storage fees, reloading fees, and high short-haul rates from the cities to the nearest small town. These specific resentments, together with the land policies of the Southern Pacific, contributed directly to a bloody confrontation between agents of the company and a group of farmers at Mussel Slough in the San Joaquin Valley.

On May 11, 1880, several U.S. marshals broke up a meeting of farmers at Mussel Slough. A settler fired the first shot. When the smoke cleared, eight men lay dead. Forty settlers were arrested and charged with conspiracy and resisting a federal officer. Of the forty settlers, five were found guilty and sentenced to eight months in jail. Public sentiment was polarized in their favor: the jailers treated them royally, a group of four hundred church members called on them, and sympathetic letters, cables and telegrams poured in from the East and from Europe. Public sentiment was ripe for the emergence of a heroic figure, one following the example set years earlier by the James Gang in Missouri.

On February 22, 1889, a Southern Pacific train was halted in the San Joaquin Valley and robbed by two masked men. The robbery was well executed: the men seemed to know exactly where the money was. They shot and killed one crewman who attempted to stop them, and escaped into the Sierras. On January 20, 1890, a second robbery, this time outside of Goshen, was executed by the same two men. And on February 6, 1891, two men, said to be the same pair, robbed a Southern Pacific train at Alila, killing a fireman and escaping into the Sierras. There followed a fourth robbery at Ceres on September 3 of that same year, and a fifth at Collis in early August of 1892. All descriptions pointed to the same two men, one short and one tall, both apparently at home in the Sierras. In late 1892 official suspicion began to focus on Christopher Evans and John Sontag.

Both men lived with Evans' family, which by this time included seven children. Evans was known to be a devoted father who placed great value on family life. He was particularly affectionate toward his daughter Eve, who happened to answer the door when George

Wells, Fargo and Southern Pacific posted the conditions of the hunt:

Whereas said Wells, Fargo and Southern Pacific have heretofore offered large rewards for the arrest and conviction of any of the parties named in the above named robberies; Now, therefore, the said rewards are hereby withdrawn and in lieu thereof the said companies do hereby

The first structure erected by the builders of Central Pacific when they started work at Sacramento in 1863 on the western link of the first transcontinental railroad.—*Southern Pacific photo*

Witty, a deputy sheriff, and Will Smith, a railroad detective, arrived to question Evans. When Eve refused to disclose her father's whereabouts, Smith, it was later claimed, called her a liar and pulled his gun. Evans and Sontag appeared from the back of the house, and as the lawmen retreated Evans wounded one of them in the leg and the other in the shoulder. Then he and Sontag commandeered the sheriff's buckboard and drove quickly away. They returned in the evening to collect supplies, only to meet a posse. In the ensuing gunfight they shot and killed Oscar Beaver, a local man out to collect the offered reward of "ten dollars and an oyster supper." Wounded themselves in the battle, the two men limped off toward the foothills of the Sierra Nevadas.

Thus began one of the most colorful manhunts in American history. Acting jointly,

jointly offer a reward of $10,000 for the arrest and delivery to the sheriffs of Fresno and Tulare Counties of said John Sontag and said Chris Evans, or $5,000 for the arrest and delivery to either of the said sheriffs of either John Sontag or Chris Evans [later changed to "dead or alive"]; the said rewards to be payable upon delivery. Signed, A.N. Towne, general manager of Southern Pacific, and E.M. Cooper, manager of Wells, Fargo & Company. September 6, 1892.

The bounty hunters began gathering in Visalia. United States Deputy Marshal Vernon C. "Vic" Wilson came in from Arizona to lead the posse. "I've got twenty-seven notches on my gun," he is reported to have said, "and I'm going into the mountains tomorrow and Evans and Sontag will make twenty-nine." He brought with him from Arizona two Apache trackers, Pelon and Jericho, a string of bloodhounds, and as many outside men as wanted to join the chase. There were many who did: in 1892 the country was going through a depression. During their search the badly organized mob shot at each other, terrorized innocent hunters, and so annoyed the settlers in the San Joaquin Valley as to polarize their sympathies toward Evans and Sontag.

The outlaws hid in the foothills of the Sierras for several weeks, relying on friendly mountain people to keep them posted about the movements of the posse. The mountaineers were Tennesseeans, clannish folk who did not trust any government authority. The outlaws were safe with them. But on September 13 they were surrounded by the posse while hiding in the cabin of a Tennesseean named Jim Young. In this battle Deputy George Witty and another man were killed, and Evans and Sontag were wounded; but they escaped again, moving further up the mountain to the cabin of another Tennesseean named Jane Downing. They settled into the Downing cabin for the winter while the frightened posse members went back to town.

The Battle of Young's Cabin, as it was called, attracted the attention of the newspapers. It was of special interest to William Randolph Hearst, publisher of the San Francisco *Examiner.* Hearst might not have admired the outlaws as much as he disliked "the Big Four" of the Southern Pacific. His father, George Hearst, had never gotten along with Leland Stanford. While George Hearst was a Missourian and a Democrat, Stanford was a Yankee and a Republican. When George Hearst went to the United States Senate as the Democratic senator from California, Leland Stanford went as a Republican. William Randolph Hearst inherited his father's policies. When California Governor Markham was pressured by Southern Pacific to call out the state militia to help in the search for Evans and Sontag, Hearst ordered his best writers to produce sympathetic articles on the two men. In those days the *Examiner* had a stable of very good writers: the acerbic Ambrose Bierce; Cincinnatus Hiner Miller, the local-color writer who called himself Joaquin Miller; Charles Michelson; Henry Bigelow; Edward Morphy; and Orren and Winifred Black. Most of these writers were hostile to the Southern Pacific; all wrote favorably of Evans and Sontag.

Henry Bigelow's story of October 7, 1892, describing an interview with the two outlaws, was accompanied by sketches of Evans posed nobly with his right hand grasping the barrel of a shotgun and holding a shell said to be from the cartridge with which Evans tried to kill a detective at Young's cabin. The story contained the outlaws' protestation of their innocence, their expressions of determination to remain in the Sierras all winter, and a warning that they had passed up many opportunities to ambush the posse in pursuit of them. Possibly aware of the interest in them, Evans cast himself and Sontag in the role of moral agents: ". . . we have never killed anyone except in self-defense. We are entirely guiltless of the train robbery and are thoroughly conscious of our innocence. As to the killing we have done, it seems to me it has been a pretty good riddance for this country of the so-called 'bad man.' Take Oscar Beaver. He killed 'Sheepman Kripe' near Lemoore in cold blood, and another time he shot a fellow in the Laurel Palace saloon in San Francisco. As for Andy McGinnis, he shot a young negro lad who was sleeping in a box car at Modesto and was con-

In a daring holdup of the treasure car of the Texas Central, patriotically staged on Washington's Birthday, 1878, masked miscreants made off with $2,000 in gold currency.—*New York Public Library Picture Collection*

A character scene in the emigrant waiting-room of the Union Pacific Depot at Omaha. Photocopy of wood engraving in Frank Leslie's Illustrated Newspaper, (1877).—*Library of Congress*

cerned in the whitecap business there. I never kept track of Vic Wilson's graveyard, but everybody always knew that he was terribly dangerous."

Ambrose Bierce accepted the outlaws' personal myth. "If there were brave men before Agamemnon," he wrote in the *Examiner,* "there is certainly none behind Chris Evans." In the weeks and months which followed, a series of stories by Joaquin Miller and others built up the reputations of the two men. There was speculation that they had left the mountains and escaped to South America, Italy, Hawaii. Joaquin Miller's romanticized and fictitious interview with Evans, "The Bard and the Bandit," presented a very sympathetic picture of Evans and his family.

On June 11, 1893, the two men were trapped again, this time by a posse under U.S. Marshal George E. Gard at Stone Corral, near Yettem, California. The men were in the open and the posse fired a hundred and thirty rounds at them. Sontag was shot through the chest and his remaining lung was pierced. Evans received bullet wounds in the back; three buckshots lodged in his skull; one shot tore out his right eye and left it dangling by an ocular muscle; another bullet shredded his left arm

below the elbow; his right arm received two bullets, one ripping his flesh from wrist to elbow and the other passing through. Unable to move, Sontag attempted to kill himself but succeeded only in grazing his scalp. He was taken alive by the posse. But Christopher Evans crawled away, eluding the posse and moving seven miles through the mountains to the cabin of some Tennesseeans named Perkins. From there he sent word down the mountain that he would surrender if his family received part of the reward money.

Several posses descended on the Perkins home and began fighting over the money, which by this time had increased to $11,200 due to an additional $1,200 offered by the State of California. Evans was taken back to Visalia, where his left arm was amputated. While he was awaiting trial the newspapers rallied around him. The *Examiner* sent out a reporter to trace the path of Evans' retreat through the mountains from Stone Corral to the Perkins cabin. A San Francisco playwright wrote and produced a melodrama about the outlaws, paying Evans' wife and daughter to act in it; the money was used to defray the outlaws' legal expenses. John Sontag died in jail before the trial. Evans was tried and found guilty of

64

1. Union Pacific construction crews in Nebraska.—*Photo courtesy of Kansas State Historical Society, Topeka*

2. The caboose served as office, bedroom and kitchen den for the train crews. This picture was taken shortly before the turn of the century. Note the antlers over the door.—*Courtesy of the State Historical Society of Colorado Library*

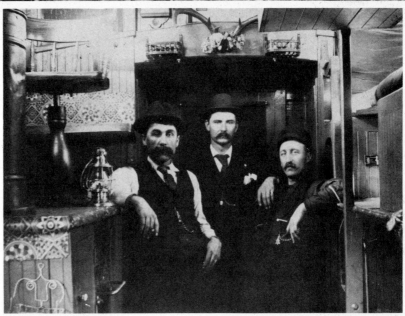

3. Survey engineers for the Denver & Rio Grande Junction Railway sit for a picture at their field camp.—*Courtesy of the State Historical Society of Colorado Library*

murder. He was not found guilty of the train robberies. On December 14, 1893, he was sentenced to life in Folsom Prison.

On December 28 Eve Evans slipped a gun to her father and he escaped. The newspapers resumed their speculations as to his whereabouts: he was back in the Sierras, in Petaluma, aboard a boat bound for Hawaii to marry Queen Liliuokalani. Evans, however, was hiding out with the Yakuts Indians up in the Sierras. On February 19, 1894, he returned to his home in Visalia, lured there by a false message of family illness sent by U.S. Marshal George Gard. He was captured, resentenced and put into Folsom Prison. An estimated two thousand people, 10 percent of the population of Fresno County, watched him board the train for Folsom Prison.

During his years in prison Christopher Evans became known as the Good Samaritan to his fellow inmates. He worked in the library and continued his reading, and wrote a utopian novel called *Eurasia*. It was published by the James H. Barry Company of San Francisco, in 1924, with the following preface:

> In *Eurasia* the author describes an ideal republic where many of the problems that confront us are worked out. The book describes in an interesting and readable way how government is administered in this ideal republic. The government is one in which women take their full share of responsibility, the school children are trained in the problems they will meet in life, and more emphasis is laid on character building than on the dead languages. The children of both sexes are taught useful trades. All school children are taught to swim. The idle are employed in the construction of roads, canals and irrigation works. The problems of distribution are so arranged that the worker receives a more equitable reward for his labor.

In Christopher Evans' *Eurasia* all areas of government are under the control of thirteen Ministers of State: Justice, Railways, Education, Finance, Information, Agriculture, Health, Commerce, Manufacturing, Mines, War, Foreign Affairs and Labor. The novel consists of interviews by the narrator with each of these Ministers. The Department of Information, headed by a woman, keeps watch on all public officials. The Department of Education, also run by a woman, operates free schools and "one great university for orphan children and those without a name, and from it all the departments of the government are supplied with secretaries, clerks, type-writers and messengers." The Department of Health looks after the physical, mental and moral welfare of the people. To be a doctor, a man has to be examined physically, mentally and morally. He has to answer certain questions: "Do you believe in the Brotherhood of Man? Will you do unto others always as you would desire that others should do unto you? Do you promise . . . to maintain the honor of the country?"

Beneath the simplicity of its language and ideas, Christopher Evans' *Eurasia*, which was written in Folsom Prison between 1894 and 1911, anticipated many of the major reforms that were later to be made in American society. It spoke of camps for poor young boys (C.C.C. camps during the Depression); a woman in a government post at the highest executive level (Frances Perkins); the income tax (legalized in 1913); universal military training, followed by education at government expense (the G.I. Bill); old-age pensions; the eight-hour day; accident insurance; collective bargaining; retirement of workers after age sixty. Christopher Evans may have been an outlaw, but he was also a man of vision.

In 1908 the reform-minded Lincoln-Roosevelt League was formed in California to chase the Southern Pacific out of the state's politics. In 1910 it helped Hiram Johnson become governor of California. Between 1904 and 1911 all of Evans' petitions for parole had been vetoed by California governors. They may have been vetoed because Evans had steadfastly refused to confess that he had robbed Southern Pacific trains. Among his first acts as governor was Hiram Johnson's pardon of Evans. He was released from Folsom Prison on May 1, 1911. He joined his family in Portland, Oregon, and died there in 1917.

Christopher Evans has seldom been compared to Jesse James.

J.A.M.

RAILROAD BILL

Chorus:

D
Railroad Bill, Railroad Bill,
              G
He never worked and he never will
        D   A7   D
I'm gonna ride old Railroad Bill.

Verses:

D
Railroad Bill he was a mighty mean man
                                  G
He shot the midnight lantern out the brakeman's
  hand
             D   A7   D
I'm going to ride old Railroad Bill.

Railroad Bill took my wife,
Said if I didn't like it, he would take my life,
I'm going to ride old Railroad Bill.

Going up on a mountain, going out west,
Thirty-eight special sticking out of my vest,
I'm going to ride old Railroad Bill.

Buy me a pistol just as long as my arm,
Kill everybody ever done me harm,
I'm going to ride old Railroad Bill.

I've got a thirty-eight special on a forty-five
  frame,
How in the world can I miss him when I got dead
  aim,
I'm going to ride old Railroad Bill.

Buy me a pistol just as long as my arm,
Kill everybody ever done me harm.
I'm going to ride old Railroad Bill.

Honey, honey, think I'm a fool,
Think I would quit you while the weather is cool,
I'm going to ride old Railroad Bill.

The transcontinental railroad dream is realized as Central Pacific's Jupiter touches Union Pacific's No. 119 in the Gold Spike Ceremony at Promontory, Utah, May 10, 1869. The men in the center shaking hands are the chief engineers of the two lines—Samuel Skerry Montague of Central Pacific on the left and General G.M. Dodge of Union Pacific—*Southern Pacific photo*

SIDETRACK REACHING

Over half a century passed between the chartering of the nation's first railroad and the laying of track from one coast to the other. It took only twelve more years to build a second transcontinental railroad, this one running through New Mexico to Southern California. Two years later a third connection was laid through St. Paul, Minnesota, to the Pacific Northwest.

Five more years, and the Southern route was completed between Chicago and California. Then five more, and the Great Lakes were linked to Puget Sound.

Between 1870 and 1890, 110,675 miles of road were added to the nation's rail system.

To stimulate the use of the rails, the railroads carried on a great promotional campaign to sell Easterners and new immigrants on the advantages of Western life. They were responsible, in great part, for the settling of the West.

The rail system reached its peak in 1916, when 254,000 miles of road tied the nation's towns and cities together. The system was gradually reduced to its present size as more and more highways were built and improved technology made possible an increasingly efficient use of the rails.

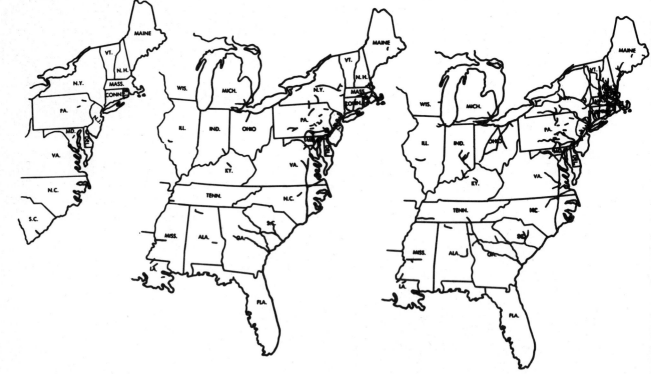

The early stages of railway development in America are shown by this set of maps. During the decade 1830-1840, the total length of completed railroad lines increased from 23 to 2,808 miles, and during the next ten years, more than 6,200 miles of railroad were opened, bringing the total network up to 9,021 miles in 1850. The most intensive growth during this period was in the Atlantic Seaboard states. In 1850, a trip from Boston or New York to Chicago was made by rail and lake steamers or by stagecoaches, and required several days. One could travel all the way from Boston to Wilmington, North Carolina, by rail, with several changes of cars and a few ferry trips en route. During the first twenty years of railway development, covered by these maps, the population of the United States nearly doubled.

—Courtesy of the Association of American Railroads

The decade 1850–60 was a period of rapid railway expansion, marked by the extension of many short lines. The nation's network increased to a total of 30,626 miles by 1860. — *The Association of American Railroads*

1890. The period of 1880–90 was one of rapid expansion. More than 70,300 miles of new lines brought the total network to 163,597 miles. — *The Association of American Railroads*

Although the Civil War temporarily halted railway development, many projects were resumed or initiated soon after the end of the conflict. The nation's network increased from 30,626 miles in 1860 to 52,922 miles in 1870. — *The Association of American Railroads*

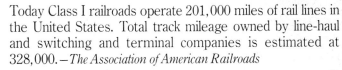

Today Class I railroads operate 201,000 miles of rail lines in the United States. Total track mileage owned by line-haul and switching and terminal companies is estimated at 328,000. — *The Association of American Railroads*

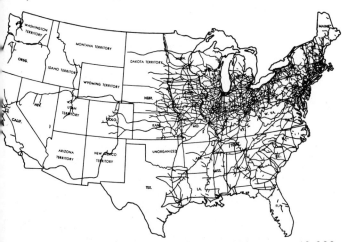

1880. In the ten-year period prior to 1880, some 40,000 miles of railroad were built, bringing the total network up to 93,267 miles. — *The Association of American Railroads*

PAYDAY HUSSEY'S CAMP BB RRR

BACK EAST AND DOWN SOUTH
1865-1900

Courtesy Library of Congress

I been workin' on the railroad
Just to pass the time away....

— *folk song*

HOW KATE SHELLEY SAVED
THE MIDNIGHT EXPRESS

The midnight coaches from the west
Plunged in the ripping rain;
West of Moingona ties were sound—
East was a broken train—
(East in the bite of Honey Creek)
In one drowned, "creaking" curl,
Lay ninety tons of twisted steel
Between them was a girl.

          —MacKinlay Kantor

Railroading can sometimes be colorless, fashioned by a repeated routine. But there are other times when the ever-present danger looms big and captures the stage. Those are times when tales of heroism stir the soul and become a part of our heritage. Such a tale—a true one—is the story of 15-year-old Kate Shelley, who through her own efforts saved from certain disaster a Chicago & North Western "Midnight Express" with 200 aboard.

Kate Shelley lived in Moingona, Iowa, a

Artist Karl Rittmann's impression of Kate's ordeal.—
*Courtesy Order of Railroad Conductors and Brakemen,
Cedar Rapids, Iowa*

coal-mining town near the banks of the Des Moines River. Her Irish father, a native of Tipperary, was a section foreman on the C&NW who died at an early age, leaving Kate to help her ailing mother run the family farm and care for the younger children.

Kate became the strong right arm of the family, doing the chores, sending the youngsters off to school, ploughing and harvesting. Her early maturity and independence of thought played a big part in the drama that was to change her life.

The oppressive tropical heat of July 6, 1881 in that section near Boone, Iowa gave hint of the trouble that was to come later. At noon, Mrs. Shelley observed to her family, "This heat will bring a bad storm by night." During the afternoon menacing clouds mounted the southwest sky. By late afternoon the sun had vanished.

Thunder muttered and the wind swelled. Kate hurried the children into the house. The first few raindrops soon gave way to a violent downpour. A hard midsummer storm was in full force.

A lecture manuscript, written by Kate herself, takes the eventful story from there:

"It was as dark as midnight. We watched the water come down in sheets until fright took possession of us. It drove us from the windows through which the lightning flashed dreadful pictures of destruction.

"There was no house near us save the little cottage of the old watchman at the entrance of the bridge, and if we were to have help, we must furnish it ourselves.

"Our slender stock, the cows and horses, driven by the storm, had taken refuge in the stable halfway down the slope. The pigs and chickens were housed in the same neighborhood, and we could see in the blinding flashes of lightning that Honey Creek was swollen to a torrent and growing in force and volume.

"The streams of water that washed down the hills behind us had poured into the house and through it and we saw that something must be done for the poor dumb beasts, and I made the effort to relieve them . . .

"Honey Creek was loaded with all kinds of burdens—picket fences, lumber, trees and stumps and rubbish swept down and heaped up against the piling of the bridge. The storm had raged from 6 o'clock to 11 p.m. when, in a lull, the rumble of a train was heard crossing the long bridge, slowly pulling out going east. It was the pusher obeying an order to cross and go to Boone."

Fearing for the safety of the bridges and track in the area, local C&NW officials had dispatched pusher engine number 11 with a crew of four to check the track. Engineer Ed Wood carefully picked his way along the flooded right-of-way. In the cab also were A. P. Olmsted, fireman, Adam Agar, brakeman, and Patrick Donohue, foreman. Wood stopped the engine at the Honey Creek bridge and, at a word from Donohue who indicated that everything looked safe, inched the engine onto the bridge.

Kate and her mother heard the engine. Her story continued: "I heard the bell toll twice distinctly as she swayed on the uprooted bridge, and then came the horrible crash and the fierce hissing of steam as tender and engine went down in 25 feet of water."

The shock of the crash left Kate and her mother dumb with fear, and then Kate thought of the Express which would soon come bearing down from the west—with no one to warn them.

The girl snatched her father's old railroad lantern, reassured her frantic mother, flung a jacket about herself, grabbed an old straw hat and was gone out into the raging tempest.

The Shelley dooryard ran kneedeep in swirling water. Kate scaled the slippery bluff behind the house, circled until she reached a wagon road and followed it to the tracks. Once on the tracks, she ran to the end of ruined Honey Creek bridge.

Fitful lightning showed Kate the forms of Engineer Wood and Brakeman Agar clinging to tree limbs. Water tugged at them and their shouts were lost in the roar of the torrent. The other two crewmen? Lost in the flood.

One mile away lay Moingona. The Des Moines River, now utterly berserk, stormed the high bridge. "Five hundred feet of bridging lay before me," continued Kate. "A misstep would send me down below the ties into the flood that was boiling there. The Des Moines River into which the hundred streams of its watershed had been pouring all that evening and night—each one swollen like Honey Creek—was a furious flood that had passed all bounds and covered all the lands about that were lower than the village, and was now straining hard at the bridge.

"It was loaded with all kinds of rubbish, even trees carried down by the landslides and swept away by the streams, the sod yet clinging to the roots."

The girl walked lightly for a few feet outward on the trestle. She fancied she could feel the ties sag. A blast of wind almost lifted her into the torrent. Because the railroad company had removed the planking to balk pedestrians, the ties, a full pace apart, were carpeted with nails and twisted spikes where the planks had been removed. Hardly a welcome sight under the best of conditions. Kate dropped to her hands and knees and began to creep forward.

The gale battered the girl; she tried to hold fast. As she flung out an arm to keep her balance her lantern globe struck a tie with a crunch—and the light went out. In the pitch blackness Kate felt cold sweat beneath her drenched clothing.

Tweetsie in Doe River Gorge-1882.—*New York Public Library Picture Collection*

She fumbled forward. Nails and spikes caught at her clothing and tore it. Her knees and legs became scratched and her hands began to fill with splinters of soggy wood. She didn't stop. Darkness seemed almost a sanctuary but too often stark lightning showed her imminent death in the boiling waters below.

Suddenly, near midstream, Kate saw a massive shape plunging toward her. The grotesque roots of an uprooted tree seemed to tower over her. Paralyzed, she stared as the shape grew larger. Now the bridge would go, she thought as she hung on tighter than ever. But the silent monster darted under the bridge with a sweeping rush and its branches scattered foam and water over her.

Death clutched at Kate Shelley with a thousand hands. Was that a whistle or only the screaming wind? Was that the headlight up ahead or only the afterglow of a lightning flash? Were these minutes or was this eternity? Was that the throb of the rails or just the pierce pulse of the flood?

Kate Shelley prayed, sobbed and staggered ahead in the blackness. Suddenly she felt cinders and earth. She had crossed the bridge.

With hysterical relief she stumbled and plunged on, only a quarter of a mile to the Moingona depot. Would she make it in time? Her heart throbbed wildly.

A storm-borne apparition burst into the depot. A stumbling girl, hatless, bleeding, disarrayed . . . the fantastic figure of a girl with a smashed, dead lantern, in dripping tatters and choking with excitement.

"Stop the Express! Honey Creek bridge is out!" Then Kate fainted.

The group huddled in the small depot stared at each other, then someone blurted out: "The girl is crazy!" But the night operator knew Kate and said: "My God, that's Kate Shelley. She ought to know." He promptly dropped the signal to "stop." In the distance the whistle of the Midnight Express sounded.

The drama was over. The express was stopped in time, and a relief engine was sent out to rescue the two crew members still clinging to the branches.

But for Kate it wasn't all over. She was ill-prepared for the fame that followed. The public had found a new idol as her story reached across the country. Crowds thronged the Shelley dooryard and swarmed about the scene of her exploit. Whether it was this sudden fame or the ordeal of her exposure to the elements, Kate fell violently ill and did not recover for three months.

At the end of that time she found that the world had not forgotten her. Passengers on the express train raised a purse of several hundred dollars for her. The State of Iowa added $200. Dubuque school children gave her a medal. The North Western awarded her $100, a half-barrel of flour, a half-load of coal and a lifetime pass. And the Order of Railway Conductors gave her an inscribed gold watch.

Kate was awarded a year's college tuition, and after she finished her studies she taught school for several years. The Iowa legislature voted Kate a $5,000 grant. She served for a time as a bill clerk for the Iowa legislature and she accepted a long-standing offer from the Chicago & North Western to serve as station agent at Moingona. She was one of the few women agents on the company rolls and served until a year before she passed away in 1912.

The legend of Kate Shelley lives on in railroad lore and in Iowa history as an outstanding act of selflessness and bravery by a nineteenth century "liberated" woman.

Today there is no track past the Shelley homestead. Originally the North Western's main line, it became a branch line when the new Des Moines River brige was completed in 1900, the longest doubletrack viaduct in the world at that time—2,685 feet long. Towering 185 feet above the river, the steel structure is known as "The Kate Shelley Bridge," a permanent monument to a young girl's heroism.

JOHN HENRY

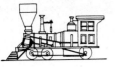

John Henry was a little baby boy,
You could hold him in the palm of your hand,
He gave a long and a lonesome cry,
"Gonna be a steel-drivin' man, Lawd, Lawd,
Gonna be a steel drivin' man."

They took John Henry to the tunnel,
Put him in the lead to drive,
The rock was so tall, John Henry so small,
That he lied down his hammer and he cried,
    Lawd, Lawd,
Lied down his hammer and he cried.

John Henry started on the right hand,
The steam drill started on the left,
" 'Fo' I'd let that steamdrill beat me down,
I'd hammer my fool self to death, Lawd, Lawd,"
    etc.

John Henry told his captain,
"A man ain't nothin' but a man,
'Fo' I let your steamdrill beat me down
I'll die with this hammer in my hand, Lawd,
    Lawd," etc.

John Henry had a little woman
Her name were Polly Anne,
John Henry took sick and he had to go to bed,
Polly Anne drove steel like a man, Lawd, Lawd,
    etc.

Now the Captain told John Henry,
"I b'lieve my tunnel's sinkin' in."
"Stand back, Captain, and doncha be afraid,
That's nothin' but my hammer catchin' wind,
    Lawd, Lawd," etc.

John Henry he told his shaker,
"Now shaker, why don't you sing?
I'm throwin' nine pounds from my hips on down,
Just listen to the cold steel ring, Lawd, Lawd,"
    etc.

John Henry he told his shaker,
"Now shaker, why don't you pray?
For if I miss this six-foot steel
Tomorrow'll be your buryin' day, Lawd, Lawd,"
    etc.

John Henry he told his Cap'n,
"Looky yonder, boy, what do I see?
Your drill's done broke and your hole's done
    choke,
And you can't drive steel like me, Lawd, Lawd,"
    etc.

John Henry hammerin' in the mountain
Till the handle of his hammer caught on fire,
He drove so hard till he broke his po' heart,
Then he lied down his hammer and he died,
    Lawd, Lawd, etc.

Women in the west heard of John Henry's death
They couldn' hardly stay in bed,
Stood in the rain, flagged that east-bound train
"Goin' where that man fell dead, Lawd, Lawd,"
    etc.

They took John Henry to the tunnel,
And they buried him in the sand,
An' every locomotive come rollin' by
Say, "There lays a steel-drivin' man, Lawd,
    Lawd," etc.

Now some say he come from England,
And some say he come from Spain,
But I say he's nothin' but a Lou'siana man,
Leader of a steel-drivin' gang, Lawd, Lawd, etc.

C & O maintenance crew spike down tie plates north of Columbus Grove, Ohio.—*C & O Chessie News photo*

RAILROADS AIN'T NO GOOD

Collected by Vance Randolph

One time there was a bunch of surveyors come down here, and the word got around that they was going to build a railroad. Some of the town people thought it would be a fine thing, but us country folks was against railroads. There was a fellow name of Bib Tarkey run the blacksmith shop in them days, and we listened to him because he knowed all about machinery. "Them heavy trains shakes the gound," says Bib, "and the acorns will be jarred off'n the trees. The razorbacks can't say it makes the cattle so jumpy they won't eat." Bib just nodded his head, and he says the engine throws so many sparks it is bound to set the woods afire, and burn up the crops anyhow.

Bud Standlee says it is bad enough when the train kills pigs and cows and horses, but if little children get on the track accidental it will run over them too, and even old folks going to church in their buggy. It's enough to make your blood run cold, he says. And also them steel rails draw lightning like a dog's tail,

The modern ship of the plains. Drawn by R. F. Zogbaum. Wood engraving in *Harper's Weekly*, Nov. 13, 1886.

fatten without mast, and we won't have no hog-meat."

"There's a lot of steam comes out of them contraptions," says old man Ledbetter. "Live steam wilts grass and spoils the pasture. The stink off a train will poison every fish in the creek. Them steam whistles scares the deer and turkeys plumb out of the country. Some and they always string telegraph wires along the track besides. And who knows what will happen with all that electricity running loose in the ground? Some say it is magnetism that causes dry weather, or maybe brings on chills and fever, too.

There was a jackleg preacher come along while the boys was a-talking, and he says railroads is wrong on principle, because there ain't no Bible for it. Oxen and horses and wagons and boats is mentioned in the Book, but the Lord don't say nothing about railroads. It is natural for wagons to run and boats to float. But a iron machine that goes a-screaming through the woods with fire in its belly is against nature, and there won't no good come of it.

Well, the city people had the money, so they went ahead and built the railroad anyhow. They fetched in gangs of foreigners to lay the tracks, and there wasn't nothing we could do about it. The first passenger train come through in nineteen-and-six. They've been a-running regular ever since, except the time the bridge washed out. Lots of old-timers just sold their farms, and moved somewheres else. But most of us have got used to the steam cars by now, and don't pay no attention to 'em.

Maybe the railroad ain't so bad as the boys figured, but it sure did bring a lot of no-good people into the country. We had to put locks on our doors, and even the smokehouse. There was a long time that the folks slept with one eye open, and the shotgun handy. And right down to this day a man has got to watch his girl mighty close, to keep her out from under them loud-talking Yankees that come in with the railroad.

In the earliest days of railroading in America, passenger trains ran only in the daytime and did not require artificial lighting. As railroads developed and journeys became longer, night travel came into vogue, and as was the custom in stagecoaches, passengers brought their own candles. Later candles were provided by the railroads and protected from drafts by glass shields. In 1850 oil lamps were introduced and contined in use until superseded by gas, first employed about 1875. Oil lamps were generally used until the 1890's. Pintsch gas was introduced in 1890 and was extensively used until about 1909. Experiments in electric lighting began in the early 1880's. The first passenger train in America to be lighted entirely by electricity was operated in 1887.

THE BAGGAGE COACH AHEAD

One stormy night as the train ran along,
  All the passengers had gone to bed,
Except a young man with a babe on his knee
  Who sat with a bowed down head;
The innocent babe began crying just then,
  As though its poor heart would break.
"Make that child hush its noise," an angry man
    said.
    "It's keeping us all awake."
"Put it out," said another, "We don't want it in
    here.
  We've paid for our berths and want rest."
But never a word said the man with the child,
  As he folded it close to his breast.
"O where is its mother? Go take it to her,"
  One young lady softly said.
"I wish that I could," was the man's sad reply.
  "But I can't though, for she's dead."

As the train rolled onward, a husband sat in
    tears,
Thinking of the happiness of just a few short
    years.
A baby's face brings pictures of a cherished hope
    now dead,
And the baby's cries won't wake her, in the
    baggage coach ahead.

Every eye filled with tears as the story he told
  Of a wife who was faithful and true;
He told how he'd saved up his earnings for years,
  Just to build a home for two;
How when heaven sent them their sweet little
    babe,
  Their young happy lives were blest;
His heart seemed to break when he mentioned
    her name,
  And in tears tried to tell them the rest.
Every woman arose to assist with the child;
  There were mothers and wives on that train.
And soon was the little one sleeping in peace,
  With no thought of sorrow or pain.
Next morning at the station he bade all goodbye,
  "God bless you," he softly said,
And each had a story to tell in their homes
  Of the baggage coach ahead.

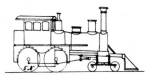

SLOW TRAIN THROUGH ARKANSAS

Collected by Vance Randolph

One time there was a fellow named Jackson that lived over in Missouri somewhere. He was knowed as Three-Finger Jackson, because one of his hands got crippled up when he used to be a brakeman on the railroad. This fellow Jackson was always cracking funny jokes, and the folks all said he ought to go on the stage or something, because they didn't have no radio in them days. Jackson couldn't hardly write

train stopped away out in the woods a drummer says "Conductor, what is the matter now?" and the trainman answered "There is some cows on the track." So after while the train stopped at another place, and the fellow says "Well, we must have caught up with them cattle again." And then they took the cowcatcher off the engine and put it on the hind end, to keep bulls from jumping on the caboose. A woman kept hollering how the cars

A number of people lost their lives riding the rails on velocipede handcars until they were outlawed. The private handcar was invented by George Sheffield at Three Rivers, Michigan, in 1879. This model was manufactured by the Sheffield Velocipede Co., now Fairbanks, Morse & Co.—*The Association of American Railroads*

his own name, but he married a girl that was plenty smart, and she wrote down a lot of jokes just like he told 'em. After while they got this stuff printed in a little yellow book, and the name on the cover was *A Slow Train through Arkansaw,* by Thos. W. Jackson.

It was all about how the trains in Arkansas was no good, or the roadbed neither, and the passengers have to get out and push when they come to a steep grade. One time the cars run mighty smooth for a while, so everybody knowed they had run off the track. The train whistled at every house, and if it was a double house they had to whistle twice. When the

was slower than cold sorghum, so the brakeman says "Well, why don't you get off and walk?" The woman says she would, only her folks was not expecting her till the train got there. And one of the passengers wanted to commit suicide, so he run half a mile ahead and laid down on the track, but the train was so slow he couldn't wait, as he had to get up and find something to eat. Also there was a man with whiskers three foot long a-riding on a half fare ticket, because he was a little boy when he got on the train. The whole book was full of stories like that, and some of 'em worse yet.

PLESSY v. FERGUSON—
"OUR CONSTITUTION IS COLOR-BLIND"

The life of the law has not been logic," Justice Oliver Wendell Holmes perceived in his famous *The Common Law*. "It has been experience." Perhaps the most fascinating experience in the evolution of American law has been the slow, certainly illogical way in which citizens of the United States who are very often relatives have been segregated from each other on the basis of color. This custom gained the sanction of law as early as 1849, when the Supreme Judicial Court of Massachusetts in *Roberts* v. *City of Boston* first embraced the doctrine that it was within the power of the state, and not violative of the Constitution, to provide separate educational facilities for members of the two groups called "black" and "white." Almost half a century later, during the period of national reconstruction following the Civil War, certain progressive people in the United States Congress sought to abolish the two categories, and the caste system they supported, by creating a third and neutral category for purposes of legal classification: that of citizen of the United States. This hypothetical person, neither black nor white, male or female, would enjoy all the rights of citizenship and would be expected to meet all the responsibilities required of such a citizen. When such rights and responsibilities were assessed, the categories "black" and "white" would be meaningless. This was the purpose of Section 1 of the Fourteenth Amendment to the Constitution:

> All persons born or naturalized in the United States, and subject to the jurisdiction thereof, are citizens of the United States and of the State wherein they reside. No State shall make or enforce any law which shall abridge the privileges or immunities of citizens of the United States; nor shall any State deprive any person of life, liberty, or property without due process of law, nor deny to any person within its jurisdiction the equal protection of the laws.

During the betrayal of democratic ideals following the Reconstruction, a series of decisions by the United States Supreme Court began stripping away the muscle of the Fourteenth Amendment and dismantling the concept of paramount nation citizenship. This process of reinterpretation began in the *Slaughterhouse Cases* (1879), was continued in the *Civil Rights Cases* (1883), and set the stage for reintroduction of the old "black-white" categories in *Plessy* v. *Ferguson* (1896), which allowed the State of Louisiana to segregate passengers on railroad coaches.

The seating in railroad coaches was an ideal place for the legislature of Louisiana to reintroduce discrimination based on color. Traditionally, American railroad coaches have provided a greater degree of democratic interaction than any other mode of transporta-

tion in the history of the world. All persons seated in a train coach are members of the same class from the time they begin their trip until they reach their destinations. A person cannot sit in a coach and not allow his imagination to wander into the life and experiences of the person seated next to him or across the aisle. The human imagination is integrative, even when a person is against such a process. Since American trains never recognized more than two classes of passengers—coach and sleeper car—the exclusion of Negroes from coaches occupied by whites was the perfect way for the State of Louisiana to reintroduce a caste system under the guise of law.

There was only one flaw in the arrangement: the reductive categories "white" and "black" created by statute did not conform to the objective reality of the color situation in Louisiana. Homer Plessy, a mulatto with seven-eighths European ancestry and one-eighth African ancestry, perceived that the statute ordering segregation in the coaches had not taken into account his identity as neither black nor white. It made no provision for the many millions like him of mixed ancestry who had no choice but to call themselves citizens of the United States. Recognizing the unfairness of this arrangement, he sued the state judge, John H. Ferguson, who had upheld his removal from the "white" coach, on the ground that since he was more white than black he had been denied a vested property interest which the Fourteenth Amendment, as well as the Louisiana statute ordering segregation in the coaches, granted to citizens of the United States of the white group. Homer Plessy's loss of his suit against Judge Ferguson is one of the best-known, and lamentable, facts of American history. What made the defeat a disaster was the interpretation given to the Thirteenth and Fourteenth Amendments by the United States Supreme Court when the case, *Plessy* v. *Ferguson,* reached its chambers. The Court ruled—Justice Henry Brown writing the majority opinion—that these amendments did not prevent the legislature of Louisiana from ordering segregation by color on railroad coaches. In answer to Homer Plessy's argument that he had been denied a property interest by being forced into the "colored" coach, Justice Brown wrote:

If he be a white man, and assigned to a colored coach, he may have his action for damages against the company for being deprived of his so-called "property." Upon the other hand, if he be a colored man, and be so assigned, he has been deprived of no property, since he is not lawfully entitled to the reputation of being a white man.

This one decision opened the way for every Southern state to segregate all their public facilities, from drinking fountains, restaurants and housing to rest rooms and schools. It would not be overturned until fifty-eight years later, by *Brown* v. *Board of Education* in 1954. This much is history.

What is little known is the origin of the phase made famous by the opponents of *Plessy* v. *Ferguson* in their efforts to get that decision reversed: "Our Constitution is color-blind." It was admitted into the language of the law by Justice John Harlan in his eloquent dissent from the majority opinion in *Plessy:*

The white race deems itself to be the dominant race in this country. And so it is, in prestige, in achievements, in education, in wealth, and in power. So, I doubt not, it will continue to be for all time, if it remains true to its great heritage, and holds fast to the principles of constitutional liberty. But in view of the constitution, in the eye of the law, there is in this country no superior, dominant, ruling class of citizens. There is no caste here. Our constitution is color-blind, and neither knows nor tolerates classes among citizens.

"Our Constitution is color-blind." These words, written in passion by a Southerner who was using, according to legend, the same inkwell used by Justice Roger B. Taney in writing the infamous *Dred Scott* decision, have shaped the course of legal theory from 1896 to the present. "Our Constitution is color-blind." It is a phrase of art borrowed by Justice Harlan from the brief of Homer Plessy's lawyer, the multitalented, brilliant lawyer-novelist Albion W. Tourgée. In his brief to the Supreme Court, Tourgée wrote: "Justice is pictured blind and her daughter, the Law, ought at least to be color-blind." Tourgée was stating an ideal, not an absolute; it was a metaphor from the imagination of an artist. Justice Harlan, incorporating the metaphor, transformed the statement of an ideal into the statement of an absolute. "Our Constitution is color-blind." It is still a phrase of art.

The issues which gave rise to *Plessy* v. *Fer-* *guson* are still with us. Only this time they have been removed from the possibility of preventing democratic interaction inside a railroad coach.

J. A. M.

Horse Shoe Curve, near Kittanning Point, on the Pennsylvania Railroad.—*New York Public Library Picture Collection*

TO A LOCOMOTIVE IN WINTER

Walt Whitman

Thee for my recitative,
Thee in the driving storm even as now, the snow,
   the winter-day declining,
Thee in thy panoply, thy measur'd dual throb-
   bing and thy beat convulsive,
Thy black cylindric body, golden brass and sil-
   very steel,
Thy ponderous side-bars, parallel and connecting
   rods, gyrating, shuttling at thy sides,
Thy metrical, now swelling pant and roar, now
   tapering in the distance,
Thy great protruding head-light fix'd in front,
Thy long, pale, floating vapor-pennants, tinged
   with delicate purple,
The dense and murky clouds out-belching from
   thy smokestack,
Thy knitted frame, thy springs and valves, the
   tremulous twinkle of thy wheels,
Thy train of cars behind, obedient, merrily
   following,
Through gale or calm, now swift, now slack, yet
   steadily careering;

Type of the modern—emblem of motion and
   power—pulse of the continent
For once come serve the Muse and merge in
   verse, even as here I see thee,
With storm and buffeting gusts of wind and
   falling snow,
By day thy warning ringing bell to sound its
   notes,
By night thy silent signal lamps to swing.

Fierce-throated beauty!
Roll through my chant with all thy lawless
   music, thy swinging lamps at night,
Thy madly-whistled laughter, echoing, rumbling
   like an earthquake, rousing all,
Law of thyself complete, thine own track firmly
   holding,
(No sweetness debonair of tearful harp or glib
   piano thine,)
Thy trills of shrieks by rocks and hills return'd,
Launch'd o'er the prairies wide, across the lakes,
To the free skies unpent and glad and strong.

THOMAS EDISON TELLS ABOUT HIS DAYS AS A TRAIN BUTCH

I became deaf when I was about twelve years old. I had just got a job as newsboy on the Grand Trunk Railway, and it is supposed that the injury which permanently deafened me was caused by my being lifted by the ears from where I stood upon the ground into the baggage car. Earache came first, then a little deafness, and this deafness increased until at the theater I could hear only a few words now and then. Plays and most other "entertainments" in consequence be-

Stationmaster, U.S. 1876.—*N.Y. Public Library Picture Collection*

came a bore to me, although I could imagine enough to fill in the gaps my hearing left. I am inclined to think I did not miss much. After the earache finally stopped I settled down into steady deafness.

There were no great specialists, I presume, in that region at the time, but I had doctors. They could do nothing for me.

I have been deaf ever since and the fact that I am getting deafer constantly, they tell me, doesn't bother me. I have been deaf enough for many years to know the worst, and my deafness has been not a handicap but a help to me.

While I was a newsboy on the Grand Trunk I had a chance to learn that money can be made out of a little careful thought, and, being poor, I already knew that money is a valuable thing. Boys who don't know that are under a disadvantage greater than deafness. That was a long time ago. The Civil War was on and the Battle of Pittsburgh Landing, sometimes called the Battle of Shiloh, was in progress—and I was already very deaf. In my isolation (insulation would be a better term) I had time to think things out. I decided that if I could send ahead to outlying stations a hint of the big war news which I, there in Detroit, had learned was coming, I could do a better than normal business when I reached them.

I therefore ran to the office of the Detroit Free Press and asked Mr. Seitz, the man in charge, if he would trust me for a thousand newspapers. He regarded me as if perhaps I might be crazy, but referred me to Mr. Story. Mr. Story carefully considered me. I was poorly dressed. He hesitated, but finally told Mr. Seitz to let me have the papers.

I got them to the station and into the baggage car as best I could and then attended to my scheme. All along the line I had made friends of the station-agents, who also were the telegraphers, by giving them candy and other things which a train-boy dealt in in those days. They were a good-natured lot of men, too, and had been kind to me. I wired ahead to them, through the courtesy of the Detroit agent, who also was my friend, asking them to post notices that when the train arrived I would have newspapers with details of the great battle.

When I got to the first station on the run I found that the device had worked beyond my expectations. The platform literally was crowded with men and women anxious to buy newspapers. After one look at that crowd I raised the price from five cents to ten and sold as many papers as the crowd could absorb. At Mount Clemons, the next station, I raised the price from ten cents to fifteen. The advertising worked as well at all the other stations. By the time the train reached Port Huron I had advanced the price of the Detroit Free Press for that day to thirty-five cents per copy and everybody took one.

Out of this one idea I made enough money to give me a chance to learn telegraphy. This was something I long had wished to do, for thus early I had found that my deafness did not prevent me from hearing the clicking of a telegraph instrument when I was as near to it as an operator always must be. From the start I found that deafness was an advantage to a telegrapher. While I could hear unerringly the loud ticking of the instrument, I could not hear other and perhaps distracting sounds. I could not even hear the instrument of the man next to me in a big office. I became rather well-known as a fast operator, especially at receiving.

It may be said that I was shut off from that particular kind of social intercourse which is small talk. I am glad of it. I couldn't hear, for instance, the conversations at the dinner tables of the boarding-houses and hotels where after I became a telegrapher I took my meals. Freedom from such talk gave me an opportunity to think out my problems. I have no doubt that my nerves are stronger and better today than they would have been if I had heard all the foolish conversation and other meaningless sounds that normal people hear. The things that I have needed to hear I have heard.

I think it is because my nerves have not been bothered that now I am able to write without tremor. Few men of my age can do that. Steady nerves are perhaps an advantage of themselves great enough to offset impaired hearing. To me, when I go over there from Orange, New York seems rather a quiet place. Not even that city is a strain upon my nerves.

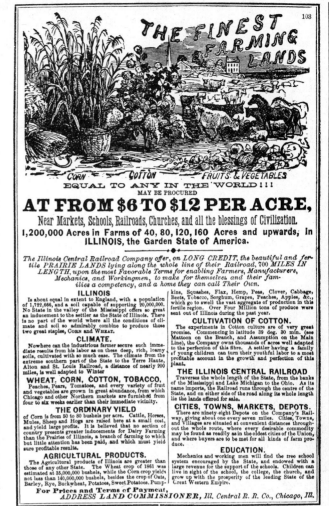

Most nerve strain of our modern life, I fancy, comes to us through our ears.

When the Ninth Avenue Elevated Railway first began its operation in New York there was much complaint about its noisiness. Some people were literally up in arms. I was hired to go to the metropolis to make a report on it. The fact that my hearing was not perfect enabled me to find out what the trouble really was. I heard only the worst of it, you understand, and this helped me to determine that the difficulty lay in the rail joints. Other experts had not been able to make sure of that because they had heard too much general uproar to make it possible for them to make sure of details.

There is almost no American music untouched by the machine, and by the train especially. Rudi Blesh tells about a Scott Joplin rag made of the sounds of a railroad collision.

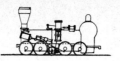

Along came the F.F.V., the fastest on the line,
Running along the C & O road, just twenty
minutes behind,
A-running into Sewell yard, quartered on the
line,
Awaiting for strict orders from the station just
behind.

And when she blew for Hinton, her engineer was
there.
George Alley was his name, with bright and
wavy hair;
His fireman, young Jack Dickson, was standing
by his side,
Awaiting for strict orders and in the cab to ride.

George Alley said to his fireman, "Jack, a little
more steam;
I intend to run old number 4, the fastest ever
seen;
So over this road I mean to fly, as angels' wings
unfold,
And when we see the Big Bend Tunnel, they'll
hear my whistle blow."

George Alley said to his fireman, "Jack, a rock
ahead I see,
And I know that death is lurking there, awaiting
for you and me;
So from this car, dear Jack, you leap, your
darling life to save,
For I want you to be an engineer, when I'm
sleeping in my grave."

Payday Hussey's Camp BB&BRR.

George Alley's mother came to him with a
bucket on her arm;
She said, "My darling boy, be careful how you
run,
For many a man has lost his life in trying to
make lost time,
But if you run your engine right, you'll get there
just on time."

George Alley said, "Dear Mother, you know I'll
take your heed.
I know my engine, it's all right, I know that she
will speed.
So over this road I mean to run with a speed
unknown to all,
And when I blow for Clifton Forge, they'll surely
hear my call."

Then up the road he hurtled, against the rock he
crashed;
The engine it turned over, poor George's chest
was mashed.
George's head in the firebox lay; the flames were
rolling high.
"I'm glad I was born for an engineer, on the
C & O road to die."

George Alley's mother came to him, in sorrow
she did sigh,
When she looked upon her darling boy and saw
that he must die.
"Too late, too late, dear Mother! My life is almost
done,
And I know that God will let me in when I've
finished my last run."

The doctor said, "Dear George, my darling boy,
  be still;
Your life may yet be spared, if it is God's
  precious will."
"Oh no!," said George, "That cannot be. I want
  to die so free,
I want to die on the engine I love, 143."

The doctor said, "George Alley, your life cannot
  be saved.
Murdered upon the railway, to lie in a lonesome
  grave."
His face was covered up with blood, his eyes they
  could not see;
The very last words George Alley said were
  "Nearer, my God, to Thee."

John Harrington Cox, folklorist, gathered these facts of the wreck from Ernest and Margaret Alley, George's brother and sister, and from R. E. Noel, a retired C & O engineer.

George Alley was born in Richmond, Virginia, July 10, 1860, was married and became the father of four children, and lived five hours after his engine (No. 143, pulling train No. 4, the Fast Flying Vestibule) hit a landslide at 5:40 A.M., October 23, 1890. Jack Dickson was not working that run; the engine was fired by Lewis Withrow, and Clifton Forge, another fireman, was in the cab deadheading. Forge and Withrow both went out the left side of the cab. George Alley stayed with the engine.

The discrepancies don't matter, of course, to the spirit or meaning of the song. Folk music tells its own truth.

The Big Bend Tunnel is the one where John Henry died beating out the steam drill two decades earlier.

The best evidence is that the ballad was composed by a Negro engine-wiper who worked in the roundhouse in Hinton. It would be another engine-wiper who, in a few years, would clean out the cab in which Casey Jones died, and make up a song about that wreck.

Fatal Railway Accident at Kentish-Town, on the North and South Western Junction Line: Scene of the disaster on Monday night.—*New York Public Library Picture Collection*

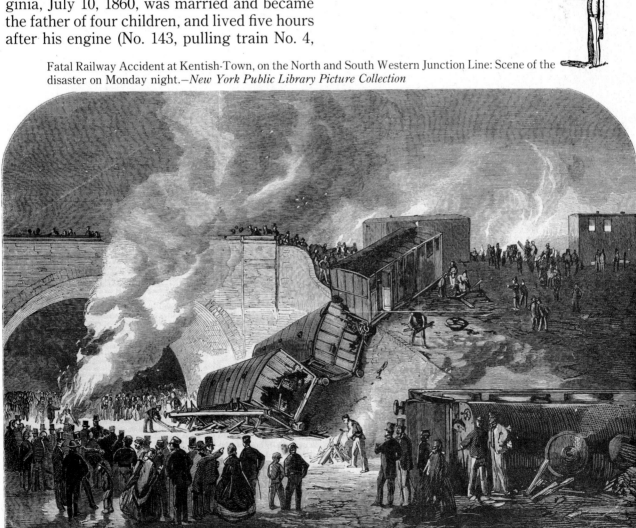

SIDETRACK
THE BRIDGES

Bridges—like the depots and the engines themselves—carry us into the nation's past. We see one far from the city, built of rough cut beams and densely placed stilts, and we know what the men who put it there were wearing. We see a suspension bridge with massive towers of great stone blocks, and we know that the builders had time and cheap labor.

We see a bridge with I-Beam supports and we know the steel mills were working in Pittsburgh.

And then there are bridges that translate our thoughts immediately into the thirties or the forties, though we can't always say what it is about the bridges that does this. Or maybe we don't pay that much attention to bridges anymore. We ought to. A railroad bridge is the purest combination of the aesthetics and mathematics of architecture: form and strength, naked and open.

Iron bridge and tunnel, Johnson's Canyon, Arizona.—*Santa Fe Railway photo*

Union Pacific's Engine No. 119, with a full head of steam, works her way up to the meeting with the Central Pacific over the newly completed Promontory trestle. A. J. Russell photo (1869).—*Union Pacific Railroad Museum Collection*

Heavy traffic on an early wooden bridge. Note the diamond-stack on the front engine, and the barefoot boy on the hillside in the foreground taking it all in.—*Courtesy of Southern Railway System*

Canyon Diablo bridge near Winslow, Arizona.—*Santa Fe Railway photo*

Dale Creek bridge, erected entirely of wood to span Dale Creek in Wyoming. It was 125 feet high and 500 feet long, and almost all the timber used to build it was transported from Chicago. The bridge was completed in thirty working days. It was torn down years later and replaced by a steel structure. Later the line was abandoned. (A.J. Russell photo)—*Union Pacific Railroad Museum Collection*

PAYDAY HUSSEY'S CAMP B.C. R.R.

UNIONISM AND THE CZARS
1865-1912

New York Public Library Picture Collection

Our cause is just, the great public is with us, and we have nothing to fear.

— Eugene V. Debs

CARNEGIE TELLS ABOUT TAKING OVER

I made the acquaintance of an extraordinary man, Thomas A. Scott, one to whom the term "genius" in his department may safely be applied. He had come to Pittsburgh as superintendent of that division of the Pennsylvania Railroad. Frequent telegraphic communication was necessary between him and his superior Mr. Lombaert, general superintendent at Altoona. This brought him to the telegraph office at nights, and upon several occasions I happened to be the operator. One day I was surprised by one of his assistants, with whom I was acquainted, telling me that Mr. Scott had asked him whether he thought that I could be obtained as his clerk and telegraph operator, to which this young man told me he had replied: "That is impossible. He is now an operator."

But when I heard this I said at once: "Not so fast. He can have me. I want to get out of a mere office life. Please go and tell him so."

The result was I was engaged February 1, 1853, at a salary of thirty-five dollars a month as Mr. Scott's clerk and operator. A raise in wages from twenty-five to thirty-five dollars per month was the greatest I had ever known.

"He strives to please." Pen and ink drawing by W. A. Rogers, 1906.—*Library of Congress*

The public telegraph line was temporarily put into Mr. Scott's office at the outer depot and the Pennsylvania Railroad Company was given permission to use the wire at seasons when such use would not interfere with the general public business, until their own line, then being built, was completed.

* * * * *

It was not long after this that the railroad company constructed its own telegraph line. We had to supply it with operators. Most of these were taught in our offices at Pittsburgh. The telegraph business continued to increase with startling rapidity. We could scarcely provide facilities fast enough. New telegraph offices were required. My fellow-messenger boy, "Davy" McCargo, I appointed superintendent of the telegraph department, March 11, 1859. I have been told that "Davy" and myself are entitled to the credit of being the first to employ young women as telegraph operators in the United States upon railroads, or perhaps in any branch. At all events, we placed girls in various offices as pupils, taught and then put them in charge of offices as occasion required. Among the first of these was my cousin, Miss Maria Hogan. She was the operator at the freight station in Pittsburgh, and with her were placed successive pupils, her office becoming a school. Our experience was that young women operators were more to be relied upon than young men. Among all the new occupations invaded by women I do not know of any better suited for them than that of telegraph operator.

Mr. Scott was one of the most delightful superiors that anybody could have and I soon became warmly attached to him. He was my great man and all the hero worship that is inherent in youth I showered upon him. I soon began placing him in imagination in the presidency of the great Pennsylvania Railroad—a position which he afterwards attained. Under him I gradually performed duties not strictly belonging to my department and I can attribute my decided advancement in the service to one well-remembered incident.

The railway was a single line. Telegraph

orders to trains often became necessary, although it was not then a regular practice to run trains by telegraph. No one but the superintendent himself was permitted to give a train order on any part of the Pennsylvania system, or indeed of any other system, I believe, at that time. It was then a dangerous expedient to give telegraphic orders, for the whole system of railway management was still in its infancy, and men had not yet been trained for it. It was necessary for Mr. Scott to go out night after night to break-downs or wrecks to superintend the clearing of the line. He was necessarily absent from the office on many mornings.

One morning I reached the office and found that a serious accident on the Eastern Division had delayed the express passenger train westward, and that the passenger train eastward was proceeding with a flagman in advance at every curve. The freight trains in both directions were all standing still upon the sidings. Mr. Scott was not to be found. Finally I could not resist the temptation to plunge in, take the responsibility, give "train orders," and set matters going. "Death or Westminster Abbey," flashed across my mind. I knew it was dismissal, disgrace, perhaps criminal punishment for me if I erred. On the other hand, I could bring in the wearied freight-train men who had lain out all night. I could set everything in motion. I knew I could. I had often done it in wiring Mr. Scott's orders. I knew just what to do, and so I began. I gave the orders in his name, started every train, sat at the instrument watching every tick, carried the trains along from station to station, took extra precautions, and had every thing running smoothly when Mr. Scott at last reached the office. He had heard of the delay. His first words were: "Well! How are matters?"

He came to my side quickly, grasped his pencil, and began to write his orders. I had then to speak, and timidly said: "Mr. Scott, I could not find you anywhere and I gave these orders in your name early this morning."

"Are they going all right? Where is the Eastern Express?"

I showed him the messages and gave him the position of every train on the line—freights, ballast trains, everything—showed him the answers of the various conductors, the latest reports at the stations where the various trains had passed. All was right. He looked in my face for a second. I scarcely dared look in his. I did not know what was going to happen. He did not say one word, but again looked carefully over all that had taken place. Still he said nothing. After a little he moved away from my desk to his own, and that was the end

Southern & Western Railroad Station at Broad and Prime Streets, Philadelphia.—*Library of Congress*

of it. He was afraid to approve what I had done, yet he had not censured me. If it came out all right, it was all right; if it came out all wrong, the responsibility was mine. So it stood, but I noticed that he came in regularly and in good time for some mornings after that.

Of course I never spoke to any one about it. None of the trainmen knew that Mr. Scott had not personally given the orders. I had almost made up my mind that if the like occurred again, I would not repeat my proceeding of that morning unless I was authorized to do so. I was feeling rather distressed about what I had done until heard from Mr. Franciscus, who was then in charge of the freighting department at Pittsburgh, that Mr. Scott, the evening after the memorable morning, had said to him: "Do you know what that little white-haired Scotch devil of mine did?"

"No."

"I'm blamed if he didn't run every train on the division in my name without the slightest authority."

"And did he do it all right?" asked Franciscus.

"Oh, yes, all right."

This satisfied me. Of course I had my cue for the next occasion and went boldly in. From that date it was very seldom that Mr. Scott gave a train order.

RASCALITY RIDES THE RAILS:
Daniel Drew, Cornelius Vanderbilt, Jim Fisk and Jay Gould

Agnes C. Laut

When Gould came into the big rail world, utterly unknown, he was between his twenty-fourth and twenty-sixth years. When Vanderbilt came as a power in the same arena, he was well on in his sixties and one of the richest men in America. Legend has it that his sudden conversion to rails at an age when other men usually seek repose resulted from a chance ride on a railroad, when in spite of a minor accident entailing delay, steam on steel went racing past his river steamer at a pace that opened his eyes to the future of rails. It is also true that he became involved in rails because in the slump of prosperity after the Crimean War, many crippled, poorly built rails with interest on debts they could not pay came to him as a rich man with ready cash to endorse their otherwise quite worthless promissory notes. Also his son William—to Vanderbilt's amazement—had made a dinky little suburban road on Staten Island pay. This was the son to whom legend has ascribed the classic phrase, "the public be damned"; and, it may be added, there is no authority for that legend. The old

Commodore might explode in anger almost to apoplexy. The son was of another stripe—sharp as his father but reticent as a clam.

Vanderbilt had endorsed bad paper on the Erie's chattel mortgage stock for more than four hundred thousand dollars; but Daniel Drew had endorsed up to nine hundred and eighty thousand and held in addition bonds between three and four millions, which he could at any time either change into stock or foreclose as a mortgage is foreclosed on a farm—and toss the whole road into bankruptcy.

Two questions should occur here.

When the Erie had reached the Lakes in such a blaze of triumph, how came it that its bonds had swollen to thirty-four millions with stock of only ten millions? That was as dangerous a proposition as to mortgage a thousand-dollar house for thirty-four hundred. The thing seemed inexplicable. Here was the Erie, with huge immigration traffic west and huge coal traffic east, going back financially every year. How came it the Erie was at one and the same time making money and losing it? Solely from those early blunders. The gauge had

The great race for the Eastern stakes, 1870. Currier & Ives, 1870.—*Library of Congress*

been made six feet. It had to be changed to the standard guage. Though that was at first done by laying a third rail, it meant changes in one hundred and thirty-two engines and sixteen hundred cars. Iron rails, too, were being replaced by steel. The charter did not permit crossing New Jersey; so expensive docks had to be bought to connect with New York. Telegraph and machine shops and rail stations and water tanks added to the outlay on a railroad

times almost six millions; and certainly at one time when Erie shares were down to 17, he held, in addition to these mortgages, bonds as double security, twenty-eight thousand shares in one block and fifty-eight thousand shares in another. If the directors did not keep him as treasurer, he could ruin the road. If they kept him, though they could not prove it, "the Street" was aware something sinister was the matter with the jumpy Erie shares. How many

A railway track crew lays quarter-mile lengths of continuous welded rail.—*The Association of American Railroads photo*

that had really begun on capital far below its costs. Side roads had to be built to feed the main line; and when these crossed a New Jersey or Pennsylvania boundary, they had to be under separate charter. The fact that Daniel Drew, the treasurer of the Erie, held some of these properties and sold them to his own line under cover did not make them a particularly cheap investment; and the sly old scamp took mighty good care that properties so bought for the Erie had bonds that could be converted into Erie stock. At this very time, too, the Erie suffered heavily from floods, from strikes, from hard winters that hampered traffic.

The second question is—how did an ignorant old man like Drew, a cattle drover, a driveling, tobacco-chewing, evil-faced country skinflint—ever get such bulldog grip, such sinister, unbreakable power on a road financed and sponsored by the best minds of his generation? How do rats in a great ship gnaw holes that may engulf it? The question is already answered. Drew held the mortgages. At times he held three and a half millions of bonds, at

shares of Erie were out on the market anyway? Nobody knew. All the public knew was when Erie went from 80 to 43, and from 43 down to 17 and 8, and everyone was flinging it wildly to the dogs, an unseen hand was buying up the cheap shares, and woe betide the speculator who couldn't deliver what he had sold at the low price. The price would run up mysteriously to 80 again, and the speculator had to deliver or go to ruin. He often did both. Drew, of course, was the explanation. By changing bonds to stock, he could flood the market beyond its buying power. When the price went down, he was the buyer. When the price swung up from scarcity of stock, Erie soared; and the speculative public followed as stampeding sheep follow a bellwether over a precipice; and Drew was at the bottom of the precipice to shear them well. He sheared friends and foes alike. He would "tip off" church friends that Erie was "a good buy"; and when each friend "tipped off" circle after circle of other friends, Daniel Drew was on hand to let them have all the shares they wanted.

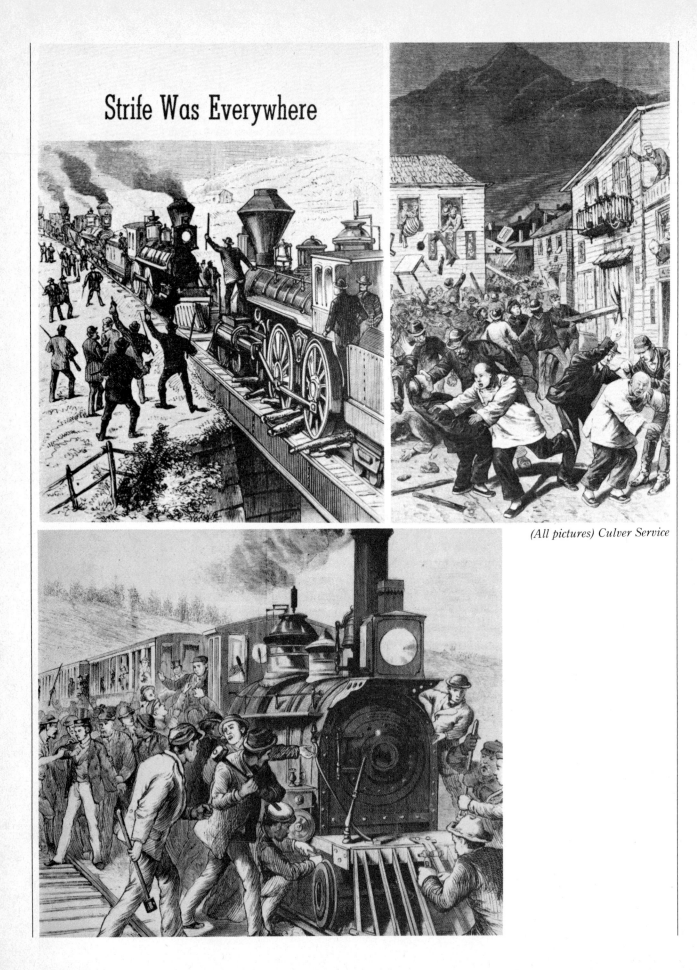

Strife Was Everywhere

Drew and Vanderbilt did not love each other. Both had begun as what we would call "roughnecks"; but while Drew's faults became more glaring and shameless with age, Vanderbilt was no longer a crude ferryman. He had gone to Europe in the fifties on a yacht that was the wonder of the world. "Upstart," they had called him at first and refused to receive him in high circles; but when he left Europe, half the royal courts of the Old World had groveled at his feet and all society was feeding out of his hand. He had learned more on that trip than he perhaps acknowledged. He had learned diplomacy. No longer did he send back such a terrific ultimatum as he had once delivered to a rival steamship line: "You have undertaken to cheat me. I will not sue you because the law takes too long. I will ruin you." And he did. He had learned that you can't fight a skunk in the open and not come out damaged. He must also have realized that American carriers, which were independent, could not stand up against European water carriers heavily subsidized by their governments.

Vanderbilt and Drew had been rivals in the Hudson River steamship business. They had slashed rates; and again legend has it—Drew had come out best and taken a good slice out of Vanderbilt's millions; and now Vanderbilt came into rails. He had added vastly to his fortune from steamships in the wild stampede to California; but he was quick to see that a gold camp is only transient as an earner. It either attracts rival roads, or if short-lived, peters out; but a railroad through densely settled territory is an earner for all time. He had begun to buy Harlem when its stock had sunk to $9 and bought it all the way up to $100, to which it ascended in less than four years under his careful management of scrapping poor engines, which the crew called "tea pots," "tin kettles," selling the old slat-seated cars to new lines in the West, and putting on cars that could carry as many as eight passengers, and inducing the City Council of New York to extend his right of way through the heart of the city, which in the sixties was still very largely suburbs and truck farms. Undoubtedly he used Boss Tweed as his tramway tool with the City Council; but before these tricky rascals could rescind the permission in order to pound his Harlem stock down, he took good care to have his workmen on the streets day and night getting the tracks down; so when the motion came up before the finance committees, there lay the rails, and when Drew allied himself with the Tammany gang and tried to force Harlem down by selling what one historian calls "imaginary shares," Vanderbilt's orders were to buy every share offered at any price. Before the Tammany gang realized, Harlem shares were at 179, and Vanderbilt demanded delivery of the "imaginary shares." No one knows what he took out of Drew's tight pockets by this bold stroke, but certainly enough to make up all Drew had cost him in the old steamship days.

Many legends cluster round this first clash of the two masters of finance in Wall Street, one the ruthless, despotic builder; the other the rat gnawing ruin for others in the dark; but all agree Vanderbilt was unmoved by the whining tears for mercy and bade the Drew gang "pay up or shut up." Then it dawned on the Street, that Vanderbilt was in rails, not to smash them and speculate, but to build them up in great permanent systems.

Parallel to the Hudson and the Harlem, another road—the New York and Hudson—had crept in decrepit joints to Albany and was now, like other roads after the Crimean War, crippled by finance. Vanderbilt began buying

CENTRAL PACIFIC RAILROAD.
NO. 1, TIME CARD No. 1.
To take effect Monday June 6th, 1864, at 5 A. M.

TRAINS EASTWARD.			STATIONS.	TRAINS WESTWARD.		
Frt and Pass No 3	Frt and Pass No 2	Pass & Mail No 1.		Frt and Pass No 1	Pass & Mail No 2.	Frt and Pass No 3.
5 PM leave	1 PM leave	6-15 A M, L	Sacramento	8.45 A M arr	12 M arr	6.40 P M ar.
5.50 } mt frt 5.55 }	2.15	3.55	18 Junction	18 3	11.20	5.55 } mt. Frt 5.50 }
6.09	2.38	7.05	22 Rocklin	4 7.40	11.07	5.37
6.22	2.55	7.15 m set F	25 Pino	3 7.15 mt	10.56	5.25
6.40	3.30 PM arr	7.30 A M arr	31 Newcastle	6 3.45 A M, L	10.30 A M, L	5 P M, L.

Trains No. 2 and 3 east, and 1 and 3 west, daily, except Sunday.
Trains No. 1 east and 2 west, daily.

LELAND STANFORD, President.

it at 25. What could he do with it? men asked. Vanderbilt's next step was to go to Albany and obtain authority in the charters to consolidate his rail holdings for a vast system to carry immigrants, now arriving in America by the thousands, to the roads west of the Lakes. Bribery as a fine art had not yet been perfected in Albany, but with Boss Tweed's help he got the authority; and his Hudson stock went to

Jay Gould's private bowling alley showing the speculators in famous manipulations.—*The Bettmann Archive*

150. Again poor old Drew tried to pound Hudson down, and again Vanderbilt bought every share offered right down to 90. Again many legends cling to this episode—Vanderbilt standing at his office windows signaling and shouting for his brokers and swift messengers—there were no telephones in those days—"to buy every blank, blank, blank share offered" right up to 285. Again Drew wept and cringed and pleaded and dogged the Commodore to his residence in Washington Square. "Pay up or shut up" was Vanderbilt's pitiless reply. Drew lost another million to Vanderbilt.

Now Vanderbilt did exactly what Eleazer Lord did back in the thirties. He looked at the rail map. His system covered one straight leg of a triangle south to north, then at right angles, another leg of the triangle east to west. Obviously, though Vanderbilt knew nothing about geometry, a problem over which most of us tripped in our schooldays would have told anyone the base of that triangle would complete his system cheaper, quicker, straighter, without this slashing of rates between Erie and New York Central from nine dollars to five,

and in some cases with secret discounts for big shippers to four. There was no sense in that. What is more—there was senseless loss; and Vanderbilt hated loss and he hated senseless, stupid blunders. His first step was always to make a rail pay on its merits; and this slashing of rates below cost of service, this paying of big shippers secret discounts (rebates), this system of employing "runners," or agents, to go out and get freight from rivals at any cost—wasn't sense. It was crazy folly, that killed the little shipper, who didn't get discounts; and Vanderbilt knew the prosperity of his lines depended on the prosperity of the shippers along the lines. Ruin them and the traffic would decrease.

So Vanderbilt cast his wise old eyes on the Erie; and the tragedy crashed from the blue in a storm that rocked and wrecked the rail world for more than twenty years. He was a holder of some of its bad papers and he rightly guessed whence the floods of worthless stock were emanating—from Drew. His first measure was to dam those floods; and I doubt not he did it in pretty vigorous language. Erie's bonds were down to thirty-five dollars and when Drew advanced more loans on more bonds, he handed over only sixty dollars for hundred-dollar bonds and took the difference in stock, more stock. All this did not happen in one year. It ran on from 1857 to 1869. The Erie, which was to cost only ten millions, had now cost in actual outlay thirty-seven millions.

When the bonds were at 35, the stock was at 8; and Drew continued to suck it down alive. He was eating it up at that price; for Erie had to borrow from the old curmudgeon. It couldn't pay its wages. It couldn't pay its taxes. It couldn't pay interest on its debts. It did not seem that any power on earth could pry it loose from Drew's coils. Directors tried to pry it loose by forcing it into a receivership. Who bought it? A representative of the bondholders—for two hundred and twenty thousand dollars in 1861—which meant Drew; but Vanderbilt and Vanderbilt's friends were on the new board of directors; and one would give a good deal for a snapshot of those two old enemies with masked faces looking at each other across the big table—Vanderbilt now showing the signs of age with side-burn whiskers and high forehead topped by a fluff of whitening hair but as brainy, as dominant and determined as in his ferry days; Drew stooped, leaning on a cane, suave, self-righteous to the point of being bullet-proof, sniveling, but shifty of eye as ever. There was only one way to guess what Drew would do. He would pretty nearly always do the very opposite of what he was pretending to do. Whereas with Vanderbilt, he would do what he set out to do, or smash what tried to stop him, or smash himself trying to smash obstructions. One was a fighter in the open, the other was an assassin who struck in the dark; and it seems ridiculous to add, the banks of New York shrank in sheer terror before the power of these two battling men. Drew realized he needed younger men; so he was using Fisk, the showman, and Gould, the silent young free lance, just as Vanderbilt had not scrupled to use Tweed. Both Gould and Fisk were new names to the Street as late as 1867; but because Tweed and Fisk played the same game with Tammany Hall to elect judges pliant to their chiefs' will, the Street had an erroneous idea that Vanderbilt and Drew were playing a game in collusion to shear the public in frenzied speculation. The Street guessed wrong. It was rather that each like a wrestler was playing the foolish Street to catch the other unawares and crush him.

It seems outrageous, incomprehensible, unbelievable, that a great rail system, on which two or three million shippers were dependent, in which thousands of innocent people had invested their hard-earned savings, could become the prey in a disgraceful prize ring of rascality. It seems to point to the inference that all rails should be taken out of private ownership and placed under national management. But wait a bit! The darkest shadow overhanging Erie's fate was that the railroad had got into politics and politics had got into the railroad. Public rights were ignored as the bleating of fool sheep. Votes were bought in mobs. Legislators offered themselves on the auction block to the highest bidder. Judges obeyed orders from the rail fighters as from the nod of a god's head and in reward got fees running from fifty thousand dollars for a decision to one hundred and fifty thousand for a referee's action; and sheriffs were beaten up by Bowery toughs and thugs who were never so much as arrested. That the judges were later impeached and the legislators relegated to the disgrace of defeat and infamy—did not restore the losses to the ruined.

Ugly pages in the history of democracy and it doesn't commend rails in politics, or politics in rails. It harks back to the earliest experiences of New York and Massachusetts that the farther those two are separated, the better for each.

Records before the courts and state investigations cover literally thousands of pages. One need relate only one or two of the high spots to grasp the iniquities now working under cover to use the Erie as the speculative football of thugs, gamblers, bribe givers and bribe takers.

Vanderbilt's first move was to go openly to the courts to stop Drew from issuing stocks for bonds as fast as the printing presses could grind out shares. He asked an injunction stopping the directors from paying interest or principal on the bonds held by Drew till he would restore the bonds and shares held as additional security. Judge Barnard, who came under black enough cloud himself, granted the petition. Vanderbilt then demanded the withdrawal of Drew as treasurer. Here, Judge Barnard delayed his decision. Did he delay for a bribe? The question cannot be answered. He was later impeached and stock profits or fees totaling fifty thousand dollars were finally

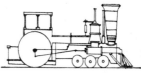

traced to his doorstep. Vanderbilt went on fearlessly buying Erie stock; and Drew gave him all he wanted at mounting and soaring prices. But while Vanderbilt was appealing to a New York City court, Drew hopped across the Brooklyn ferry and asked another injunction from another judge to restrain Judge Barnard and Vanderbilt from using the courts to speculate in Erie stocks. The Brooklyn judge granted the petition. The Erie directors were permitted by the court of Brooklyn to go on turning bonds into stocks.

Here were two courts in one state giving absolutely contradictory decisions.

In twenty-four hours, Drew and his crowd issued ten millions more of stock and hurled them on the market in defiant triumph. The stock fell fifteen points in one thud.

Was Vanderbilt stopped from buying Erie? He was not. He flung his whole fortune into the fight, and the press kept quiet, and the banks trembled. Later, the Brooklyn judge cleared himself by acknowledging frankly he had given his decision to Drew on insufficient evidence and was unaware it was to be used for stock-jobbing purposes. In the interval—and it was only twenty-four hours—"at ten on the morning of the 11th, a panic stricken Drew, Gould and Fisk bearing in their hands account books, desk drawers, packages of paper, bonds, assets, archives, bales of greenbacks in hackney coaches ... fled to Jersey City ... followed by others like themselves in the night to place the Hudson between themselves and" Judge Barnard. If Drew's judge was going back on him, Drew was going to be safe across the river in Jersey; and the printing press went on grinding out more shares for Vanderbilt to buy. . . .

Vanderbilt demanded that a receiver be appointed for all the Erie.

The receiver named was Vanderbilt's son-in-law. A judge from yet another court on petition of Drew's lawyers forbade Mr. Vanderbilt's son-in-law from becoming a receiver; but in any case, what was he to receive? All the

Maryland. The Baltimore and Ohio Railroad strike, 1877.—*Library of Congress*

Erie papers were over in New Jersey beyond reach of New York court officers and both sides were now ignoring injunctions and Daniel's printing presses were busy as ever grinding out Erie stock.

A Tammany party heeler was appointed to referee what decisions were to stand; and while he never refereed anything, he was paid for his services—and, of course, that came out of the poor Erie's treasury; for the treasurer was Mr. Drew.

The thing was now becoming such a public scandal that the judges found themselves in the witness box. Barnard did acknowledge he had talked things over with friends of both sides in taverns and clubs. It was proved there were plans to have thugs from New York kidnap Drew in Jersey City; but these plans had miscarried.

A secret meeting was now arranged between Drew and Vanderbilt on a Sunday, when Drew knew the process men were off duty and he could venture to New York. Drew agreed to take back his Erie stock from Vanderbilt, but Vanderbilt was insistent Drew should go out of Erie. Drew was allowed to come back to New York unmolested and his overissue of stock no longer questioned. Peter Sweeney, a Tammany man, was named receiver and was paid one hundred and fifty thousand dollars for his services. The lawyers pocketed their fees. The judges pocketed their bribes, and the might of the law was the laughing stock of the Street. So dropped the curtain on the fevered year of 1866–67.

But where were Fisk and Gould in this wild scrimmage of iniquity? Acting for Drew from beginning to end as brokers in the rail market. Gould went up in 1868 to Albany "to induce" the legislature to legalize the stock issues of Drew. The legislators required a lot of "inducing." There, Gould met Boss Tweed of Vanderbilt's Tammany Ring. Tweed had unaccountably one hundred and eighty thousand dollars of the stock delivered by Drew to Vanderbilt. Naturally, he wanted that made legally valid. Under oath Tweed later swore "the inducing" process emptied "a little black satchel" of a half million which Mr. Gould had brought with him. One senator's vote wouldn't stay put. At the last moment, when it looked like a tie, he raised his price to twenty thousand dollars. The law was passed legalizing the stock issue but forbidding any consolidation of the New York Central system with the Erie. This killed Vanderbilt's plan to consolidate the two systems.

One wonders what would have been the fate of the Erie if Vanderbilt had won.

Gould had been brought down from Albany under arrest on that prior charge of overissuing Erie stock; but when the sheriff went to seize the body of said Jay Gould, Tammany thugs interfered with the process of the law. While the lawyers kept up a show of argument to midsummer of 1868–largely to placate an enraged public–Jay Gould emerged from the scrimmage as president of the Erie, age thirty-four. What influences put him in, it is hard to guess. Perhaps Drew, forced out, wanted his man in to hold the loaded dice for future tricks. If so, he reckoned wrong on Gould. Once clear of that "old man of the sea," Gould charted his own course. Perhaps the legislators of Albany and the Tammany Ring wanted as president a man who could not tell all he knew of "rings inside rings" because he dare not. They were all heavy holders of Erie stock and did not want to see it footballed down again by Drew. Perhaps Gould's own consummate ability in handling men, and his still more consummate ability in keeping his lips sealed, commended him to all sides as the best compromise candidate to disentangle the Erie from the awful plight into which it had fallen.

As poor old Drew mournfully wailed, "there ain't nothin' more in Airy for eny ov us–Corneel."

It was an ominous sign that Fisk, Tweed, Sweeney, were now directors. Anyway, judges would obey their nod and the Erie would be free of contradictory injunctions and ravenous politicians demanding "blackmail" for votes. Cheaper to buy the voters, who created the judges and politicians!

But the banks had become gunshy. No more loans to Erie. It had at least forty millions of common stock on the market instead of the ten millions with which it had begun. In 1868, it could not sell a bond, and the Exchange could not exclude it for fear of a universal panic. Up and down, wiggle-waggle went Erie stock. With Fisk as auditor, wilder and wilder went the spendings–eight hundred and fifty thousand dollars for the Grand Opera House; a million and a half for nine brownstone houses in Twenty-third Street, some of which housed Erie offices, some of which housed Fisk's show ladies. Old Drew must have taken fright at the

One of the first of the streamliners.—*Milwaukee Road Photograph courtesy of* Trains *Magazine*

wild pace; for he now turned on Gould and besought the courts to enjoin and remove the new directors. He was ghastly short of Erie stock, which he had again been trying to pound down. He was indeed almost down to the penury in which he died, dependent on poor relatives. Gould and Fisk were through with the pitiful old harpy. He was tossed aside as a worn-out tool, a victim of his own plots. The receivership came as already told with Gould as receiver and later as president of the reorganized Erie. Again a block of genuinely furious stockholders tried to oust what they called the Tammany Gang; but the Tammany toughs camped in the halls of the Erie offices and the minions of the law did not find it healthy to pass them, though it is a commonly accepted tradition that Jay Gould made exit from his offices several times over desks and through windows and down fire escapes, till fresh decisions ensconced him securely in the saddle. Henceforth, Tweed and Fisk and Sweeney were his office boys. They had simply changed their boss from Drew to Gould.

Gould meanwhile went ahead restoring the dilapidated Erie as revenues permitted.... The prices were so very low that English investors came buying in tempted by the reputation of Gould's abilities to restore a ruined line; and this led to one of the most amazing fiascos in all Gould's spectacular career.

A wife of Fisk's partner visiting in Minneapolis met a lion from the Old Country posing as a "Lord Gordon Gordon." True, he didn't say he was, or sign himself as "Lord" Gordon. What titled man would? But letters came to his hotel addressed "Lord Gordon Gordon," stamped with the Aberdeen crest. The little frontier city, now in the first mad scramble of its Northern Pacific Railroad boom, pricked up its ears and all social doors were thrown wide open to the suave, deferential, charming addition to polite circles. He was simply an accomplished swindler from Europe—living by his wits which were sharper than his courage and no remote relative to the Aberdeen Gordons; but the son of a poor man, with a past few knew except that he had had the knack of picking up such a veneer of polished manners as any sharp valet or hotel waiter could acquire. He did not say so, but he let drop mysterious, casual hints of being a scout to look over cheap Western lands for fifty thousand or

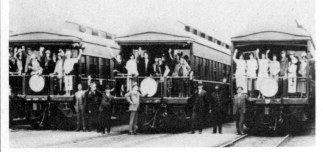

Three sections of the California limited before departure from Los Angeles in 1930.—*Santa Fe Railway Photo*

more British colonists. Cheap lands! The Northern Pacific had oodles of cheap lands—land grants. Forthwith, he was supplied with a private train to look over cheap lands. That entertainment cost the Northern Pacific fifteen thousand dollars. He selected his land and in his quiet way proceeded to a bigger field for operations—New York—where mysteriously enough he took quarters in a hotel owned by Tweed's son; and mysteriously, the whisper leaked out he was in New York with power of attorney to negotiate sixty thousand or more of Erie stock owned by English banks for the best value they could get; and again forthwith he became a lion in New York. Horace Greeley was taken in by the impostor. So was the president of the Pennsylvania Railroad. So were Vanderbilt and his family; but it was to the Erie crowd he drifted, though he at first questioned "whether it were wise to meet the Erie people when he was negotiating terms for English stockholders in the Erie." He was a wise boy—was "Lord" Gordon Gordon; and a keen student of human psychology long before character analysis had come in vogue. One

can see Jay Gould pretty nearly jump out of his boots! *Sixty thousand more shares of Erie* tossed on the market would have smashed Erie values to the dust. Gould met him almost as a suppliant. Gordon treated Gould with scant and royal condescension. He would "refrain" from tossing these shares on the market provided Gould would resign the presidency of the Erie. The certificates were on the way from London, and, on second thought, Gordon consented to refrain from ruining the Erie by such a move if he were compensated a million in good securities, half down to pay his expenses and negotiate delays with the English crowd. Now Gould was at this time having real enough trouble with genuine English shareholders, who had a beastly stolid British way of wanting facts, not explanations. The American Ambassador to England was plaguing his very soul. Like lightning Gould handed over to "Lord" Gordon two hundred thousand dollars in greenbacks and three hundred thousand dollars in other securities of the Erie's holdings.

What pricked Jay Gould's suspicions, he never told. He may have seen the British consul; but within twenty-four hours, early in the day, he stepped into Boss Tweed's offices on Duane Street with the astounding announcement: "Tweed, that Gordon is a scoundrel—I want him arrested."

Within half an hour, the Tammany chief of police, Gould, a judge, and a sheriff were in Gordon's hotel. Admitted to his parlor, they told him he must restore the securities instantly or he would be railroaded to prison till he disgorged. Gordon handed back the cash and gave an order on his broker to restore the securities; but Gould hadn't finished with him. He swore out an order for his arrest, and Gordon countered by entering suit against Gould for intimidation and breach of contract, but he was shy of court proceedings, was "Lord" Gordon Gordon. Leaving his friends thirty-seven thousand dollars in the lurch for bonds for his appearance in court, he disappeared; and a year later turned up in the settlement of Headingly, just west of Winnipeg, Manitoba. His bondsmen were furious and dispatched two American detectives using fake Canadian badges and warrants to kidnap Gordon and slip him back across the border. At this time, just after the Riel Rebellion of 1871, Manitoba was not feeling particularly kindly to Minnesota for harboring Fenians and rebels. The detectives knocked on the door of Gordon's little farmhouse. He begged not to be taken back East through the United States and, on promise that he would not, asked leave to retire to his room and pack. A revolver shot sounded, and "Lord" Gordon was found with his brains blown out. If he had had as much daring as cunning, he might still have been a most dangerous foe to Gould; but he probably knew the reputation of those Tammany thugs towards a man in jail. Of course, such a violation of international law as fake detectives or kidnaping a man across a friendly neighbor's border provided leather-lungs with a theme for some months; but though Manitoba had no love for Fenian raids, she had less for fake English adventurers. Being an old Hudson's Bay Company town, Winnipeg had suffered too much from such gentry herself. After lying in jail a few weeks to teach them to observe the law, the detectives were quietly tried and sentenced to twenty-four hours' imprisonment. Discounting all the leather-lung rantings, it was pretty much regarded as a good joke on Jay Gould.

The early years of Gould's presidency of the Erie continued hectic. Fisk fell by an assassin's bullet in January of 1872, killed by a young

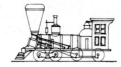

man jealous over one of the showman's ladies. The Tweed Ring was driven from public life by the fury of an outraged public. The fearful crash of 1873 was hanging over the financial world like a sword suspended by a thread. In thirty years, the Erie passed through four receiverships; but all dated back to that era of lords of misrule, dictated by an ignorant old man, who died a pauper in the midst of senile dreams that he would go back to the Street and "lick the gang." There was never a scintilla of evidence at any time that Daniel Drew realized he had ever done wrong.

In his leisure, which was little, Gould retreated to his flowers, to his books, to his family. It was his appalling misfortune to fall into the coils of a Daniel Drew and gain his admission to the great financial center of the subterranean channels of the most corrupt city government New York ever knew. If he had had Vanderbilt's physique, he might have fought it and lived long enough to triumph over it, but he hadn't. He was frail of body and came to a prematurely foreshortened end by taking on his back greater loads than he could carry. He died a burned-out candle at fifty-six.

JAY GOULD'S DAUGHTER

A
Jay Gould's daughter said before she died,
E7
Papa, fix the blinds so the bums can't ride.
    A
If ride they must, they got to ride the rod.
     E7 A
Let 'em put their trust in the hands of God.
 D
In the hands of God.
 A
In the hands of God.
     E7   A
Let them put their trust in the hands of God.

Jay Gould's daughter said, before she died,
There's two more trains I'd like to ride.
Jay Gould said, "Daughter, what can they be?"
The Southern Pacific and the Santa Fe.
The Santa Fe, etc.

Jay Gould's daughter said, before she died,
There's two more drinks I'd like to try.
Jay Gould said, "Daughter what can they be?"
They's a glass o' water and a cup o' tea.
A cup o' tea, etc.

On a Monday morning it begin to rain.
'Round the curve come a passenger train.
On the blinds was Hobo John.
He's a good old hobo, but he's dead and gone.
Dead and gone, etc.

Charlie Snyder was a good engineer
Told his fireman not to fear
Pour on your water, boys, and shovel on your coal
Stick your head out the window, see the drivers roll
See the drivers roll, etc.

It was 1882, and the freight handlers on the New York Central & Hudson River Railroad and the New York Lake Erie & Western Railroad were earning seventeen cents an hour. With no union and almost no organization, they decided to strike for a raise to twenty cents. They walked off their jobs during the summer, and the railroad officials (Vanderbilt, Gould and Field) brought in strike breakers. The strike was a failure.

(Tune: "Rambling Rake of Poverty")

It was at Cooper's Institute, Jack Burke and I chanced to meet;
It's years since last we parted, leaving school on Hudson Street.
He introduced me to his friends, the Doyles, the O's, the Macs,
And the subject of the evening was about the railroad strike.

Refrain: We're on the strike and we won't go back,
    Our claims are just and right;
    Trade unions and the public press
    Will help us with all their might.

There's Field, Jay Gould, and Vanderbilt, their millions they did save
By paying starvation wages and working men like slaves;
They hum round honest labor as the bee does round the flower,
And suck the sweetness of your toil for 17 cents an hour.

They advertised in English, French, Irish, and Dutch,

They got a sample of all nations to work in place of us;
They marched them to the depot and told them not to fear,
And to shake their courage up in them, they gave them lager beer.

The lager beer and sandwiches with them did not agree;
In place of handling merchandise they all got on the spree.
The Russian Jews soon spread the news about their jolly times,
And all the bums from Baxter Street rushed for the railroad lines.

The Italians made themselves at home and soon began to call
For William H., the railroad king, to pass the beer along;
Jay Gould was making sandwiches and Field began to cry
Because he couldn't snatch the man that blew up his English spy.

Those mean monopolizers had the cheek to take the stand
And ask to get protection from the honest working man
Who tries to sell his labor in a manly upright way,
And will not handle railroad freight for less than two a day.

Does the devil make those fools believe that they are smart and clever—
Does he tell them wealth will bring them health and make them live for ever;
Does he lead them from their gambling dens and to some shady bower,
To make them fix a workman's pay at 17 cents an hour?

THE OTHER MAGNATE

If you had been standing by the roadside in western New York State in October of 1844, you might have seen the fourteen-year-old son of Reverend Isaac and Jane Flagler carrying a carpetbag and wearing the rough clothes his mother had sewn, heading for the Erie Canal. If you had asked him where he was headed, he might have said, "I am going away to seek my fortune." That's what he was doing. He was not a rambler. He knew that he was going off to work in a store and learn business and be successful. With hardly a side step and never a back one, this is what he did. But nothing in his early life—or his middle life, for that matter—would match the final achievement of his old age.

Henry Flagler did learn the ways of business in his half brother's store in Republic, Ohio, then greatly profited from the grain business during the Civil War, then lost money experimenting with salt mining, and then followed John D. Rockefeller from grain into oil. What became the Standard Oil Company was for a while Rockefeller, Andrews and Flagler. But making fortunes and consorting with the shapers of the century quickly became routine for the tall preacher's son who didn't want to stay poor.

The great adventure of his life began when he took his second wife to Florida on their honeymoon in 1883. His first wife, Mary, had died of bronchial trouble, and Alice was to fill the emptiness of his middle years. (As it happened, she was not the companion he hoped for and needed, and eventually died in a private sanitarium for the insane.) He fell in love with Florida on that trip and came to spend an increasing amount of time there.

He noticed that there was not much found in Florida in the way of tourist accommodations, so he set about correcting that lack. By the time he returned on his private railroad car in 1885, he was able to take Alice to their own hotel near completion in St. Augustine. Then, because he felt there was insufficient rail service, he got into that business with the Jacksonville, St. Augustine & Indian River Railroad. By 1895 its name was changed to the Florida East Coast Railway, and it was under this banner that Flagler pushed his main line out to sea in the most incredible feat of railroad building in America's history.

The same year in which the company's name was changed, Alice Flagler was confined to a mental institution in New York State, and Henry took up residence in Florida without her. When she had been insane for six years, he decided he had a right to dissolve the marriage so long as he saw to her continued care. Faced with Florida and New York laws that prohibited divorce from insane spouses, he used his money and political influence to have a law passed by the Florida legislature which allowed such divorce, and amid a statewide storm of protest in the newspapers and pulpit he filed suit and won his freedom. On August

24, 1901, he married Mary Lily Kennan, a North Carolinian of thirty-four. He was seventy-one.

As with the hotels and the railroad, he had seen something he thought ought to be different, and he changed it. He was getting ready for the undertaking that engineers around the world would refer to, when they first heard about it, as Flagler's Folly. What he saw now and didn't like was the inaccessibility of the Florida Keys, stretching from the mainland 128 miles to Key West. Flagler decided that he was going to connect Miami and each of the Keys with an extension of his Florida East Coast Railway. When he finally found engineers who didn't think he was crazy, he was seventy-five years old. By the time he found enough workmen who didn't think he was

crazy or who didn't care, and saw the first rails being laid, he was seventy-six. He was told over and over again by friends and by strangers that the wild tides and the tropical storms would make the laying of such a line impossible. Flagler's Folly was talked about and laughed about everywhere.

There was not much laughing, though, among the men who were building the extension. The demands on the skills of the engineers and the stamina of the workmen were staggering to the body and the spirit and seemed endless. Thirty-seven miles of the track were actually to bridge the sea, and twenty miles had to be set on embankments, or beds built up with rock fill. Miles of track were ripped out by hurricanes almost as soon as they were laid; rock fill was swept away and embankments collapsed.

On October 18, 1906, the workers were caught off guard by a hurricane that tore away a giant pile driver with a full crew and sank the houseboats the crews were quartered in. At least seventy-five and perhaps over a hundred workers were lost. Another hurricane, in 1909, destroyed a great deal of track and equipment.

The four thousand who spent seven years

taking Flagler's railroad out to sea may have known—if they cared—that the purpose of the extension was to make Key West the main gateway for trade with Cuba and the rest of Latin America. All anyone cared about on January 22, 1912, was the grand celebration when Henry Flagler, a physically weakened but alert and good-humored man of eighty-two, rode from the mainland to Key West in his private railroad car. He was accompanied by dignitaries from Washington and Central American and European countries, and the speeches at Key West went on and on. If the old man grew tired from this, he didn't show it. Flagler's Folly had become "the eighth wonder of the world."

When he died in 1919, Henry Flagler believed his dream would stay true and that he had made Key West the permanent Gibraltar of America. But on Labor Day 1935 a hurricane destroyed much of the track and threw a whole train into the water with great loss of life. The Florida East Coast Railway didn't try to rebuild, and abandoned the extension. For a while it looked as if Flagler's work would be for nothing, then the State of Florida took charge and replaced the steel with pavement. The roadway that now links Miami and the Keys rests on the embankments and bridges that Flagler's engineers and laborers laid for his seagoing railroad. It still belongs to him, in a way, and even more to the thousands who built it and the scores who died trying.

M. W.

EUGENE V. DEBS AND THE
AMERICAN RAILWAY UNION

Ray Ginger

The fierce, hard-fought Pullman boycott of 1894, named The Debs Rebellion by the commercial newspapers, began as a local dispute in the small Chicago suburb of Pullman, Illinois. During the previous year, more than sixteen thousand business firms had gone bankrupt, including fifty companies with a capital of more than a half million dollars each. Thousands of other firms were threatened with failure. The continued drop of wholesale prices made it increasingly difficult to produce goods at a profit. Companies, in a frantic attempt to cut their production costs and salvage their investments, repeatedly slashed the pay of their workers. These wage cuts and layoffs burst with a peculiar fury upon the residents of Pullman, where the Pullman Palace Car Company was the only employer and the only landlord. Since there was no competing demand for labor, and since most of the Pullman workers lacked the money to migrate elsewhere in search of better jobs, they were forced to submit or starve.

Just as wages were lower in Pullman, so rents were higher there. Jane Addams of Hull House, who investigated the town for the Civic Federation of Chicago, said that an eighteen-dollar-per-month cottage in Pullman could be rented for fifteen dollars in Chicago. In the words of the Federal commission: "If we exclude the aesthetic and sanitary features at Pullman, the rents there are from 20 to 25 per cent higher than rents in Chicago or surrounding towns for similar accommodations. The aesthetic features are admired by visitors, but have little money value to employees, especially when they lack bread." But the company refused to cut rents when it reduced wages, claiming that its rental of houses was a separate business from its manufacture of sleeping cars, and that there was no connection between the two enterprises.

Every foot of ground, every house, every church in the town was owned by the company, and they were run on a purely commercial basis. Even the sewage from the workers' homes was pumped to George M. Pullman's truck farm as fertilizer. Adults paid three dollars and children one dollar per year for the use of the town library, but the company said this charge was levied "not for profit, but to give the subscribers a sense of ownership."

The town was similar in many ways to a feudal manor, with George Pullman as absolute monarch. Since he believed that saloons and trade unions tended to inflame the workers, both were banned from the community. The eight-hour day was also banned, because Pullman thought that idleness would promote mischief. Professor Richard T. Ely and a Chicago judge both charged that the company hired spies to inform against the workers, and Mr. Carwardine wrote: "I am in a position to know that information of everything going on in the town of Pullman . . . is conveyed by letter every week to headquarters from the town proper." In order to maintain this absolute domination, the company freely interfered in local elections. Intimidation at the polls was common. The residents were advised how to vote, and the advice also held a poorly concealed threat. On one occasion a foreman was ordered to withdraw his name as a candidate for public office; when he refused he was fired.

Although most employees continued to live in Pullman because residents there were the last to be laid off and the first to be rehired, they deeply resented the destruction of their dignity. With grim humor one man declared: "We are born in a Pullman house, fed from the Pullman shop, taught in the Pullman school, catechized in the Pullman church, and when we die we shall be buried in the Pullman cemetery and go to the Pullman hell." Mr. Carwardine added that an awareness of George M. Pullman, not an awareness of God, ruled the community: "An unpleasant feature of the town is that you are made to feel at every turn the presence of the corporation. . . . This is a corporation-made and a corporation-governed town, and is utterly un-American in its tendencies." Four years later, the Supreme Court of Illinois agreed. Ordering the Palace Car Company to sell all property in the town of Pullman not needed for its manufacturing business, the Court declared that company towns were "opposed to good public policy and incompatible with the theory and spirit of our institutions."

The Pullman Company also exploited its monopoly position by charging exorbitant prices for its services. Since its formation in 1867, the company had paid an annual dividend of 8 per cent, and during the depression dividends were increased while wages were being cut 25 per cent. For the year ending July 31, 1894, the corporation had an undivided surplus of $2,320,000, exceeding its total wage outlay for six months.

As early as December, 1893, the Pullman Company was forced to issue a public statement denying the existence of extreme distress among its workers. The denial was easy to read, and easy to believe for men who had their own distress. Nobody cared much about poverty in Pullman except the residents of Pullman. During the harsh Illinois winter, want and suffering there became unbearable. Children lacked the money to buy school

The Louisville & Nashville Railroad's crack passenger train, The Humming Bird, shown at Birmingham, Ala., in 1954. The train ran between Cincinnati, Ohio, and New Orleans, La. It was discontinued in 1969.—*Louisville & Nashville Railroad Photo*

books, but that didn't matter—they also lacked the shoes and coats needed to go to school. In some homes they were kept in bed all day because there was no coal in the house; in others they were sent to bed early because there was no food for dinner. All joy passed from life. Sullen, tight-lipped women walked lead-footed through their worries. Men stood day after day by their windows and looked at the dirty black snow in the street—no work, no money, little

King Debs.—*Library of Congress*

hope. They erupted into violent rage, kicking the dog, swearing at the children, berating the wife for unmentionable evils. Nothing to do but stand at a window all day, looking at the dirty black snow and hearing a baby's whine from the next room.

Spring brought back hope, not much but a little. Men began to talk about striking one good blow against Pullman. During March and April, a majority of the employees joined the American Railway Union—they were eligible because the company operated a few miles of track near the factory. Finally on May 7, 1894, a committee of forty employees visited vice-president Wickes to present their complaints about wages and working conditions. Wickes told the committee to return two days later with their grievances down in writing; but on May 9 Wickes again delayed, promising to personally investigate the shop abuses. The men were not satisfied. Words were cheap,

they thought; you couldn't trust Wickes. The next night the grievance committee held an all-night session at the Turner Hall in Kensington, an adjoining town, to discuss the advisability of a strike. George Howard and Sylvester Keliher were both at the meeting to urge delay until Wickes had completed his investigation. Howard had previously wired to Debs [leader of the American Railway Union], who was in Terre Haute, that a walkout might occur. Debs, knowing nothing of conditions in Pullman, had advised caution until the union could learn the facts. But Howard's oratory, Keliher's ebullient charm, and Debs' influence all went for nothing. The workers were mad. God Himself could not have stopped them. On the third ballot they voted unanimously to strike.

At noon on May 11, three thousand workers left their jobs in the Pullman shops, and the remaining three hundred men were quickly laid off by the company. The walkout was calm, with no hint of violence. The strikers posted guards around the plant to make certain that vandals would have no chance to damage corporation property. Driven to the end of the tether, these men had snapped the chains and struck, but they struck without much hope. Resigned desperation was the major key in a May 13 statement by Thomas Heathcote, the strike committee's chairman: "We do not expect the company to concede to our demands. We do not know what the outcome will be, and in fact we do not care much. We know that we are working for less wages than will maintain ourselves and families in the necessaries of life, and on that proposition we absolutely refuse to work any longer."

Notified that the strike had begun, Debs at once hurried to Pullman to investigate its causes. The ARU had neither called nor authorized the walkout, but these men were members of the union and Debs' clear responsibility was to ascertain the justice of their action. Seven years earlier he had protested against George Pullman's labor policies, but he was ill prepared for what he found in 1894. The Pullman employees told incredible but truthful stories of hardship. One skilled mechanic worked ten hours a day for twelve days, and then received a pay check for seven cents;

his wages had been $9.07, but nine dollars rent for his company-owned house had been deducted in advance. A fireman worked "428 hours per month or about sixteen hours per day, and receives therefrom $40.00 per month pay," according to Mr. Carwardine. A blacksmith, paid forty-five cents for working six hours, declared that he was not willing to starve and wear out his clothes on Pullman's anvil at the same time. "I have a wife and four children," another employee said, "and it was for them that I struck, as I think that when a man is sober and steady, and has a saving wife, one who is willing to help along, and after working two and a half years for a company he finds himself in debt for a common living, something must be wrong."

On May 14, Eugene Debs spent the entire day wandering through the town of Pullman, inspecting the houses, talking with the women and children, noticing the size of pay checks, hearing complaints by the score, by the hundred. That night Debs left for St. Paul, but four days later he was back in Pullman and spent most of the day and evening there. As one link clutched the next to form an ugly chain of greed and injustice, his hesitation disappeared. Finally he told a meeting of Pullman employees:

> If it is a fact that after working for George M. Pullman for years you appear two weeks after your work stops, ragged and hungry, it only emphasizes the charge I made before this community, and Pullman stands before you a self-confessed robber ... The paternalism of Pullman is the same as the self-interest of a slave-holder in his human chattels. You are striking to avert slavery and degradation.

When the first national convention of the American Railway Union met in Chicago on June 12, 1894, the entire labor movement was in a critical situation. Layoffs and wage cuts had aroused fierce resistance, but strike after strike had been beaten down by strikebreakers, injunctions, Federal and state troops, starvation. The glorious promise of the unemployed march on Washington had ended a ludicrous shambles, with General Jacob S. Coxey arrested for walking on the Capitol lawn. Only the American Railway Union had managed to beat its way forward. Debs had

been ridiculed ten months earlier when he predicted three hundred lodges within a year, but his estimate had been exceeded; the convention held more than four hundred delegates from four hundred sixty-five local unions.

On June 15 the convention began its consideration of the Pullman dispute. Many of the delegates had already made inspection trips to the suburb and talked to the workers there. They had returned to Chicago angry, resentful. Now a committee from the strikers presented a lengthy statement to prove the greed and despotism of George M. Pullman. The statement concluded with a passionate appeal for support from the convention:

> We struck because we were without hope. We joined the American Railway Union because it gave us a glimmer of hope. ... We will make you proud of us, brothers, if you will give us the hand we need. Help us make our country better and more wholesome. ... Teach arrogant grinders of the faces of the poor that there is still a God of Israel, and if need be a Jehovah—a God of battles.

Thus was the stage set for a moving statement by Jennie Curtis, a seamstress at Pullman, who lifted to reckless heights the growing excitement among the delegates. Miss Curtis, thin and tired, said that after her father died she had been forced to repay the sixty dollars back rent that he owed the company, even though her father had been a Pullman employee for thirteen years. The Rev. William Carwardine

The private railroad car of George Jay Gould has found a resting place in Jefferson, Texas, the town he once cursed. The car is located across the street from the Excelsior House, where the financier wrote in the guest register, "The end of Jefferson," because the city preferred "grass growing in the streets" to Gould's railroad.—*Courtesy Marion County (Texas) Chamber of Commerce*

testified that the residents of Pullman were on the brink of starvation, but his plea was not needed. The story of Jennie Curtis was irresistible to the sentimental railroaders.

Debs now used every rein of control in the hands of a chairman. His shrewdness, his eloquence, his influence, were all thrown into battle against headstrong action, and, in the end, they all went for nothing. The entire hall was filled with muffled, bitter comments: George Pullman had gone too far. It was time to show the bloodsucker. The ARU should boycott all Pullman cars, not move a single sleeper until Pullman settled with his workers. By God, it wasn't right to rob a girl. No, by God. Finally one man spoke for dozens of men: A boycott against Pullman cars should be declared immediately. Debs, in his calmest voice, refused to entertain the motion. He suggested that a committee be appointed to confer with the Pullman Company.

Determined to settle the dispute peacefully, Debs fervently hoped that the company would agree to the proposal. Above everything else, he wanted to avoid a boycott on Pullman cars.

But the Pullman Company refused to yield an inch. The company claimed that wages and working conditions should be decided by the management, with no interference by labor. George Pullman was in business for profit, and the decreased sale of his product made it necessary to cut wages. That was his position. And, from the company's viewpoint, it was undeniably true. On June 16, the mediation committee from the convention reported that the company refused to confer with any members of the American Railway Union. This news fairly exploded in Uhlich's Hall. Pullman's intransigeance infuriated the delegates, who were now ready for any action. Again a boycott was proposed, with overwhelming support. Again Debs blocked the move. At his suggestion a second committee, composed entirely of Pullman employees, was sent with a request for arbitration. Within a few hours the committee returned; vice-president Wickes

had said there was "nothing to arbitrate." The committee had then asked whether the company would consider restoring wages to the May, 1893, scale. The vice-president's answer wiped out all hope for a peaceful settlement: "Mr. Wickes replied that we had no right to ask him that question, as he thought we stood in the same position as the man on the sidewalk."

Realizing that the dispute could not be settled promptly, the convention tried to alleviate the suffering at Pullman. Mayor John P. Hopkins of Chicago was thanked for his fifteen-hundred-dollar donation to the relief fund. The delegates also voted a two-thousand-dollar contribution to the strikers, and a weekly assessment of ten cents on every member at the discretion of the executive board. Then attention returned to the strategy to be used against the Pullman Company. The delegates wired to their local unions for instructions and the replies gave them blanket authority to use their own judgment. Finally a special committee was chosen to recommend a plan of action.

On June 22, this committee made its report: Unless the Pullman Company agreed to begin negotiations within four days, the Pullman shops at Ludlow, Kentucky, and at St. Louis, would be struck, and the ARU would refuse to handle Pullman cars. George Howard opposed this plan by arguing that mere cessation of work at Ludlow and St. Louis would force the company to yield. The delegates brushed aside this proposal. They knew that a major part of the company's revenue came from rental of its Palace Cars; it would surrender only if its income were completely cut off. Debs announced his readiness to accept the convention's verdict, but he again emphasized the need for caution. In no mood for caution, the delegates accepted the committee's report. The committee was then sent for a final conference with Mr. Wickes, who still refused to settle the dispute by peaceful means, so the convention unanimously voted the boycott, to begin at noon on June 26 unless the corporation changed its mind. . . .

The Pullman Company did not retreat, nor did the workers. At noon on June 26, the deadline set by the convention, Debs ordered all sleep-

ing cars cut from the trains and sidetracked. The railroads at once took an active rôle in the conflict; they refused to move any trains without Palace Cars on the grounds that their contracts with Pullman were inviolable. The General Managers Association,* which was the employers' general staff throughout the boycott, welcomed a showdown fight with the ARU. The railroads had consistently discriminated against ARU members, and they had

The great railway strikes—the first meat train leaving the Chicago stock-yards under escort of U.S. Cavalry, July 10, 1894.—*Library of Congress*

refused to give Debs and his colleagues the free passes which they handed out to officials in the Brotherhoods. Thus the ARU came into immediate conflict with one of the strongest groups of employers in America; The Managers represented the twenty-four railroads terminating or centering in Chicago, which had a combined capital of eight hundred and eighteen million dollars, operated forty-one thousand miles of track, and had two hundred twenty-one thousand employees.

Foreseeing opposition from the railroads, Debs had already asked for assistance from the AFL and the Brotherhoods. A return wire from Samuel Gompers showed the reluctance in that sector: "Just received telegram signed your name. Verify same by letter giving full particulars." Only president John McBride of the Mine Workers promised full co-operation;

_____
* Hereafter called The Managers.

the others replied evasively or negatively, and most of the Brotherhoods worked against the boycott. . . .

But Debs had no time to send Gompers "full particulars" or to negotiate with the Brotherhood leaders. . . . Co-ordination of five hundred local unions and thousands of men rested in the hands of Debs, Howard, Keliher, Rogers, a few organizers, and Theodore Debs, who was again working side by side with his brother. The boycott began slowly. In spite of the convention orders, each ARU lodge was constitutionally forced to hold its own vote to determine whether it would support the boycott. Every lodge voted to enforce the convention's decision. The boycott was not called solely from sympathy with the Pullman workers; the railroad employees were also suffering from blacklists, short hours, wage cuts, discrimination. Also the feeling was widespread that, if the corporations succeeded in conquering the unorganized workers, they would next move against the organized men. Even among skilled workers there was agreement with Debs' statement: "Every concession the railway companies have ever made, has been wrung from them by the power of organized effort." As lodge after lodge voted to quit work, Debs sent them all the same instructions: Use no violence. Stop no trains. Elect a strike committee and send me the name of the chairman. In this way he hoped to keep control over the entire boycott.

By June 27 only five thousand men had left their jobs, but fifteen railroads were tied up. The Managers opened offices in Pittsburgh, Cleveland, Philadelphia, New York, and Buffalo, to recruit strikebreakers; they also opened a central publicity office in Chicago to furnish information to the newspapers. Soon the commercial press raised the cry of "Anarchy"; this charge was doubly effective because President Sadi Carnot of France had been assassinated by an anarchist just two days before the boycott began. The third day, more than forty thousand men had quit work. Traffic was stopped dead on all lines west of Chicago. In spite of Debs' orders to move mail trains, the Postal authorities reported that mails were obstructed at Chicago, St. Paul, and on the Southern Pacific in the Far West. United States Attorneys were instructed by the Justice Department to ask for warrants against all offenders.

One day later, nearly a hundred twenty-five thousand men had joined the boycott. Twenty roads were tied up. A crowd of a thousand strikers and sympathizers stopped a train on the Chicago & Erie at Hammond, Indiana, and forced the crew to detach two Pullmans. The head of the Switchmen warned that any member of his union supporting the strike would be subject to expulsion, and the Conductor's chief attacked the boycott in the public press.

But several unions rallied to the ARU. J. R. Sovereign pledged aid from the Knights of Labor. The Chicago Federation of Labor, with one hundred fifty thousand members, offered to call a city-wide general strike to enforce the boycott. In view of the probable effects on public opinion, Debs refused to sanction such an extreme measure at that stage. During the entire boycott he divided his attention between the need to maintain the strikers' morale and the equal need to win support among other trade unions and the general community.

On June 30, in spite of Debs' orders to the contrary, minor violence again occurred. Crowds in Chicago temporarily halted two express trains on the Illinois Central and Pan-handle lines. Union leaders were arrested in Indiana and Missouri. The first demand for militia in Illinois came from the Illinois Central, which claimed that its property in Cairo was endangered. Under the laws of Illinois, the governor could call out state troops when the legislature was not in session, but only at the request of the mayor or sheriff. As soon as he had secured permission from these local authorities, Governor Altgeld sent three companies of militia to Cairo. Thomas Milchrist, the Federal district attorney in Chicago, telegraphed to Washington that strikers had stopped mail trains in the suburbs the previous night. He also reported that conditions in Chicago were so bad that special deputies were needed, and recommended that the United States marshal in Chicago be empowered to hire such deputies. This wire by Milchrist exaggerated the actual situation. Five days after he sent the telegram, total strike damages were still less than six thousand dollars. There

had been no major riots. The trains halted on the Chicago & Erie, Illinois Central, and Pan-handle had soon been allowed to proceed. The telegram from Milchrist was contradicted by a simultaneous telegram from the Superintendent of Railway Mail Service in Chicago, telling the Postmaster General that no mail had accumulated in the city.

Opposition to the boycott was gathering intensity. The railroads began deliberately to disrupt their schedules, hoping that the resultant inconvenience to the public would force government intervention. Pullmans were attached to trains that did not customarily carry them—freights, suburbans, and, most important of all, mail trains, trying to force the strikers to halt the mails. The Brotherhoods accelerated their campaign against the ARU. Conductors in Fort Wayne, Indiana, denounced the strike, declaring that they would not aid in any way. P. M. Arthur announced that he did not care whether the railroads employed union or nonunion engineers and firemen; any engineers who refused to work with strikebreakers could be fired without protest from the Brotherhood. Frank Sargent declared that any fireman who joined the strike would have to look to the ARU for help—he would get none from the BLF.

Never before had there been such a strike in the United States. More than a hundred thousand men had voluntarily quit work. Between Chicago and the Golden Gate, only the Great Northern was maintaining a semblance of its regular schedule. Everybody in the country had taken sides in the dispute. Debs clearly stated the situation in a speech to the railroaders:

> The struggle with the Pullman Company has developed into a contest between the producing classes and the money power of the country. . . . The fight was between the American Railroad Union and the Pullman Company. . . . Then the railway corporations, through the General Managers' Association, came to the rescue, and in a series of whereases declared to the world that they would go into partnership with Pullman, so to speak, and stand by him in his devilish work of starving his employees to death.

A. PHILIP RANDOLPH
AND THE BROTHERHOOD
OF SLEEPING CAR PORTERS

Jervis Anderson

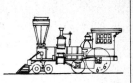

(Editor's note: By the time this story begins, A. Philip Randolph had been one of the great black radical leaders for fifteen years, and the founding editor of the Messenger, *the "Only Radical Negro Magazine in America." He was thirty-six, and everything he had tried to accomplish—except the magazine—had ended in defeat.)*

One morning in June, 1925, two months past his thirty-sixth birthday, and with his political future apparently behind him, Randolph was walking from his new apartment, at 314 West 133rd Street, up Seventh Avenue, on his way to the *Messenger*'s office. At the corner of 135th Street, he was stopped by a man who doffed his white Panama hat, introduced himself as Ashley Totten, and asked to have a word.

Totten further introduced himself as someone who had read the *Messenger* for several years and who had once been a regular listener at Randolph's soapbox forums. What he had on his mind was this: would Randolph consider coming to the Pullman Porters Athletic Association one evening, and speaking to the members on the subject of trade unionism and collective bargaining? Randolph said he would be glad to. He made a date, and resumed his walk to the *Messenger*'s office, carrying away the image of Totten's manner that had most impressed him: "a sort of fearlessness."

Randolph's talk to the Porters Athletic Association was well received, and it encouraged Totten in his resolve. Yet he and his colleagues in New York knew only too well the dangers and difficulties of what they wanted to attempt; every previous effort by Pullman porters to organize themselves had been crushed by the company and the ringleaders fired. Historically, it was not the policy of the Pullman Company to recognize bona fide labor organizations. The company simply fixed its wage rates and working conditions, and employees were free either to accept them or to quit.

In the early 1850's, railroads in the United States linked only the East Coast and the Middle West. To get from California to New York, for instance, it was necessary to take a steamboat down the Pacific coast to San Juan del Sur, in Nicaragua, travel by mule, wagon, and boat across the jungle to the eastern shore, and sail from there to New York. The journey, when not impeded by bad weather, could take as much as four weeks. Even the railroad trip from Chicago to New York City was something of an ordeal. A passenger rode one train from Chicago to Cleveland, changed there to another, for Buffalo, transferred at Buffalo to one headed for Albany, and took another from Albany to New York City. And if, in the process, he had to change from one primitive sleeping car to another, it was a still greater ordeal.

One cold night in 1853, George Mortimer Pullman, twenty-two-year-old woodworker, living in Albion, New York, was traveling in a sleeping car between Buffalo and Westfield, a distance of some fifty-eight miles. It was an uncomfortable experience. The car had neither sheets, blankets, nor pillows. Lying in his clothes and shoes, and trying to sleep on the rough mattress, the young Pullman—who, according to one observer, grew up "conveying the impression that the world rested on his shoulders"—was thinking to himself how such a car might be improved.

It was one of the earliest sleeping cars. Stanley Buder, a Pullman historian, describes them as

> ordinary coaches with a few crude extras added. Three wooden shelves were permanently fixed to the sides in a tier arrangement so that the sleeper could not be used for day travel. Lacking privacy and adequate bedding, the passenger would climb fully dressed onto a shelf. . . . Everyone knew that the problem was to build a sleeping car that could be used comfortably day and night. What was lacking, however, was the know-how.

George Mortimer Pullman provided that know-how. His first chance at doing so came in

1858, when he went to Bloomington, Illinois, and converted two old passenger coaches into sleeping cars, for the Chicago and Alton Railroad. Though they were not much of an improvement upon the existing sleepers, he converted several more, and persuaded a few railroads to use them. When passenger travel fell off, during the Civil War, Pullman left for the gold fields of Colorado, where he ran a trading post from 1862 to 1863, and saved his money. With his savings, he returned to Chicago toward the end of the war, determined to build "the biggest and best car ever."

This turned out to be the "Pioneer." It was built at a cost of $20,000, five times more than any previous sleeping car had cost. Many who had seen it under construction had laughed it away as "Pullman's Folly." But when Pullman unveiled the "Pioneer," it was hailed as "the wonder of the age." "Never before," writes Joseph Husband, one of Pullman's biographers, "had such a car been seen; never had the wildest flights of fancy imagined such magnificence." The floor was covered with a rich red carpet, the seats upholstered with brocaded fabrics, the doorframes made of polished woods, the berths paneled with ornamented wood, and the entire car lit with silver-trimmed oil lamps and hung with gilt-edged mirrors. Arthur Dubin, of Chicago, a collector of Pullman memorabilia, says, "There was a sense of order about this man which must have

The first California Limited into Los Angeles, November, 1892.—*Courtesy of Santa Fe Railway*

been in his personal life. He was a very religious man. He built seminaries and left money to churches. George Pullman was a lover of beautiful things. That's an interesting facet to a man considered by so many to be ruthless."

For a time, the "Pioneer" seemed to be the wonder of the age in more ways than one. Because it was too large to fit between any of the existing station platforms, the railroad companies displayed little interest in it, and people started wondering what on earth Pullman was going to do with his sleeper. It was the assassination of President Lincoln that provided an answer, and opened up a future for the "Pioneer." When the body of the slain President arrived in Chicago, on its way to Springfield, Illinois, state officials looked around for the most splendid conveyance to bear Lincoln on the final leg of his journey. And, of course, there was nothing more splendid in Chicago at the time than the "Pioneer." Platforms along the way were hurriedly widened. The dead President was placed aboard the "Pioneer," and the magnificent sleeper received everywhere an outpouring of publicity and acclaim that exceeded even George Pullman's most optimistic dreams.

"From that day on," says Arthur Dubin, "the Pullman car was very much accepted, and somehow I feel that George Pullman always felt that this break, this accident of Lincoln's death, contributed somehow to the development of his company. So that the attorney for the company at one time was Robert Todd Lincoln. And the minute George Pullman died, Robert Todd Lincoln was elected president of the company. All kinds of romantic stories grew, many of which proved fallacious. But Robert Lincoln was very tight-lipped about anything to do with his father."

Moving quickly to exploit the publicity gained during the President's funeral, the Chicago and Alton Railroad hired the "Pioneer," on Pullman's terms, and placed it in service. Pullman now built several more cars, some even more luxurious than the "Pioneer," and hired them out to a number of other railroads. By the end of 1866, he had forty-eight cars in service, and had become the leading sleeping car builder and entrepreneur in the Midwest. People now called him "the prince of railroads" and "a missionary of civilization" who had made railroad passenger travel "both a comfort and luxury." On February 22, 1867, the Pullman Palace Car Company was incorporated, and by 1870, when the first through train crossed from the Atlantic to the Pacific, George Pullman dominated the sleeping car business in the entire United States.

At first, the comfort and luxury of a Pullman

traveler were in the hands of conductors, but conductors alone—or, perhaps because they were white—could not provide the sort of hospitality Pullman had in mind for his passengers. There had to be a few maids to render personal services to women and children; and, above all, there had to be porters to help receive and discharge passengers, handle baggage, prepare beds and berths, care for linen and equipment, keep the cars tidy, and wait upon a passenger's every wish and desire. In 1867, when he first felt the need for such service, George Pullman turned to what he considered a uniquely appropriate source: the recently freed slaves. Thus from the very beginning the porter's job was "a black man's job."

On the trains, the porters came to be trusted for their honesty, praised for their reliability, and romanticized for their unfailing politeness. And since some of them—the college graduates, no doubt—had been found remarkable for intelligence and refinement, it was not infrequently said by satisfied travelers that the porter was "a higher grade of Negro."

For several years, however, the majority of porters had not been as happy with their situation within the Pullman service as passengers and admiring friends seemed to be. A few of them had stopped smiling not only at their situation, but also at the passengers. Such men meant business; they wanted to change both their working conditions and their public image.

Consider the porter's working conditions. In 1915, when his minimum monthly wage was $27.50, the chairman of a U.S. Commission on Industrial Relations asked the company's general manager, L. S. Hungerford, "Do you consider $27.50 a month sufficient for a man who is required to discharge all the duties you have detailed here and to follow all the rules referred to?" Hungerford replied, "All I can say is that you can get all the men you require to do the work." Between 1915 and 1919, the porter's wage rose to a minimum of $47.50 a month. And in the latter year—following a ruling by William Gibbs McAdoo, Director-General of Railroads under Woodrow Wilson—the porter started making $60 a month, still considerably below what a New York Factory Commission study had set as a decent minimum for an American family. Pullman justified its policy of substandard wages on the following grounds: faced with the urgent need to supplement his wage with tips, the porter would not be able to afford any slackening in his attentions to the passenger.

A porter was also expected to run several hours or hundreds of miles a month without pay. This was called "deadheading." It worked this way. A porter scheduled to leave New York at 12:30 A.M. on a train for Washington, D.C., say, was required to report for duty at 7:30 P.M. He spent these hours preparing the train for departure and receiving passengers. His paid time, however, did not begin until 12:30, when the train pulled out. And if, at 12:30, there were no passengers, the porter was also required to "deadhead" into Washington, in the hope that there would be passengers coming back.

Then there were the times when the porter had to "double out," whether he liked it or not. That is, whenever he returned from a long run—which may have lasted for as long as a week—he could be ordered out on the very next train, without a rest period, and at a lower rate of pay. This, of course, gave him no time to see his family, or even to shower, shave, and change his clothes. But if, while "doubling out," he was found untidy, unclean, or asleep, he was either docked, suspended, or fired.

A porter could also be ordered to run "in charge." On such runs, he performed not only his own duties, but also those of the conductor. If he was "lucky" enough to run "in charge" for a month, he received $10 above his basic salary. This was a considerable saving to the company, for a conductor's salary in, say, 1920 was $150 a month.

"Then, too," a porter from Jacksonville recalls, "there was this thing of 'George.' No matter who you were, or how old, most everybody wanted to call you 'George.' It meant that you were just George Pullman's boy, same as in slave days when if the owner was called Jones the slave was called Jones. It got so you were scared to go into the office to pick up your check, for fear some little sixteen-year-old office boy would yell out 'George.'"

Randolph's decision to lead the new movement had turned mainly on two considerations. First, no one else seemed willing to take up the porters' cause. And, second, on further reflection, he saw the porters as his last and, possibly, best chance to promote the idea of labor unionism among black workers. "The Pullman porter," he told Benjamin Stolberg a year later, "seems to be made to order to carry the gospel of unionism in the colored world. His home is everywhere."

The Brotherhood of Sleeping Car Porters was launched on the night of August 25, 1925, in the auditorium of the Imperial Lodge of Elks, at 160 West 129th Street. The New York *Amsterdam News* called the gathering of 500 "the greatest labor mass meeting ever held of, for and by Negro working men." But not all were well-wishers and potential members. According to the *Amsterdam News,* there were also "a few of the Company's spies and several hat-in-hand porters, waiting to get information to carry back to the Pullman offices." Because of this, the inaugural meeting had to be a cautious and restrained affair. Randolph recalls it:

> I told the men I didn't want one porter to open his mouth in the meeting, lest the stool pigeons reported them to the Pullman Company. So I ran the whole meeting myself. I told them I would now give the invocation, and I gave it. I told them I was going to sing the Brotherhood's song, "Hold the Fort," and I sang it. I told them I was going to make the announcements and introduce guest speakers, and I did. I told them now I was going to make the main speech, and then I did. At the end of the meeting, I moved the vote of thanks, said the benediction, and told everyone to go home and not hold any discussions on the street corners.

Randolph also told the porters what the Brotherhood would be demanding: recognition of the union and abolition of the company's Plan of Employee Representation; an end to tipping, and a minimum monthly wage of $150; a basic work month of 240 hours, compensation for "deadheading," and an end to "doubling out"; conductor's pay for conductor's work; and, "by no means least, that porters be treated like men."

The following day, more than 200 porters came to the *Messenger's* office—also headquarters of the new Brotherhood—to join the union. The initial enthusiasm was so great that within two months [it] would claim a majority of the porters in New York.

But the message had to be spread. Porters in Pullman terminals all over the country had to be organized. There seemed no way, at first, for this to be done, for the Brotherhood had no money to conduct a national membership drive. The parent organization, in New York, took in just enough dues to keep itself alive. Here Randolph turned to his connections among white Socialists and liberals in New York; and the Garland Fund, a supporter of liberal causes—of which Roger Baldwin and Norman Thomas were members—came through with a grant of $10,000. In mid-October, Randolph left New York on the first leg of his first national organizational tour, on which Chicago, Oakland, and St. Louis—three of the largest Pullman terminals outside New York—would be the most important stops.

The man to see in Chicago, Totten had told Randolph, was an old porter named John C. Mills, one of the few delegates who had tried to hold out against Pullman during the 1924 wage conference. But Mills, having neither taste nor talent for organization, called, instead, upon the one man in Chicago who could get porters together: Milton Webster.

At the age of thirty-eight, Milton Price Webster was as tall as Ashley Totten—whom he knew—and even more powerfully built. Not too long before, Webster, who had worked as a Pullman porter for twenty years, had been "canned" by the company, as he put it, for attempting to organize porters in the Railroad Men's Benevolent Association. Launching the movement in Chicago proved more difficult than Randolph, buoyed by the experience in New York, had hoped. Chicago had the largest number of Pullman porters, and would, in time, become the strongest local of the Brotherhood, but the men there were nowhere near as eager to sign up as the New York men had been. And since none of the "big Negroes" would lend the prestige of their presence to the nightly meetings, the only two speakers were Webster and Randolph—"me opening," as Webster said later, "and Brother Randolph closing."

In moving against the upstart Brotherhood of Sleeping Car Porters, the Pullman Company employed three basic weapons: a spy system, in which loyal company porters—or stool pigeons, as they were called—informed upon union members; threats, firings, and suspensions; and the black church, the black press, and the "big Negroes," as the chief instruments of propaganda against the union and its leadership.

Across the country, hundreds of porters were fired as Pullman uncovered their membership in the union. There was that day in St. Louis when superintendent A. V. Burr fired more than thirty men, which crippled Bradley's organization for several years. "Sometimes when Randolph came into St. Louis to hold a meeting," an ex-porter recalls, "he would just talk with anybody he saw on the street, 'cause there were no porters there, or none that would come within a mile of him. Every porter that went to a meeting, old man Burr would just line 'em up next morning and fire 'em."

In Oakland, the company took away Dad Moore's job as caretaker of the two old sleeping cars where out-of-town porters slept. To support himself, and to keep the Oakland division of the union going, he opened his own sleeping quarters to compete with the company's. "He went up on Seventh Street," according to his successor, C. L. Dellums, "over an old saloon, got about four little rooms, and had some secondhand furniture put in. He got a big old stove put in the middle of the living-room part, to keep the place warm. The Eastern porters rented the rooms and slept in some old hammocks he had. On the ground floor, behind the saloon, Dad got another small room and set up the Brotherhood office there. But Pullman kept after him. Soon after he opened the office, the company canceled his $15-a-month pension."

A.R.U.
Carl Sandburg
Been on the hummer since ninety-four,
Last job I had was on the Lake Shore.
Lost my office in the A.R.U.,
And I won't get it back till nineteen-two.
And I'm still on the hog train flagging my
* meals,*
Riding the brake beams close to the wheels.

To break Dad Moore was to smash the Oakland organization, and the Pullman Company threatened to fire any porter seen patronizing Moore's rooming house. Without his pension and the extra income from his roomers, neither he nor the movement could survive. And both very nearly went under—but for the handful of secret union members who defied Pullman's orders. "I am going to stand by the ship, no matter what happen," Dad Moore wrote Milton Webster in Chicago, in May, 1926, while having a hard time raising money for the rent. "The sea is ruff and the wind are high but I'll stay with her until she make the harbor." A month later he wrote again: "I will not stop until the flag of the Brotherhood fly high in the breeze of victory. . . . If the ship sink I will be on the head end, with such men as yourself . . . and Mr. Randolph."

In one of its earliest attempts to scuttle the Brotherhood, the Pullman Company called in the porter representatives on the Plan of Employee Representation to a conference in Chicago—from January 27 to February 5, 1926—to "negotiate" a revision of wages and working conditions. Again, as in 1924, most of the representatives were loyal company men, and their sentiments were perhaps best expressed by porter E. Anderson, representing the Atlanta district, who made the opening speech:

Hotels were built across from railroad depots as motels grow up around airports. This one is in San Marcial, N.M. 1901.—*Santa Fe Railway photo*

115

We are here today to join with the Pullman Company and not some outside organization.... Our hands are extended to the Pullman Company in the interest of good fellowship.... We are not here to demand, but requesting.... We are not here in an arrogant way, but submissive to the degree that we desire that our wishes be complied with as far as possible.... We are quite cognizant of the fact that the Pullman Company has done and are doing more for the Negro race than any corporation in the world.

Nothing so illustrated the need for an independent union. And there can scarcely be any surprise that the loyal porters—far from getting even what they humbly requested—had to take what Pullman offered: a $5 increase, raising their minimum salary from $67.50 a month to $72.50. Still, no serious complaint was recorded. All but two of the delegates signed the "agreement," and before the conference broke up, porter W. A. Hill, from Cincinnati, rose to applaud "the fairness" the company had displayed "by laying your cards on the table for us to read openly," and pledged to "do all in our power to discredit radicalism." The Pull-

man Company, Hill said, "has been our greatest benefactor and friend from the dawn of freedom down to the present day." One delegate who had refused to sign was Benjamin ("Bennie") Smith, of the Omaha district, a fact that Pullman would not forget.

Bennie Smith was a tall man of medium build, with a military bearing that accentuated his three-piece suits and the watch chain running across his vest. But his distinguishing physical features were a cool, dark, and solemn face and a head of thick, carefully groomed hair parted in the center—all of which made him appear to be of predominantly East Indian rather than African strain. His grave mien seems to have been deceiving, for, as an officer of the Brotherhood has said, no one was capable of more humor. He was an old friend and colleague of Milton Webster, the two having run together between Chicago and Omaha when Webster was a porter. Smith was a militant, undercover union man. During the Chicago conference, he had served not only as the porters' delegate from Omaha, but also as a spy for the Brotherhood. At the end of each day's session, Smith had taken a taxicab from the Pullman headquarters, at 79 Adams Street, to the Vincennes Hotel, on Chicago's South Side, where Randolph and Webster were waiting to receive his reports. And it was at their instigation that he had refused to affix his signature to the results of the conference—the strategy being for the Brotherhood to claim a victory if Smith succeeded in blocking a settlement.

Less than a year later, however, Pullman evened the score with Bennie Smith—firing him, after several months of harassment. But since no porter of Smith's caliber could be wasted, Randolph immediately hired him, and sent him to help Ashley Totten organize the Kansas City division.

In April, 1927, Randolph recalled Smith from Kansas City and sent him to Jacksonville, with a view to setting up the first division of the Brotherhood in the South. The plan failed, however. Posing as a salesman of the *Messenger* in Jacksonville, Smith was reported to the local authorities by a Pullman stool pigeon, and one day, while holding a secret meeting in the basement of a private home, he was arrested and charged with "preaching social equality in the South." According to Randolph, "social equality then was like communism now." Smith reported later, "I hired a young colored lawyer, and we had a fight on the courthouse steps. He told me to run. I said, 'I paid you $50 to defend me.' He said, 'Well, you'll find out what's going to happen.' . . . The judge said, before he adjourned, 'We know what you're doing down here, and you won't get away with that stuff. We're going to send you to Blue Jay prison farm, and from there we're going to take you to a tree.' "

That night Smith telegraphed his plight to Randolph, in New York, who ordered him to get out of Jacksonville immediately. But leaving so unceremoniously did not appeal to Smith, and he wired Randolph again:

AM FULLY MINDFUL OF GRAVE SERIOUSNESS OF SITUATION AND PERSONAL DANGER. CONSCIENTIOUSLY FEEL BROTHERHOOD CAUSE IS SO RIGHTEOUSLY IMPORTANT THAT A FIRM STAND SHOULD BE TAKEN. HAVE FULLY DECIDED TO REMAIN AND MEET CONSEQUENCES. THIS MEANS THAT I'M WILLING TO MAKE SUPREME SACRIFICE. HAVE SACREDLY DEDICATED MY ALL TO THE BROTHERHOOD'S NOBLE CAUSE. ADVISE AT ONCE.

The advice was the same, but this time it came from Webster, accompanied by $40 for train fare: "Get the hell out of Jacksonville. You can't beat no case down there." Smith was then sent to organize Detroit, where he has remained ever since.

The Pullman Company had no more formidable allies in the black community than the "big Negroes," the church, and the press. As Milton Webster would put it, "Everything Negro was against us."

"Any Sunday you went to church," recalls a Chicago porter, "the preachers touched on the Brotherhood. Their slogan was 'Don't rock the boat, don't bite the hand that feeds you.' They said Randolph was just a glib orator, whereas the Pullman Company was a million-dollar outfit. 'The company will never sit down with a man like that,' they told us. 'Look at his record. He was drafted in World War I and accused of treason. Look at the little radical magazine he's putting out. Way out of line.' "

"Randolph's interference in Pullman porters' affairs," said a writer in the *Louisiana Weekly*, "is dangerous to industrial colored America." To counteract the influence of the *Messenger* as mouthpiece of the organized porters, the Pullman Company subsidized the publication among its loyalists of a journal called the *Pullman Porter Messenger*. This journal, in its May, 1926, issue, called Randolph "a lamp post orator," and the members of his union "wormy Pullman fruit, poor, disloyal, yellowed, spotted out, ungrateful, undesirable, beggars for a job, not wanted, exiled, abandoned, slipping around here and there under cover."

The company saw to it that the porters were supplied with the pro-Pullman newspapers from the black community. According to Ulas Crowder, of Chicago, "the *St. Louis Argus,* the *Denver Star,* the *Seattle Enterprise,* the *Chicago Whip,* and the *Chicago Defender* were stacked up high in our sign-out offices. They were full of nothing but Pullman propaganda. All you had to do was walk in and pick up your copy. You didn't need to pay for any, 'cause Pullman was providing them free. And if you didn't pick up a copy, a clerk or somebody like that would yell after you, 'Hey, where's your paper?' "

The Railway Labor Act, passed on May 20, 1926, provided for "the prompt disposition" of all disputes between railroad carriers and their employees. To avoid "any interruption in the operation of any carrier," the act called upon both sides to meet in joint conference to "make and maintain agreements" on rates of pay, rules, and working conditions. Employee and employer representatives were to be designated without "interference, influence, or coercion," and disputes that could not be resolved in conference were to be submitted to a Board of Mediation. The leaders of the Brotherhood were joyful. The Railway Labor Act seemed a clear affirmation of the porters' right to *independent* self-organization. It would be merely a matter of time, they felt—the time it would take to exhaust the due process of the act—before their union was recognized as the bona fide bargaining agent of the porters.

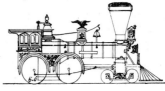

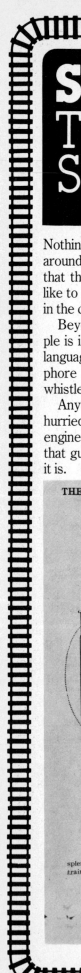

SIDETRACK THE SIGNALS

Nothing is more fascinating than a code. Spy stories revolve around them. Schoolchildren sit in class and devise them so that their club can be secret and therefore significant. We like to have private signs, handshakes and passwords, to be in the circle, to know what's going on.

Beyond this, any means of communication between people is interesting to us. We like to hear—and see—another language at work: the hand language of the deaf, the semaphore of the sailor, the dit-dah of the telegrapher, the whistles and lights of the railroad engineer.

Any code carries a hint of important things going on, of hurried contacts with fortunes and lives at stake. When an engineer decodes the signs and whistles, bells and lights that guide him through the countryside, that's exactly how it is.

THE HANDLAN PATENT ENGINE AND TRAIN TAIL SIGNAL LAMPS.

This new and improved pattern Signal Lamp is adapted to any place or position, its patented feature of the revolving slide for obscuring either signal as desired, being a marked improvement. The change in signal can be made without removing the lamp from its socket.

Fig. E-838.

This lamp is perfectly ventilated, burns splendidly and is easily operated by any trainman.

Any color of lenses furnished.

Fig. E-839.

THE WHISTLES

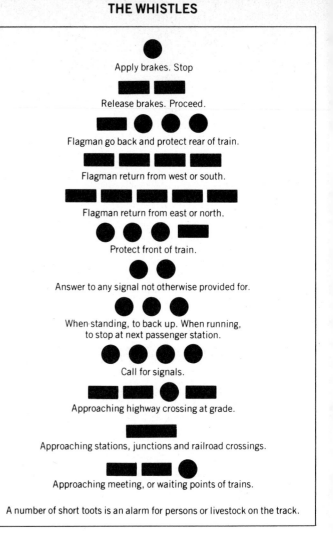

Apply brakes. Stop

Release brakes. Proceed.

Flagman go back and protect rear of train.

Flagman return from west or south.

Flagman return from east or north.

Protect front of train.

Answer to any signal not otherwise provided for.

When standing, to back up. When running, to stop at next passenger station.

Call for signals.

Approaching highway crossing at grade.

Approaching stations, junctions and railroad crossings.

Approaching meeting, or waiting points of trains.

A number of short toots is an alarm for persons or livestock on the track.

—*Courtesy Association of American Railroads*

THE BELL-CORD COMMUNICATING SIGNALS FROM TRAIN TO ENGINE CAB

Two shorts: When standing, start.

Two shorts: When running, stop at once.

Three shorts: When standing, back up.

Three shorts: When running, stop at next passenger station.

Four shorts: When standing, apply or release air brakes.

Four shorts: When running, reduce speed.

Five shorts: When standing, recall flagman.

Five shorts: When running, increase speed.

Six shorts: When running, increase train heat.

One short, one long, one short: Shut off train heat.

One long: When running, brakes sticking; look back for hand signals.

1. A lamp swung vertically in a circle across the track, when the train is standing, is the signal to move back.

2. A lamp raised and lowered vertically is the signal to move ahead.

3. A lamp swung vertically in a circle at arm's length across the track, when the train is running, is the signal that the train has parted.

—New York Public Library Picture Collection

1   2   3

NAME	INDICATION	SEMAPHORE	COLOUR LIGHT	SEARCHLIGHT	POSITION LIGHT	COLOUR-POSITION LIGHT
CLEAR	PROCEED					
APPROACH	PROCEED PREPARING TO STOP AT NEXT SIGNAL. TRAIN EXCEEDING MEDIUM SPEED MUST AT ONCE REDUCE TO THAT SPEED					
STOP AND PROCEED	STOP, THEN PROCEED AT RESTRICTED SPEED		50008	13727		
STOP	STOP					

STANDARD AMERICAN SIGNAL INDICATIONS AND ASPECTS

Lamp colours: G, green; Y, yellow; R, red; W, white. The three columns under ''Semaphore'' show how the same indication may be given with one, two or three signal heads on the same mast (any of the other types of signal may also be combined in the same fashion); two- and three-head signals ordinarily are used at junctions, passing sidings, etc. A stop-and-proceed signal is designated by a number plate on the mast below the signal head, by a marker light, by a pointed semaphore blade or by a combination of these features.

PAYDAY HUSSEY'S CAMP B.R. R.R.

THE GOLDEN AGE OF IRON
1900-1930

Courtesy Missouri Pacific Railroad

**Let the Midnight Special Shine its everlovin
light on me.**

— a prisoner in Texas

BOOMER DAYS

Charles B. Chrysler

Howzit for camping and cutting in on the mulligan?" says I.

Mulligan, in case you don't know, is hobo stew. It consists of *hoppins* (any and all vegetables that can be bought, begged, borrowed, or stolen), together with meat acquired the same way, or maybe *gumps* (chickens) or other fowl, the whole savory mess cooked outdoors.

My question was answered by the camp bully, a big carrot-topped boomer of philosophical bent, who liked to hear himself talk. They called him "Rhode Island Red."

"The camp belongs to God almighty," says Red, "and if you're all right with Him you're all right with us. There's plenty of timber, straw, moss, water, fire, and plenty of alky [alcoholic liquor]. But mulligan—well, that's something else again. The law of compensation says you can't take something out unless you put something in. I didn't make the law—it was made by the camp—I enforce it. You can stay here as long as you like; but if you want to eat, you'll have to hustle some hoppins. Unless you're a Johnnie Newcomer you know this as well as I do."

As I said, the guy liked to chew the rag, so I listened.

"All right, all right," he says. "You're hungry. Well, I'm gonna show you how you can eat. See that tar kettle there? It holds about a barrel of anything you want to put into it. Right now it contains hot water, but tonight I'm taking a detail of men out to fill it. Now, here's the layout. . . ."

Red explained there was a carload of live chickens on a sidetrack by the depot in town. All kinds. Big ones, tall ones, fat ones, Plymouth Rocks, Leghorns—all in crates. A whole express car full. A score of volunteers would sneak out of the jungle at night, go down to the depot, and grab as many of the crates as they could get away with. Some crates had only a pair of chickens in them; others had six or eight. The plan was for each man to pick out a crate containing a large number of chickens.

"If you fail," Red warned, "don't come back

to the jungle and expect to eat. If your conscience bothers you, you needn't trail along."

So that night twenty or so unshaven stalwarts disappeared in the darkness toward San Bernardino. A war council was held in the underbrush. Red spoke up again.

"Two of you men go down the track a few blocks, pick up some dry leaves and straw, place them in an empty boxcar, and set them afire. Then return here. When it's smoking good, you, Dutch, run over to the depot and tell the agent there's a boxcar burning down the track. When they leave the station to put out the fire, the rest of us go into action. It's every bozo for himself. Grab a crate, take to the brush, and hike for camp."

New York Public Library
Picture Collection

There were two men in the station and both of them ran over to the smoking car. The denizens of the hobo camp moved with trained precision. Each grabbed a pen of squawking chickens, four men lugging the big containers, one or two lugging each of the small ones.

The raiders solemnly toted the crates down to the river bank near the jungle and there they held sacrificial rites. Then they dumped the slaughtered fowl back into the crates, took them to the campfire, and scalded them in the tar kettle. One squad neatly picked off the feathers, another degutted and cut up the poultry, a third buried the feathers and refuse. Each job was handled efficiently. After that, all hands went back to the stream and washed up in cold water. Finally, after cleaning the kettle, we plopped the chickens into the great pot. Then we broke up the crates to feed the roaring flames.

By that time the midnight prowling detail had returned with paper bags full of cabbage, potatoes, onions, chili peppers, tomatoes, and parsley. Somebody even brought along a bag of salt. At two in the morning our mulligan started to simmer. By sunrise it was prime. And we were famished! Bowls and spoons mysteriously appeared and we dug in.

The stew lasted us three days. Tramps for miles around heard of the feast and drifted into camp. They tried to wheedle us into sharing with them, but only those who brought along dessert for the gang or other food to vary our diet were permitted to more than sniff the mulligan.

Meanwhile, there was hell to pay at San Bernardino. It seems that a lot of pedigreed chickens had been stolen from an express car. The loss was terrific. Those fowl had been the result of years of scientific breeding and had been exhibited all over California. In fact, at the time of the theft, they had been awaiting shipment to the Los Angeles County Fair at Pomona, where they were expected to win medal cups, blue ribbons, and cash prizes in addition to the long list of awards they already held. These haughty birds were rare breeding stock. But by the time railroad bulls reached our camp there was no trace of them, and most of the men had scattered.

Even to-day, if you chance to visit hobo jungles on the West Coast, you are likely to hear men around campfires tell about the "Million-Dollar Mulligan," as it was called. Many a wandering brother will claim that he was either a night yardmaster at Pocatello or else was "in on" the greatest stew of all time. But Rhode Island Red, "Circus" Doyle, "Fish-mouth" Ferguson, and other famous boomers—if they are still living—will tell you there were less than twenty-five men in that raid, and Charley Chrysler was one of them.

Union pacific's No. 7038 (4-8-2), the Overland Limited.—*Union Pacific Railroad Museum Collection*

THE WABASH CANNONBALL

The Wabash Cannonball is the railroad version of the ghost ship *The Flying Dutchman.*

Now the eastern states are dandies, so the western people say
From New York to St. Louis and Chicago by the way,
Thru the hills of Minnesota where the rippling waters fall
No chances can be taken on the Wabash Cannonball.   (Cho.)

Now here's to Daddy Claxton, may his name forever stand.
He'll be honored and respected by the 'boes throughout the land.

And when his days are over and the curtains round him fall,
We'll ship him off to hell and on the Wabash Cannonball.

There are other cities, pardner, that you can go to see—
St. Paul and Minneapolis, Ashtabula, Kankakee.
The lakes of Minnehaha, where the laughing waters fall—
We reach them by no other but the Wabash Cannonball.

THE STORY OF CASEY JONES

Adapted by Miller Williams from a chapter in
Carlton J. Corliss' Main Line of America

Casey's real name was John Luther Jones. He was born in southwestern Missouri on March 14, 1864, the son of a country schoolteacher. When he was thirteen his family moved to Cayce, a small town in southwestern Kentucky. Two years later, at the age of fifteen, he became an apprentice telegrapher on the Mobile & Ohio Railroad at Columbus, Kentucky, and there his co-workers gave him the nickname "Casey," after his hometown, to distinguish him from other railway men named Jones. It was a distinction he would not need.

Casey amazed his co-workers by the ease with which he mastered telegraphy, but he was not satisfied with the job. He wanted to become a locomotive engineer, and nothing else would do. As soon as he turned eighteen he applied for a fireman's job. That was the traditional and practical way to move into the cab and eventually from the left seat into the right one. Several months later, when he passed the examination and began firing, he was happier than he had ever been in his life. But he was still not satisfied. More than ever, he wanted his own cab and he wouldn't slow down until he had it. Anyone who knew him might have suspected that he wouldn't slow down much after he had it, either.

On March 1, 1888, he moved from the Mobile & Ohio to the Illinois Central when he learned that a yellow-fever epidemic had wiped out a number of train crews on the Illinois Central, bringing about a number of unexpected promotions. He was put on as a fireman on a freight run between Jackson, Tennessee, and Water Valley, Mississippi. In February of 1890, when he was not yet twenty-six, he passed the examination and became a locomotive engineer. He was assigned to a fast freight run between Jackson and Water Valley.

Casey knew exactly where he was going. How fast he was getting there must have surprised everybody but Casey. By 1892 Casey was running freight out of Centralia, Illinois. By 1893 he was assigned to one of the fast specials which ran back and forth that summer between Chicago's Van Buren Street and the grounds of the World's Columbian Exposition in Jackson Park. More than a hundred thousand passengers rode behind Casey's engine before the fair was over.

In 1886 Casey had married Janie Brady, with whom he very happily lived the half of his life not spent in a cab of a locomotive. He wrote her from the Exposition and told her with great excitement that he had seen the most beautiful locomotive in the world. It was a huge engine with eight drive wheels and two pilot wheels, the finest achievement to that time in steam-locomotive engineering and design, and the main attraction of the Illinois Central exhibit at the fair. He knew it was the engine with which he was going to spend the other half of his life.

No one knows how he managed it, but on the last day of the fair he showed up at the exhibit

Casey Jones—*Photo courtesy of Illinois Central Gulf Railroad*

with official papers ordering that the locomotive be delivered to him personally for transfer to the shop for reconditioning and then to Water Valley, Mississippi, where it was to be assigned to him for regular freight service. It was the longest run one man had ever been authorized to make, and Casey's fame spread with the news.

He helped the spread of that fame considerably with the six-toned calliope whistle he used on the engine. It sounded something like a banshee making a whippoorwill call, and it was known to everyone working on the railroad tracks and in the cotton fields along his run.

After twelve years with the Illinois Central, Casey was offered the right seat in the cab of the prize Chicago–New Orleans passenger train officially designated New Orleans Special No. 1, but generally referred to as the Cannonball. Casey was not happy about giving up the engine he had found in Chicago, and it meant that he and Janie had to move, but it was more money and prestige and a faster run. On New Year's Day 1900 Casey reported to work at Memphis and was assigned to freight runs between there and Canton so he could become familiar with the road before taking over the passenger run.

After sundown the twenty-ninth of April 1900 Casey and Sim Webb, his fireman, backed the Cannonball's engine—No. 382—into the south Memphis yard roundhouse after the scheduled northbound run. They were told that the engineer who was scheduled to make the south run was sick, and they were asked to "double out." There wasn't time for much rest and they wouldn't get any sleep at all, but they said they would do it if they could stay with No. 382. The roundhouse crews set about making it ready for the trip but the work ran late, and Casey left the Memphis station with a train of mail, baggage, coaches and sleepers already an hour and thirty-five minutes behind on a two-hour-and-forty-five-minute run. It was

12:50 A.M., April 30. By the time he pulled out of Grenada—a hundred straight, level miles from Memphis—he had made up an hour of lost time. His orders had been to run into Grenada thirty-five minutes late, into Durant twenty minutes late, and into Canton on time. Canton was 88 miles ahead.

Passing Winona, 23 miles south of Grenada, they were only fifteen minutes behind time, and they pulled into Durant, 30 miles south of Winona, almost on schedule. Here he picked up orders to meet No. 2 at Goodman and then to "saw through" freight and passenger trains at Vaughan, 14 miles north of Canton. "Saw-

ing through" is a procedure for passing a train which is too long for the siding by pulling your train even with it until your locomotive is blocked by its intrusion onto the tracks ahead of you, and then waiting while it backs along the siding onto the tracks behind your train, clearing the tracks ahead. It was a routine procedure.

Casey met No. 2 at Goodman, as scheduled, then pulled the throttle wide and headed for Vaughan 70 miles an hour with his six-tone calliope whistle going full blast all the way.

"We're going into Canton on time!" Sim remembered him saying. "If we're not delayed by that mess of trains at Vaughan."

That mess of trains at Vaughan was going to kill him. This is the scene at the Vaughan station as the people at Illinois Central reconstruct it. The station was about two thousand feet south of the north switch. On the east side of the main track was a passing track, and on the west side of the main track, near the station, was a short business track used for loading, unloading and storage of freight cars. Just north of the north switch was a curve.

There were two other southbound trains ahead of Casey that night—freight train No. 83 with forty-four cars and a caboose pulled by two locomotives, and New Orleans-bound passenger train No. 25.

Somewhere south of Vaughan, headed north, were freight train No. 72 with thirty-six cars and a caboose; northbound Cannonball No. 2; and two sections of another Chicago-bound passenger train, No. 26. All of the trains were running late.

This was before the days of modern signaling systems. A train's safety at the turn of the century depended upon strict obedience to rules and train orders, constant surveillance of the track, luck and quick thinking. Sometimes these were not enough.

The first train to reach Vaughan was southbound freight No. 83. It turned into the passing track at the north switch. When northbound 72 arrived it took the same passing track to the south switch. The two freights together were four car-lengths too long to clear both switches.

A flagman named Newberry from 83 was sent north to place warning torpedoes on the track and signal the two southbound passenger trains that they were to be "sawed" through Vaughan. Southbound passenger train 25, warned by Newberry, who was 3,200 feet north of the north switch, and by a torpedo which had been placed about 500 feet south of Newberry, pulled cautiously into Vaughan and executed the "saw." The two freights remained in a "north-saw" position, to leave the main line clear at the south switch for Cannonball No. 2 to pull past and begin "sawing through" on its way north. The "saw" was executed quickly and No. 2 met Casey's Cannonball at Goodman, 14 miles up the line. Instead of remaining in their "south-saw" position to wait for Casey's Cannonball to pull parallel to them, the two freights on the siding were "sawed north" so that Chicago-bound passenger No. 26 could get to the business track and out of the way of the Cannonball. When they started to "saw south" again, to make ready for Casey and the Cannonball, an air hose burst near the rear of No. 72 and four cars of 83 were unable to move off the main track at the north switch.

Three thousand feet north of switch, around the curve just out of sight of the station, Newberry waved his lantern frantically as Casey shot past at 70 miles an hour, apparently taking the signal as confirmation of his previous order, to be prepared for 83 and 72, which would be blocking the south switch. He had no reason to suspect that they were on the north switch instead. A hundred feet farther on, the engine detonated the torpedo which Newberry had placed on the track.

According to Sim, Casey hit the brakes immediately after passing the torpedo, but for some reason his famous whistle was silent as he passed the whistling board a few hundred feet beyond. When he heard the torpedo, Sim went to the left side of the cab and looked out. As they rounded the curve he saw the lights of 83's caboose a few hundred feet ahead. He yelled at Casey to jump.

"You jump," Casey yelled back and hit the emergency brakes. "I'll stay."

Casey had cut the speed from 70 to about 50 miles an hour by the time Sim leaped, and managed to cut it considerably more before he tore through 83's caboose and a car of hay.

When Casey's body was found in the wreckage, one hand was clutching the throttle and the other the air-brake control of the overturned engine. He was the only person killed. Some passengers and crew members sustained a few injuries, but nothing serious. It had always been a matter of pride to Casey that although he had been disciplined nine times for infractions of the rules, and suspended as many times for anywhere from five to thirty days, all of the infractions had occurred in freight service and he had never been involved in a train accident that resulted in the death of a fellow railroader or a passenger. If Casey had jumped when he had the chance, he would probably have lived—as Sim did—but he would have lived with a different record. He chose not to.

Adam Hauser, a newspaper man formerly with the New Orleans *Times Democrat,* was on board the Cannonball. This is from his account, which appeared in the *Times Democrat* the day after the wreck.

> The marvel and mystery is how Engineer Jones stopped the train. The railroad men themselves wondered at it, and of course the uninitiated could not do less. But stop it he did, in a way that showed the complete mastery of his engine, as well as his sublime heroism.

> I imagine that the Vaughan wreck will be talked about in roundhouses, lunchrooms, and cabooses for the next six months, not alone on the Illinois Central, but [on] many other roads in Mississippi and Louisiana.

It was talked about. But it was left for Wallace Saunders, a Negro engine-wiper in the Illinois Central shops who cleaned up the cab of 382 after the wreck, to make Casey Jones immortal. Saunders knew and liked Casey, and he refashioned an old folk song—which is the way folk music happens—to tell Casey's story. It was picked up and passed on by fellow workers and was already known around the country when two professional songwriters "polished it up a little" and had it published. It was a hit immediately and Wallace Saunders' chantey was almost forgotten.

Davy Crockett, Jim Bowie, Mike Fink, Johnny Appleseed, "Wild Bill" Hickok, Annie Oakley, Paul Bunyan, Amelia Earhart, Casey Jones. The figures of our American myth. Some, before they lived in myth, lived as we do. Or not quite as we do.

CASEY JONES

Wallace Saunders, a Negro helper in the roundhouse at Canton, Mississippi, cleaned up the engine in which Casey Jones was killed. It was he who set the Casey Jones ballad on its way by putting Casey's name into an older railroad ballad about "Po' Jimmy Jones, the Good Old Porter." Here we have the Mississippi folk song that grew out of Saunders' fragment. It was recorded in Canton in 1933 by Alan Lomax. The better-known and much less interesting version was composed by two white vaudevillians who heard the Saunders ballad and turned it into a pop tune.

Some folks say Casey Jones can't run,
Stop and listen what Casey done,
He left Memphis at a quarter to nine,
Made Newport News 'fore dinner time,
'Fore dinner time, 'fore dinner time,
Made Newport News 'fore dinner time.

Casey Jones, before he died,
Fixed the blinds so the bums couldn' ride,
"If they ride, gotta ride the rod,
Trust their life in the hands of God.
In the hands of God, the hand of God,
Trust their life in the hands of God."

There was a woman named Alice Fly,
Said, "I'm gonna ride with Mr Casey or die,
I ain't good lookin' but I takes my time,
I'm a ramblin' woman with a ramblin' mind,
With a ramblin' mind," etc.

Early one mornin', 'bout four o'clock,
Told his fireman, "Get the boiler hot,
All I need's a little water and coal,
Peep out my window, see the drivers roll,
See the drivers roll," etc.

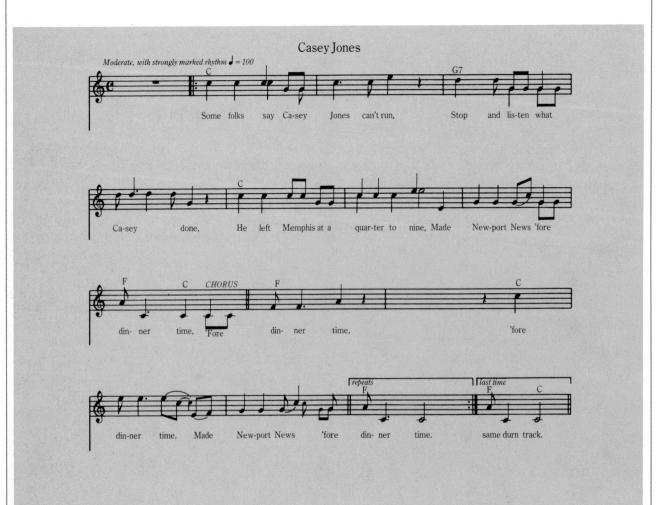

Casey Jones

Moderate, with strongly marked rhythm ♩ = 100

Some folks say Ca-sey Jones can't run, Stop and lis-ten what Ca-sey done, He left Memphis at a quar-ter to nine, Made New-port News 'fore din-ner time, 'Fore din-ner time, 'fore din-ner time, Made New-port News 'fore din-ner time. same durn track.

CHORUS

[repeats]   [last time]

Up on the mountain one cold frosty mornin',
Just watchin' the smoke from below,
It was whirlin' up from a short, black smokestack
Way down on the Southern Railroad.

It was the old '97, the fastest mailtrain,
That runs on the Southern Line,
And when she pulled into Monroe, Virginia,
She was forty-seven minutes behind.

They give him his orders in Monroe, Virginia,
Saying, "Steve, you're way behind time.
It's not '38 it's old '97,
You must put her in Danville on time."

"Just one more trip," said the sleepy conductor,
As he kissed his loving wife,
"I've stole enough money from the railroad
  comp'ny
To last us all through life."

"Goodbye, sweet wife," said the drunken
  brakeman,
As he waved his cap with delight,
"If the wheels will roll and the engineer stays
  sober,
We'll all reach home tonight."

Steve turned to his black and greasy fireman,
Said, "Shovel in a little more coal,
And when we cross the White Oak Mountain,
You can watch old '97 roll."

He was going down the grade, makin' ninety
  miles an hour,
When his whistle broke into a scream,
He was found in the wreck with his hand on the
  throttle,
And scalded to death with the steam.

O, a sad farewell, when we heard the signal,
And the brakeman dropped the pin,
And for hours and hours the switchman waited
For the train that will never pull in.

Young ladies, you must take warning
From this time now and on,
Never speak harsh words to your true-lovin'
  husband,
He will leave you and never return.

Did she ever return? No, she never returned,
Though the train was due at one,
For hours and hours the watchman stood waitin'
For the train that never returned.

Wreck of "Old 97," Stillhouse Trestle north of Danville, Virginia, September 27, 1903.—*Courtesy of Southern Railway System*

THOMAS WOLFE ON THE TRAIN

At night, great trains will pass us in the timeless spell of an unsleeping hypnosis, an endless, and unfathomable stupefaction. Then suddenly in the unwaking never sleeping century of the night, the sensual limbs of carnal whited nakedness that stir with drowsy silken warmth in the green secrecies of Lower Seven, the slow swelling and lonely and swarmhaunted land—and suddenly, suddenly, silence and thick hardening lust of dark exultant joy, the dreamlike passage of Virginia!—Then in the watches of the night a pause, the sudden silence of up-welling night, and unseen faces, voices, laughter, and farewells upon a lonely little night-time station—the lost and lonely voices of Americans:—"Good-bye! Good-bye, now! Write us when you get there, Helen! Tell Bob he's got to write!—Give my love to Emily!—Good-bye, good-bye now—write us, soon!"—And then the secret, silken and subdued rustling past the thick green curtains and the sleepers, the low respectful negroid tones of the black porter—and then the whistle cry, the tolling bell, the great train mounting to its classic monotone again, and presently the last lights of a little town, the floating void and loneliness of moon-haunted earth—Virginia!

Also, in the dream—thickets of eternal night—there will be huge steamings on the rail, the sudden smash, the wall of light, the sudden flarings of wild, roaring light upon the moon-haunted and dream-tortured faces of the sleepers!

—And finally, in that dark jungle of the night, through all the visions, memories, and enchanted weavings of the timeless and eternal spell of time, the moment of forever—there are two horsemen, riding, riding, riding in the night.

Who are they? Oh, we know them with our life and they will ride across the land, the moon-haunted passage of our lives forever. Their names are Death and Pity, and we know their face: our brother and our father ride ever beside us in the dream-enchanted spell and vista of the night; the hooves keep level time beside the rhythms of the train.

Horsed on the black and moon-maned steeds of fury, cloaked in the dark of night, the spell of time, dream-pale, eternal, they are rushing on across the haunted land, the moon-enchanted wilderness, and their hooves make level thunder with the train.

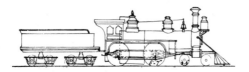

Colorado Midland train (with rider) near Hell Gate. Photo by W.H. Jackson.—*Courtesy of Denver Public Library, Western History Department*

Sitting in a cell in a Texas penitentiary, a Negro prisoner hears a cross-country train roar past every night. He imagines his sweetheart coming with his pardon, and dreams of freedom.

Yonder come Miss Rosie,
How'n the world d'you know?
Well, I knows her by her apron
And the dress she wo',
Umbereller on her shoulder,
Piece of paper in her hand,
Well, she come to tell the gov'nor,
"Turn loose-a my man."
> Let the midnight special shine its light on me,
> Let the midnight special shine its everlovin'
>   light on me.

Well, you wake up in the mornin',
When the ding dong ring,
Go marchin' to the table,
See the same damn thing.
Knife and fork-a on the table,
Nothin' in my pan,
If you say anything about it,
Haves trouble with the man.   *(Chorus)*

If you ever go to Houston
Boys, you better walk right,
Well, you better not stumble
And you better not fight.
Cause the police will arrest you,
And they'll carry you down,
You can bet your bottom dollar,
"Penitentiary bound."   *(Chorus)*

Now one of these mornin's
And the time ain't long,
That man's gonna call me,
And I'll be gone.
I'll be done all my grievin',
Whoopin', holl'in', cryin',
I'll be done all my worryin'
'Bout my great long time.   *(Chorus)*

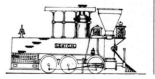

1. Conductor.
2. Modern track-laying machine at work.
3. Crew man and engine wiper.
4. Super chief engineer.
5. Train yard laborer.—*New York Public Library Picture Collection*

PHOEBE SNOW

The name "Phoebe Snow" and "The Road of Anthracite" are synonymous because in the early days coal was closely identified with the origin of the Lackawanna Railroad and anthracite was burned exclusively in all of its passenger locomotives. So general was the appreciation by the traveling public of the importance of this feature that Phoebe Snow, the Lackawanna's impersonation of this idea, became in the public's mind the synonym of cleanliness in travel. . . . While the advertising character of Phoebe Snow, as shown in the car cards and newspapers some forty years ago, was the creation of an artist's fancy, to the traveling public she [became] almost a living personage. . . .

The idea of a series of advertising jingles, exploiting the adventures of a girl dressed in white typifying such cleanliness, was originated by the Advertising Department of the Lackawanna Railroad about 1900, and was continued up to World War I, when the railroads of the country were placed under Federal control, and bituminous coal was substituted for hard coal, or anthracite, in Lackawanna passenger locomotives.

At the start of the Phoebe Snow campaign of advertising, the verses were parodies on the familiar nursery jingles:

Here is the maiden all forlorn,
Who milked the cow with crumpled horn.

The first one of the series [was] as follows:

Here is the maiden all in lawn
Who boarded the train one early morn
That runs on Road of Anthracite,
And when she left the train that night
She found to her surprised delight
Hard coal had kept her dress still bright.

Owing to the limited number of characters in this nursery epic, this meter was abandoned and a new form of verse adopted. For the sake of euphony and because of its obvious rhyming possibilities, the "maiden" was given the name of Phoebe Snow.

Years of publicity have resulted in giving "Phoebe" a foremost place among the characters in America's advertising hall of fame. Phoebe still lingers in the minds of Lackawanna travelers and shippers, and at one time the Lackawanna revived the name "Phoebe Snow" by painting on the side of box cars the inscription "Lackawanna—The route of Phoebe Snow."

[A selection from fifty-nine "Phoebe Snow" jingles follows. The first of these is printed in the original seven-line form; the others have been rearranged for space reasons.]

Says Phoebe Snow
　About to go
　　Upon a trip
　　　To Buffalo,
　　　　"My gown stays white
　　　　　From morn till night
　　　　　　Upon the Road of Anthracite."

The man in blue now helps her through
And tells her when her train is due.
"He's so polite. They do things right
Upon the Road of Anthracite."

Now Phoebe Snow direct can go
From Thirty-third to Buffalo.
From Broadway bright the "Tubes" run right
Into the Road of Anthracite.

Now Phoebe may by night or day
Enjoy her book upon the way—
Electric light dispels the night
Upon the Road of Anthracite.

The evening flies till Phoebe's eyes
Grow sleepy under mountain skies.
Sweet dreams all night are hers till light
Dawns on the Road of Anthracite.

No trip is far where comforts are.
An observation Lounging Car
Adds new delight to Phoebe's flight
Along the Road of Anthracite.

This scene reveals a chef on wheels
With care preparing Phoebe's meals.
He, too, wears white from morn till night
Upon the Road of Anthracite.

On railroad trips no other lips
Have touched the cup that Phoebe sips.
Each cup of white makes drinking quite
A treat on the Road of Anthracite.

Miss Snow draws near the cab to cheer
The level-headed engineer,
Whose watchful sight makes safe her flight
Upon the Road of Anthracite.

Miss Snow, you see, was sure to be
The object of much courtesy,
For day or night they're all polite
Upon the Road of Anthracite.

The stars now peep at her asleep,
While trackmen keen their night watch keep,
For Phoebe's flight must be all right
Upon the Road of Anthracite.

THE TRAIN

Flannery O'Connor

Thinking about the porter, he had almost forgotten the berth. He had an upper one. The man in the station had said he could give him a lower and Haze had asked didn't he have no upper ones; the man said sure if that was what he wanted, and gave him an upper one. Leaning back on the seat, Haze had seen how the ceiling was rounded over him. It was in there. They pulled the ceiling down and it was in there, and you climbed up to it on a ladder. He hadn't seen any ladders around; he reckoned they kept them in the closet. The closet was up where you came in. When he first got on the train, he had seen the porter standing in front of the closet, putting on his porter's jacket. Haze had stopped right then—right where he was.

The turn of his head was like and the back of his neck was like and the short reach of his arm. He turned away from the closet and looked at Haze and Haze saw his eyes and they were like; they were the same—same as old Cash's for the first instant, and then different. They turned different while he was looking at

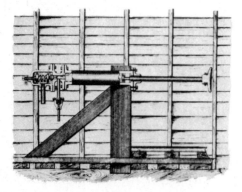

them; hardened flat. "Whu . . . what time do you pull down the beds?" Haze mumbled.

"Long time yet," the porter said, reaching into the closet again.

Haze didn't know what else to say to him. He went on to his section.

Now the train was greyflying past instants of trees and quick spaces of field and a motionless sky that sped darkening away in the opposite direction. Haze leaned his head back on the seat and looked out the window, the yellow light of the train lukewarm on him. The porter had passed twice, twice back and twice forward, and the second time forward he had looked sharply at Haze for an instant and passed on without saying anything; Haze had turned and stared after him as he had done the time before. Even his walk was like. All them gulch niggers resembled. They looked like their own kind of nigger—heavy and bald, rock all through. Old Cash in his day had been two hundred pounds heavy—no fat on him—and five feet high with not more than two inches over. Haze wanted to talk to the porter. What would the porter say when he told him: I'm from Eastrod? What would he say?

The train had come to Evansville. A lady got on and sat opposite Haze. That meant she would have the berth under him. She said she thought it was going to snow. She said her husband had driven her down to the station and he said if it didn't snow before he got home, he'd be surprised. He had ten miles to go; they lived in the suburbs. She was going to Florida to visit her daughter. She had never had time to take a trip that far off. The way things happened, one thing right after another, it seemed like time went by so fast you couldn't tell if you were old or young. She looked as if it had been cheating her, going double quick when she was asleep and couldn't watch it. Haze was glad to have someone there talking.

He remembered when he was a little boy, him and his mother and the other children would go into Chattanooga on the Tennessee Railroad. His mother had always started up a conversation with the other people on the train. She was like an old bird dog just unpenned that raced, sniffing up every rock and stick and sucking in the air around everything she stopped at. There wasn't a person she hadn't spoken to by the time they were ready to get off. She remembered them too. Long years after, she would say she wondered where the lady was who was going to Fort West, or she wondered if the man who was selling Bibles had ever got his wife out the hospital. She had a hankering for people—as if what happened to the ones she talked to happened to her then. She was a Jackson. Annie Lou Jackson.

My mother was a Jackson, Haze said to himself. He had stopped listening to the lady although he was still looking at her and she thought he was listening. My name is Hazel Wickers, he said. I'm nineteen. My mother was a Jackson. I was raised in Eastrod, Eastrod, Tennessee; he thought about the porter again. He was going to ask the porter. It struck him suddenly that the porter might even be Cash's son. Cash had a son run away. It happened before Haze's time. Even so, the porter would know Eastrod.

Haze glanced out the window at the shapes black-spinning past him. He could shut his eyes and make Eastrod at night out of any of them—he could find the two houses with the road between and the store and the nigger houses and the one barn and the piece of fence that started off into the pasture, gray-white when the moon was on it. He could put the mule face, solid, over the fence and let it hang there, feeling how the night was. He felt it himself. He felt it light-touching around him. He seen his ma coming up the path, wiping her hands on an apron she had taken off, looking like the night change was on her, and then standing in the doorway: Haaazzzzeeeee, Haazzzeee, came in here. The train said it for him. He wanted to get up and go find the porter.

"Are you going home?" Mrs. Hosen asked him. Her name was Mrs. Wallace Ben Hosen; she had been a Miss Hitchcock before she married.

"Oh!" Haze said, startled—"I get off at, I get off at Taulkinham."

Mrs. Hosen knew some people in Evansville who had a cousin in Taulkinham—a Mr. Henrys, she thought. Being from Taulkinham, Haze might know him. Had he ever heard the. . . .

"Taulkinham ain't where I'm from," Haze muttered. "I don't know nothin' about Taulkinham." He didn't look at Mrs. Hosen. He knew what she was going to ask next and he felt it coming and it came, "Well, where do you live?"

He wanted to get away from her. "It was there," he mumbled, squirming in the seat. Then he said, "I don't rightly know, I was there but . . . this is just the third time I been at Taulkinham," he said quickly—her face had crawled out and was staring at him—"I ain't been since I went when I was six. I don't know nothin' about it. Once I seen a circus there but not. . . ." He heard a clanking at the end of the car and looked to see where it was coming from. The porter was pulling the walls of the sections farther out. "I got to see the porter a minute," he said and escaped down the aisle. He didn't know what he'd say to the porter. He got to him and he still didn't know what he'd say. "I reckon you're fixing to make them up now," he said.

"That's right," the porter said.

"How long does it take you to make one up?" Haze asked.

"Seven minutes," the porter said.

"I'm from Eastrod," Haze said. "I'm from Eastrod, Tennessee."

"That isn't on this line," the porter said. "You on the wrong train if you counting on going to any such place as that."

"I'm going to Taulkinham," Haze said. "I was raised in Eastrod."

"You want your berth made up now?" the porter asked.

"Huh?" Haze said. "Eastrod, Tennessee; ain't you ever heard of Eastrod?"

The porter wrenched one side of the seat flat. "I'm from Chicago," he said. He jerked the shades down on either window and wrenched the other seat down. Even the back of his neck was like. When he bent over, it came out in three bulges. He was from Chicago. "You standing in the middle of the aisle. Somebody gonna want to get past you," he said, suddenly turning on Haze.

"I reckon I'll go sit down some," Haze said, blushing.

children if she saw them now. Her sister wrote they were as big as their father. Things changed fast, she said. Her sister's husband had worked with the city water supply in Grand Rapids—he had a good place—but in Waterloo, he. . . .

"I went back there last time," Haze said. "I wouldn't be getting off at Taulkinham if it was there; it went apart like, you know, it. . . ."

Mrs. Hosen frowned. "You must be thinking of another Grand Rapids," she said. "The Grand Rapids I'm talking about is a large city and it's always where it's always been." She stared at him for a moment and then went on: when they were in Grand Rapids they got along fine, but in Waterloo he suddenly took to liquor. Her sister had to support the house and

He knew people were staring at him as he went back to his section. Mrs. Hosen was looking out the window. She turned and eyed him suspiciously; then she said it hadn't snowed yet, had it? and relaxed into a stream of talk. She guessed her husband was getting his own supper tonight. She was paying a girl to come cook his dinner but he was having to get his own supper. She didn't think that hurt a man once in a while. She thought it did him good. Wallace wasn't lazy but he didn't think what it took to keep going with housework all day. She didn't know how it would feel to be in Florida with somebody waiting on her.

He was from Chicago.

This was her first vacation in five years. Five years ago she had gone to visit her sister in Grand Rapids. Time flies. Her sister had left Grand Rapids and moved to Waterloo. She didn't suppose she'd recognize her sister's

educate the children. It beat Mrs. Hosen how he could sit there year after year.

Haze's mother had never talked much on the train; she mostly listened. She was a Jackson.

After a while Mrs. Hosen said she was hungry and asked him if he wanted to go into the diner. He did.

The dining car was full and people were waiting to get in it. Haze and Mrs. Hosen stood in line for a half hour, rocking in the narrow passageway and every few minutes flattening themselves against the side to let a trickle of people through. Mrs. Hosen began talking to the lady on the side of her. Haze stared stupidly at the wall. He would never have had the courage to come to the diner by himself; it was fine he had met Mrs. Hosen. If she hadn't been talking, he would have told her intelligently that he had gone there the last time and that the porter was not from there but that he looked near enough like a gulch nigger to be one, near enough like old Cash to be his child. He'd tell her while they were eating. He couldn't see inside the diner from where he was; he wondered what it would be like in there. Like a restaurant, he reckoned. He thought of the berth. By the time they got through eating, the berth would probably be made up and he could get in it. What would his ma say if she seen him having a berth in a train! He bet she never reckoned that would happen. As they got nearer the entrance to the diner he could see in. It was like a city restaurant! He bet she never reckoned it was like that.

The head man was beckoning to the people at the first of the line every time someone left—sometimes for one person, sometimes for more. He motioned for two people and the line moved up so that Haze and Mrs. Hosen and the lady she was talking to were standing at the end of the diner, looking in. In a minute, two more people left. The man beckoned and Mrs. Hosen and the lady walked in, and Haze followed them. The man stopped Haze and said, "Only two," and pushed him back to the doorway. Haze's face went an ugly red. He tried to get behind the next person and then he tried to get through the line to go back to the car he had come from, but there were too many people bunched in the opening. He had to stand there while everyone around looked at him. No one left for a while and he had to stand there. Mrs. Hosen did not look at him again. Finally a lady up at the far end got up and the head man jerked his hand and Haze hesitated and saw the hand jerk again and then lurched up the aisle, falling against two tables on the way and getting his hand wet with somebody's coffee. He didn't look at the people he sat down with. He ordered the first thing on the menu and, when it came, ate it without thinking what it might be. The people he was sitting with had finished and, he could tell, were waiting, watching him eat.

When he got out the diner he was weak and his hands were making small jittery movements by themselves. It seemed a year ago that he had seen the head man beckon to him to sit down. He stopped between two cars and breathed in the cold air to clear his head. It helped. When he got back to his car all the berths were made up and the aisles were dark and sinister, hung in heavy green. He realized again that he had a berth, an upper one, and that he could get in it now. He could lie down and raise the shade just enough to look out from and watch—what he had planned to do—and see how everything went by a train at night. He could look right into the night, moving.

He got his sack and went to the men's room and put on his night clothes. A sign said to get the porter to let you into the upper berths. The porter might be a cousin of some of them gulch niggers, he thought suddenly; he might ask him if he had any cousins around Eastrod, or maybe just in Tennessee. He went down the aisle, looking for him. They might have a little conversation before he got in the berth. The porter was not at that end of the car and he went back to look at the other end. Going around the corner, he ran into something heavily pink; it gasped and muttered, "Clumsy!" It was Mrs. Hosen in a pink wrapper with her hair in knots around her head. He had forgotten about her. She was terrifying with her hair slicked back and the knobs like dark toadstools framing her face. She tried to get past him and he tried to let her but they were both moving the same way each time. Her face became purplish except for little white marks over it that didn't heat up. She drew herself stiff and stopped still and said, "What IS the matter with you?" He slipped past her and dashed down the aisle and ran suddenly into the porter so that the porter slipped and he fell on top of him and the porter's face was right under his and it was old Cash Simmons. For a minute he couldn't move off the porter for thinking it was Cash and he breathed, "Cash," and the porter pushed him

off and got up and went down the aisle quick and Haze scrambled off the floor and went after him saying he wanted to get in the berth and thinking, this is Cash's kin, and then suddenly, like something thrown at him when he wasn't looking: this is Cash's son run away;

and then: he knows about Eastrod and doesn't want it, he doesn't want to talk about it, he doesn't want to talk about Cash.

He stood staring while the porter put the ladder up to the berth and then he started up it, still looking at the porter, seeing Cash there, only different, not in the eyes, and halfway up the ladder he said, still looking at the porter, "Cash is dead. He got the cholera from a pig." The porter's mouth perked down and he muttered, looking at Haze with his eyes thin, "I'm from Chicago. My father was a railroad man." And Haze stared at him and then laughed: a nigger being a railroad "man": and laughed again, and the porter jerked the ladder off suddenly with a wrench of his arm that sent Haze clutching at the blanket into the berth.

He lay on his stomach in the berth, trembling from the way he had got in. Cash's son. From Eastrod. But not wanting Eastrod; hating it. He lay there for a while on his stomach, not moving. It seemed a year since he had fallen over the porter in the aisle.

After a while he remembered that he was actually in the berth and he turned and found the light and looked around him. There was no window.

The side wall did not have a window in it. It didn't push up to be a window. There was no window concealed in it. There was a fish-net thing stretched across the side wall; but no windows. For a second it flashed through his mind that the porter had done this—given him this berth that there were no windows to and had just a fish net strung the length of—because he hated him. But they must all be like this.

The top of the berth was low and curved over. He lay down. The curved top looked like it was not quite closed; it looked like it was closing. He lay there for a while not moving. There was something in his throat like a sponge with an egg taste. He had eggs for supper. They were in the sponge in his throat. They were right in his throat. He didn't want to turn over for fear they would move; he wanted the light off; he wanted it dark. He reached up without turning and felt for the button and snapped it and the darkness sank down on him and then faded a little with light from the aisle that came in through the foot of space not closed. He wanted it all dark, he didn't want it diluted. He heard the porter's footsteps coming down the aisle, soft into the rug, coming steadily down, brushing against the green curtains and fading up the other way out of hearing. He was from Eastrod. From Eastrod but he hated it. Cash wouldn't have put any claim on him. He wouldn't have wanted him. He wouldn't have wanted anything that wore a monkey white coat and toted a whisk broom in his pocket. Cash's clothes had looked like they'd set a while under a rock; and they smelled like nigger. He thought how Cash smelled, but he smelled the train. No more gulch niggers in Eastrod. In Eastrod. Turning in the road, he saw in the dark, half dark, the store boarded and the barn open with the dark free in it, and the smaller house half carted away, the porch gone and no floor in the hall. He had been supposed to go to his sister's in Taulkinham on his last furlough when he came up from the camp in Georgia but he didn't want to go to Taulkinham and he had gone back to Eastrod even though he knew how it was: the two families scattered in towns and even the niggers from up and down the road gone into Memphis and Murfreesboro and other places. He had gone back and slept in the house on the floor in the kitchen and a board had fallen in his head out of the roof and cut his face. He jumped, feeling the board, and the train jolted and unjolted and went again. He went looking through the house to see they hadn't left nothing in it ought to been taken.

His ma always slept in the kitchen and had her walnut shifferrobe in there. Wasn't another shifferrobe nowhere around. She was a Jackson. She had paid thirty dollars for it and hadn't bought herself nothing else big again. And they had left it. He reckoned they hadn't had room on the truck for it. He opened all the drawers. There were two lengths of wrapping cord in the top one and nothing in the others. He was surprised nobody had come and stolen a shifferrobe like that. He took the wrapping cord and tied the legs through the floorboards and left a piece of paper in each of the drawers: THIS SHIFFERROBE BELONGS TO HAZEL WICKERS. DO NOT STEAL IT OR YOU WILL BE HUNTED DOWN AND KILLED.

She could rest easier knowing it was guarded some. If she come looking any time at night, she would see. He wondered if she walked at night and came there ever—came with that look on her face, unrested and looking, going up the path and through the barn open all around and stopping in the shadow by the store boarded up, coming on unrested with that look on her face like he had seen through the crack going down. He seen her face through the crack when they were shutting the top on her, seen the shadow that came down over her face and pulled her mouth down like she wasn't satisfied with resting, like she was going to spring up and shove the lid back and fly out like a spirit going to be satisfied: but they shut it on down. She might have been going to fly out of there, she might have been going to spring—he saw her terrible like a huge bat darting from the closing—fly out of there but it was falling dark on top of her, closing down all the time, closing down; from inside he saw it closing, coming closer, closer down and cutting off the light and the room and the trees seen through the window through the crack faster and darker closing down. He opened his eyes and saw it closing

Courtesy Illinois Central Railroad

down and he sprang up between the crack and wedged his body through it and hung there moving, dizzy, with the dim light of the train slowly showing the rug below, moving, dizzy. He hung there wet and cold and saw the porter at the other end of the car, a white shape in the darkness, standing there, watching him and not moving. The tracks curved and he fell back sick into the rushing stillness of the train.

LONG GONE

Sterling A. Brown

I laks yo' kin' of lovin',
   Ain't never caught you wrong,
But it jes' ain' nachal
   Fo' to stay here long;

It jes' ain' nachal
   Fo' a railroad man,
With a itch fo' travelin'
   He cain't understan'. . . .

I looks at de rails,
   An' I looks at de ties,
An' I hears an ole freight
   Puffin' up de rise,

An' at nights on my pallet,
   When all is still,
I listens fo' de empties
   Bumpin' up de hill;

When I oughta be quiet,
   I is got a itch
Fo' to hear de whistle blow
   Fo' de crossin' or de switch,

An' I knows de time's a-nearin'
   When I got to ride,
Though it's homelike and happy
   At yo' side.

You is done all you could do
   To make me stay;
'Tain't no fault of yours I'se leavin'—
   I'se jes dataway.

I is got to see some people
   I ain't never seen,
Gotta highball thru some country
   Whah I never been.

I don't know which way I'm travelin'—
   Far or near,
All I knows fo' certain is
   I cain't stay here.

Ain't no call at all, sweet woman,
   Fo' to carry on—
Jes' my name and jes' my habit
   To be Long Gone. . . .

139

SIDETRACK
THE LANGUAGE

The end man looked down the alley, and said to the master mind, "I'm no baby lifter; I don't touch a high-wheeler."

"Okay," the master mind replied. "But you're not a head man, either, and someone has to take care of the drone cage."

"Not me," the end man said "pick up a clown in the garden. Draw bar flagging is enough for one trip. I've hit the grit twice from the doghouse."

"That might be better than dancing on the carpet for brownies."

"Well, no matter, anyway. I'm outlawed."

"If you count on that," the master mind answered, "you may as well pull the pin."

"Okay," the club winder said. "Forget the Hog Law, if you don't have a dog catcher. But leave me on the clown wagon. Let the Big O do the baby lifting."

No one, we feel sure, talks this way, but the vocabulary is there for it. No group of people—prison inmates, fighter pilots, sociologists or linguists—has a language more its own than do the people of the railroads (whether they make the trains run or ride them as hobos).

HOBO LANGUAGE

Stickers—Disguised begging by selling court plaster.

Timbers—Disguised begging by selling pencils.

Sticks—Train rider who lost a leg.

Peg—Train rider who lost a foot.

Fingy or Fingers—Train rider who lost one or more fingers.

Blinky—Train rider who lost one or both eyes.

Wingy—Train rider who lost one or both arms.

Mitts—Train rider who lost one or both hands.

Righty—Train rider who lost right arm and leg.

Lefty—Train rider who lost left arm and leg.

Halfy—Train rider who lost both legs above knee.

Straight Crip—Actually crippled or otherwise afflicted.

Phony Crip—Self-mutilated or simulating a deformity.

Pokey Stiff—Subsisted on handouts solely.

Phony Stiff—Disposed of fraudulent jewelry.

Proper Stiff—Considered manual toil the acme of disgrace.

Gink or Gandy Stiff—Occasionally labored, a day or two at the most.

Alkee Stiff—Confirmed consumers.

White Line Stiff—Confirmed consumers of alcohol.

Rummy Stiff—Deranged intellect by habitual use of raw rum.

Bindle Stiff }
Blanket Stiff } —Carried bedding.

Chronicker—Hoboed with cooking utensils.

Stew Bum
Ding Bat
Fuzzy Tail } —The dregs of vagrantdom.
Grease Ball
Jungle Buzzard

RAILROAD SLANG

A

Age—Term of time in service, usually referring to Seniority.

Air Monkey—Air brake repairman.

Alley—Clear Track.

Anchor Them—Set the brakes on still cars.

Artist—A general term usually referring to some workman, particularly adept, and usually with such prefix as brake, pin, speed, etc.

B

Baby Lifter—Passenger brakeman.

Battleship—Usually referred to the superheater type or any large locomotive.

Beanery—A railroad eating house.

Beanery Queen—Waitress

Bee Hive—Yard office.

Locomotive Lamps.

Bell Bottom Brakemen—College students.

Bend the Iron—Change the position of a switch.

Bend the Rust—Change the position of a switch.

Big Hole—Emergency position of the air brake valve; the act of abruptly applying the brakes to the full reduction.

Big Hook—Wrecking crane.

Big O—Freight conductor.

Big Ox—Conductor of either freight or passenger.

Black Diamonds—Company coal.

Blow Up—To quit a job suddenly.

Board—A fixed signal regulating railroad traffic and usually referred to as a slow board, order board, clear board (for clear tracks) or red board (stop).

Boiler Header—Riding in cab.

Boomer—The drifting type of railroad man who travels from road to road and stays but a very short time at any one place. The term was derived from the pioneer days of railroad booms along new frontiers and originally was applied to men who followed these boom camps.

Brain Plate—Trainman's badge.

Brainless Wonder—Conductor, engineer, or any official who does queer things in the opinion of their fellows.

Brains—Conductor.

Brass Collar—Applied to members of the official family.

Brass Hat—A term applicable to officials.

Brownies—Demerit marks placed against an employee's record.

Brownie Box—Superintendent's car.

Improved Frog.

Buggy—Caboose; passenger car; box car.

Bug Torch—Trainman's lantern.

Bull—Special agent or railroad police officer.

Bumper—A post at end of spur track.

C

Cage—Caboose.

Caller—Employee whose duty it is to call out a train and engine crew.

Canned—To be taken out of service.

Captain—A term applied to conductor, either passenger or freight.

Car Toad—Car repairer; there are many variations of this word, viz: car knock, car tonk, car whack, etc.

Car Whacker—Car repairman.

Caser—Silver dollar.

Century—Hundred-dollar bill.

Chariot—Sometimes applied to passenger cars, but most frequently to cabooses.

Chasing the Red—The act of a flagman who has gone back with red flag or red light to protect a train.

Cinder Cruncher—A switchman.

Cinder Snapper—A passenger who rides the open platform on observation cars.

Clown—A switchman or yard brakeman.

Clown Wagon—Caboose.

Club—Hickory pole about three feet long found on some railroads and required by the management to be carried around by a trainman in addition to his raincoat and lantern.

Club Winder—Switchman or brakeman.

Cornered—When a car, not in the clear on a siding, is struck by a passing train or engine.

Corn Field Meet—Where two trains meet head-on, both trying to use the same main line.

Cow Cage—Stock car.

Cow Catcher—The pilot.

Wrought-Iron Rail Chair.

Crib—Caboose.

Cripple—A defective car or one that needs repairs.

Croaker—Doctor.

Crowning Him—Coupling a caboose on a train when it is made up.

Crummy—Caboose.

Cupola—The observation tower on a caboose.

Cushions—A term referring to passenger cars.

Cut—A few cars attached to the goat or engine; several cars coupled together anywhere.

D.

Dancing on the Carpet—Called to the superintendent's office for investigation or discipline.

Deadhead—Employee riding over the road on company pass and on company business.

Deck—The floor part of a locomotive cab.

Detainer—Usually applied to the train dispatcher.

Diamond—Crossover.

Dick—Railroad detective.

Dinger—Yardmaster or assistant yardmaster.

Dinky—Engine without tender used around roundhouse and backshop to do the switching.

Dog Catcher—A crew sent to relieve a crew that has become outlawed.

Dog House—Caboose.

Dolly—Applied to switch stand.

Dope—Orders, official instructions.

Draw Bar Flagging—The act of a brakeman leaning up against the draw bar on the caboose to protect the rear end of his train.

Drone Cage—Private car.

Drop—A switching movement.

Drummer—Yard conductor.

Duckets—Yard checks.

Dynamiter—A car on which a defective air mechanism sends the brakes into full emergency when only service application is given from the engine.

E

Eagle-Eye—Locomotive engineer.

End Man—The brakeman or rear brakeman, usually on freight trains.

F

First Reader—Conductor's train book.

Flag—To work under an assumed name.

Flat—A type of freight car.

Flat Wheel—A car wheel that has flat spots on the tread; also applied to an employee who walks lame or limps.

Flimsy—Train Order.
Floater—Same as a boomer.
Flop—Bed.
Flying Switch—A switching movement.
Foot-Board—The step on the front end and rear end of switch and freight engines.
Freeze Hub—Cool a heated journal.

G

Gandy Dancer—Track laborer.
Gangway—The space between the rear cab post of a locomotive and the tender.
Garden—A freight yard.
Gate—A switch.
General—Yardmaster.

Glimmer—Switchman's lantern.
Glory—String of empties; death by accident.
Goat—A yard engine.
Go High—The act of decorating or climbing to the top of box cars to receive signals or to transmit signals or to apply hand brakes.
G. M.—General Manager.
Gon—A gondola or steel-sided, flat bottom coal car.
Grabber—Conductor.
Gramaphone—Telephone.
Graveyard Watch—12:01 A.M. to 8 A.M.
Greasy Spoon—A railroad eating house.
Green Backs—Frogs for rerailing cars or engines.
Gum Shoe—Railroad Policeman.

H

Hack—Another term for caboose.
Hand Shoes—Gloves.
Harness—Passenger conductor's uniform.
Hay Burner—Hand oil lantern.

Spark Arrestor.

Head Man—The brakeman who, on freight trains, rides the engine.
Head Pin—The head brakeman.
Hearse—Caboose.
Herder—A man who couples engines on and takes them off on the arrival and departure of trains.
Highball—Signal waved by the hand or by lamp in a high, wide semiarc, the meaning of which is to get out of town at full speed ahead.
Highball Artist—A locomotive engineer who is noted for fast running.
High Iron—The main line or the high speed track of a system of main tracks.
Highliner—Main line fast passenger.
High Wheeler—Passenger locomotive; a fast passenger train; a highball artist.
Hitting the Grit—Falling off a car.
Hog—A locomotive.
Hogger—A locomotive engineer.
Hoghead—A locomotive engineer.
Hog Law—The federal statute which provides that all train and engine crews tie up after 12 hours of continuous service; also called the dog law.
Hole—Term applied to passing track where one train pulls in to meet another.
Home Guard—One who stays with one railroad.
Hook—Wrecking crane or auxilliary.
Hopper—A steel-sided coal car with a hopper bottom which allows the unloading from that point.
Hop-Toad—Derail.
Hot Box—Overheated journal or bearing.
Hot Footer—Engineer or conductor in switching service who is always in a hurry.
Hot Shot—A fast train of any class. Sometimes called a highball run.
Hump—An artificial knoll at the end of a classification yard over which cars are pushed to be allowed to roll to separate tracks on their own momentum.
Hut—A term sometimes applied to a caboose and sometimes applied to the cab of a locomotive.

I

In the Hole—On a siding.
Iron Skull—A boiler maker.

J

Jack—Locomotive.
Jam Buster—Assistant yardmaster.
Jewel—Journal brass.
Jigger—A full tonnage train of dead freight.
Johnson Bar—Reverse lever on a locomotive.
Juggler—A term applied sometimes to members of the train crew of way freight runs, whose duties require them to load and unload less than carload freight at station stops.

LOOK LISTEN

K

Kangaroo Court—A hearing at which matters of main line mix-ups are investigated and disposed of.

Keeley—Water can for hot or heated journals.
Kettle—A locomotive.
Kick—Applied to switching; the act of pushing a car or cars at speed ahead or behind an engine, and then suddenly cutting the car or cars loose from the engine while the brakes are applied quickly to the engine, thus allowing the cars to be kicked free.
Kicker—A triple valve that sticks and throws brakes into emergency with application of air and sometimes by a bump of the train.
King—Freight conductor—sometimes applied to the yardmaster.
King Snipe—Foreman of track gang.
Knowledge Box—Yardmaster's office.

L

Ladder—The main track of a system of tracks which comprise a yard and from which each individual track leads off. This is also called a lead.
Lead—See ladder.
Letters—Service certificates.
Lever-Jerker—Interlocker lever man.
Lizard Scorcher—Cook.
Louse Cage—Caboose.
Lung—Drawbar.

M

Main Iron—Main track.
Main Pin—An official.
Main Stem—The main line.
Making a Hitch—Coupling two cars together.
Marker—Rear end signal.
Master—Conductor.
Master Maniac—The master mechanic.
Master Mind—Sometimes applied to trainmaster, yardmaster and conductor, also to the train dispatcher.
Mill—Steam locomotive; typewriter.
Mill Kettle—Locomotive.
Modoc—Employes' train.
Monkey House—Caboose.
Monkey Motion—Link motion.
Mud Chicken—Surveyor.
Mudhop—Yard clerk.

N

Non-Air—A non-union railroad worker.
Number Dummy—Yard clerk.
Number Grabber—Car clerk.
Nut Splitter—Machinist.

O

Old Man—Superintendent.
O.R.C.—A conductor.
Order Board—A fixed signal to indicate to approaching trains whether to pick up train orders or to proceed.
Ornament—Station Master.
O-S-ing—Reporting a train by a station to the division dispatcher.
Outlawed—A crew that has worked 12 hours, the limit allowed by law.

P

Paddle—Semaphore signal.
Palace—A term applied to the caboose.
Parlor—Caboose.
Parlor Man—The hind brakeman or flagman on a freight train.
Pig—Locomotive.
Pig Mauler—Locomotive engineer.
Pig Pen—Locomotive roundhouse.
Pin—Sometimes applied to a brakeman.
Pin Ahead and Pick Up Two Behind One—Cut off the engine and pick up three cars from the siding, put two on the train and set the first one back on the siding.
Pin For Home—To go home.
Pinhead—Applied to brakeman.
Pink—Caution card.
Pinner—Switchman that follows.
Pin-Puller—The man who cuts off the cars switching.
Play Ball—Get busy; go to work; quit fooling.
Plug—One horse passenger train.
Possum Belly—Tool box under caboose.
Pull the Pin—To resign, or quit a job.
Putty—Steam.

R

Rail—A railroad employee. Usually referred to men in transportation service.
Rattler—A freight train.
Rawhider—A conductor or engineer who is especially hard on men and equipment. This term is chiefly applied to engineers who punish locomotives to the limit without getting satisfactory results.
Red Ball—Fast freight.
Red Board—Fixed signal to stop.
Red Onion—Railroad eating house.

Reefer—Refrigerator car.
Rubberneck—Observation car.
Rule G—Thou shalt not drink.
Runty—Dwarf signal.

S

Scissor-Bill—Applied to either yard or road brakeman and a term which is not considered complimentary; a student in train service.
Scoop—The step on the front and rear-end of switch engines.
Secret Works—Automatic air brake application.
Shack—A brakeman.
Shack Stinger—Brakeman.
Shanty—A caboose.
Shining Time—Starting time.
Shuffle the Deck—Used by local brakemen for switching housetracks at every station.
Shunting Boiler—Switch engine.
Sidedoor Pullman—Box car.
Skipper—Conductor.
Slave Driver—Yardmaster.
Smart Alec—Conductor.
Smoker—Brakeman.
Snake—Switchman.
Snipe—Track laborer.
Snoozer—Pullman car.
Soft Bellies—Wooden frame cars.
Spar—A pole used to shove cars in the clear when switching.

STOP — LOOK LISTEN

Speedy—Call boy.
Spotter—A man assigned to snoop around to check up on conduct of employees.
Stick—A staff used on certain stretches of track for the purpose of controlling the block. It is carried by engine crews from one station to another.
Stinger—Brakeman.
Stopper Puller—A member of the crew that follows the engine in switching.
String—A cut of cars; several cars coupled together.
Strings—Telegraph wires.
Student—A learner in either telegraph, train or engine service.
Super—A superintendent.
Swell Head—Conductor.

T

Iron Bridge.

Tank—Locomotive tender.
Teakettle—Usually applied to leaky old locomotives.
Thousand Miler—A starched blue shirt with an attachable starched blue collar of deep hue worn by railroad men universally and especially as an insignia of rank among boomers of a bygone era.
Ticket Punch—Pair of pliers.
Tie 'Em Down—To set hand brakes.
Toad—Derailer.
Toepath—Running board.
Train Detainer—Train dispatcher.
Train Line—The pipe that carries the compressed air used to operate the air brakes.
Traveling Grunt—A road foreman of engines.
Traveling Man—Usually applied to the traveling engineer.
Trick—Applied to tour of duty.
Trip—The course of a tour of duty from one terminal to another and return.

U

Underground Hog—Chief engineer.

V

Varnished Wagons—Passenger train equipment.

W

Wagons—See buggies.
Washout—A stop signal waved violently by using both arms and swinging them in a downward arc by day, and swinging a lamp in a wide, low semicircle across the tracks by night.
Way-Car—Caboose.
Whale Belly—A type of coal car.
When Do You Shine?—What time were you called for?
Willie—Waybill.
Wing Her—Set the brakes on a moving train.
Wye—Tracks running off main line or lead, forming rough letter "Y" and used to turn cars or to reverse direction of trains. Used to reverse engines at points where no turntable is available.

Y

Yard—A system of tracks for the making of trains or the storing of cars. Boomer's version: A system of tracks surrounded by a high board fence run and inhabited by a bunch of natives that will not let a train in or out.
Y.M.—Yardmaster.

PAY DAY HUSSEY'S CAMP B.A. R.R.

YESTERDAY
1930-1970

and I shake by the thundering tracks crying hoarsely: love love love.

— Dave Etter

RR

Otto Salassi

Vicksburg

The city of Vicksburg is located on the side of a hill that overlooks the Mississippi River. In Civil War times the city was known as the Gibraltar of the Confederacy, wrongly, I might add, because Vicksburg fell to the Yankees and the real Gibraltar has never fallen to a foe. In modern times, Vicksburg has been called the Hill City, and when it hosted a professional baseball team in the Southeastern League, the team was called the Hillbillies, or Billies for short. Once every month the promoters had what they called Railroad Night when everyone who worked for the railroad was admitted for half fare. Full fare was fifty cents; half fare was a quarter. I belonged to a baseball club called the Knot-hole Gang; we wore blue baseball caps, sat in a special section, and got in the games for a nickel.

I don't believe, now when I think back on it, that railroad nights were any better attended than any other nights, but on railroad nights, sitting with the Knot-hole Gang in our little section of the bleachers behind the third-base line and watching the stands fill up, I would brag about my father who worked for the Illinois Central. I was about seven years old and it was the only time I remember actually being proud of what my father did for a living.

The Railroad

"You go up the stairs on the side of the building there, and through that door," my mother said, pointing to steps that looked like a fire escape and a big steel door at the top where a man was coming out. "Right there. Right there where the man just came out." She handed me the brown paper bag that held my father's lunch and I got out of the car. "If your daddy's not there, you wait for him. Don't ever just leave it on his locker expecting him to come get it; somebody else always walks off with it. Wait for him and make sure you give it to him in his hand."

My father got very upset if he didn't get his lunch, and my mother made sure that there were no gray areas between responsibilities.

I was about eight years old and it was my first time. She drove me in the car the first time and showed me where to go. From then on, I would be on my own and it would be dangerous. On the way there she pointed out all the things I should watch out for.

"Watch out for that track because that's the main line, and the trains don't always slow down on that one. They're likely to be coming fast." The main line track was set farther away from the other tracks like a dangerous dog or horse that is kept separate. "Watch out for trains," she said, "even if they're not moving. Never try to go under one and don't climb on them. If you got a train blocking your way, go around, no matter how far it is. Take your time, but don't take too much time. Get there before the lunch gets cold."

She didn't have to tell me not to climb through or over. The boxcars were to me as big as mountains, and I always walked around, even when I went barefooted, even with the sharp cinders hurting my feet.

This was the important thing: "Get there before the grease on the meat turns white. If the grease on the meat turns white, you get a whipping."

I climbed the stairs. I was near the top when a train passed on the track just below me, so close that I thought it was going to hit the building. The stairs shook so bad that I started crying and ran back down. My mother got out of the car and pointed for me to go back up again, which I did.

It wasn't anything but a room. The floors were concrete and very dirty; in the middle of the room was a round sink, and around the walls were lockers. I sat on one of the wooden benches in front of the lockers and waited. In a few minutes, whistles blew. The whistles were loud enough to be heard all over town; they were, in fact, heard all over town; people used to set their watches and clocks by them. One of the whistles was on the roof of the building, right over my head. It scared me so bad that I couldn't get my breath. It stopped up my ears so tight, I thought I had gone deaf.

Men came in and I watched for my father.

The men were incredibly dirty—black, almost, with grease and soot. They had been wearing goggles and their eyes were like white masks. They looked at me where I was sitting, then looked away and went about the business of washing and eating. More and more of them came in and I began to worry that my father wasn't coming. When he finally came into the crowded room, I didn't recognize him. He was the dirtiest and blackest of them all. He put his hand on my shoulder and said my name. It was the first time I had seen him like that and suddenly I was ashamed. I was ashamed of him and what he did for a living. I thrust the lunch in his hands and ran from the room.

The Smell of the Railroad

Most people, when they think about the railroads, think about the nostalgia. They remember train trips they took and think of themselves sitting very prim and proper on the seat,

Vicksburg had the only roundhouse between Memphis and New Orleans. The railroad men I saw worked in the shops and the yards. In the shops there were welders, boilermakers, mechanics and master mechanics, pipe fitters, foremen, inspectors, and supervisors. I don't remember knowing an engineer, a conductor, or a brakeman, singing or otherwise.

The railroad had two very different smells. One of the smells was the smell of the coaches: the smell of the green material that covered the seats, material that felt like coarse velvet; the smell of the white cotton antimacassars that hung on the back of them; the clean smell of the pillows that the porters gave you when you were sleepy. I only made three trips in those coaches: the trip to New Orleans when I was five, the trip to Memphis to visit my brother when I was in the seventh grade, the trip to San Antonio for basic training when I

St. Louis Union Station Waiting Room.—*Courtesy Missouri Pacific Railroad*

by the window, looking at pretty picture farms and countryside. Railroad men were brave engineers and mysterious conductors and black porters and singing brakemen like Jimmie Rogers who rambled and gambled and told their wives lies.

joined the Air Force. I can still remember the smell of them; I get it every once in a while when I'm on a library trip to Nashville and eat at the Hotel Tennessean. The Tennessean has that smell. It comes from the quality of the materials that went into the making: the wood

145

and brass and porcelain, the good carpet. The smell of things that are well-made never gets obscured by mustiness, or age, or hard use.

The other smell was the smell of coal. I can't remember the time when I didn't know what coal was, or what it smelled like. It seemed as though there was always coal around. Below our house on Speed Street, in the hollow, there was the colored town, and the colored people used almost as much coal as the railroad.

The railroad yards at Vicksburg smelled only of coal. It was stored in great pyramids; it was pulled in coal cars behind every engine that moved. It was burned and settled in the air, on everybody and everything. Coal smelled like coal. It was the cinders that was used on roadbeds and it was the mud in the yards when it rained.

The Brakeman ... takes advantage of the laugh that follows.—*New York Public Library Picture Collection*

My father smelled of coal and Borax. In the locker room there were two kinds of soap in the dispensers, Borax and the green liquid soap that smelled like barber cologne. The green stuff made you smell good, but it never got you clean, so my father never used it. The smell of the Borax never quite overcame the smell of coal.

The Poor and the Railroad

Every Easter morning my little brother and I would report to the Jackson Street Station for shoes. It was an annual thing until about 1953 when for some reason it was stopped. There would be a boxcar of shoes to be given away to every railroad kid who wanted them, but only the blacks and a few poor white kids ever showed up.

It took a whipping to make me go. There was always a photographer there taking pictures for the newspaper and I would have died if they had put my picture in the paper. There were always a few kids there from school; we knew each other in the way that the poor and the rich always know each other. We never mentioned that we saw each other there, and when we met at school we never looked at each other's shoes. The worst thing of all was the shoes themselves. They were always out of style. They always looked like little chopped-down boots, and when I got in the sixth grade I started refusing to wear them. I got a job and I bought my own shoes.

The railroad paid my father $119.00 every two weeks—more if he worked Saturday afternoons, less if he got sick and missed a day. Twice his wages were garnisheed.

He used to tell me that the reason he did not make more money than he did was because he didn't know any more than he did. I should go to school so that I wouldn't end up like him, working like a dog for no money and little thanks. He always faulted himself, never the railroad.

Growing Up with the Railroad

My father was a boilermaker. A boilermaker is essentially a welder, but more than a welder; a boilermaker works with thick-plated steel and what he welds together must be especially strong and take great pressures.

When he didn't come to the locker room for his lunch, I had to go out in the shops and find him. Sometimes I found him in the slot underneath one of the engines. Most of the time I found him working inside one of the boilers. The air inside the boilers was always bad from the torches. The only light came from a bulb at the end of a drop cord. The noise was often so great that he would not have heard the whistles, as loud as the whistles were.

The summer between the sixth and the seventh grades I stopped taking my father's lunch and my little brother started. He took it for one summer, or at least the first part of one summer; he took it until he learned that he could get out of taking it by pretending to be sick. Soon neither of us was home when it came lunchtime. My mother took it to him herself for a while, until we sold the car. My father warmed up cans of soup and stew on a hot plate.

The Santa Fe's diesel-powered streamliner, the Super Chief.—*Santa Fe Railway photo*

With the money from the car my mother bought a television set. Television was new. Jackson, Mississippi, had a station that had just started broadcasting and we could pick it up in Vicksburg. I began to watch television and I never went near the railroad shops again. I decided that I'd be a doctor or a lawyer or a private investigator. I wouldn't be like my father; I'd be like the people I saw on television. My father, for all practical purposes, had ceased to exist.

I was the kid who never told anybody where he lived. I used to ask my friends to let me out of their cars a block from my house and walk the rest of the way home.

All through junior high and high school, I had a job collecting for bingo games at the Moose Club on Monday and Friday nights. I made about ten dollars a week and spent just about all of it on shirts. At one time I must have had about thirty or forty shirts, just like the rich kids. The rich kids took English instead of shop courses at school, so I took English instead of shop. I still don't know which direction to turn a screw.

When I was in the eleventh grade, my father hit C. K. Burkle in the head with a ball-peen hammer and put him in the hospital. Burkle was an inspector and a high muck-a-muck at the First Baptist Church. The newspaper wrote it up as a news item; they didn't make it a lead story but they put it on the front page under the headline

BURKLE ASSAULTED

My father's name was given and everybody in town must have read it, whether they knew who Burkle was or not. My father wasn't in jail as they reported; he was at home in the custody of my mother's cousin, who was a deputy sheriff. I found out about it when I came home from school. I must have read the paper a hundred times; I was crying, I remember, and I told my father that because of him I could never go back to school again.

"I don't give a damn what you do," he said. "If you ain't learned anything by now, maybe you ain't never going to."

He had been in one of the boilers, cutting out a seam so he could put in a new one. Burkle didn't have anything to do, so he was in the boiler to hide out. Instead of minding his own business, Burkle started horsing around and playing grab-ass. My father told him two or three times to go away and let him do his work. Burkle didn't, and my father picked up the first thing his hand happened to light on, the hammer, and tapped him on the head with it.

"I didn't make the world," my father said. "I just try to live in it." In time I understood what he meant.

Burkle wasn't hurt that bad. He was sore. He had a concussion but it wasn't a bad one. He was back at work the next Monday, and the railroad, for punishment, sent my father home for three days without pay. The whole thing blew over.

I graduated from high school with my class in 1957, and as I say, joined the Air Force.

I have not gone back to Vicksburg but twice in all the years that followed: once for a visit when my father first found out he had cancer and was dying, the second time for his funeral.

The Passing of the Railroad

I cannot help thinking about the differences. My father worked hard for his living; I am a

Engineer John Maynard Douglas, better known as Cornbread, after his last run on Cotton Belt passenger train No. 6, the day of his retirement, March 30, 1941.—*Courtesy of Mrs. Dorothy Douglas Wood*

librarian. He lived with physical discomfort all of his life; I've seen him come home with bad burns on his face and neck, rub some kind of sulfur and grease ointment on them, sleep and go back to work the next morning. I get uncomfortable when I don't get my dinner on time.

I don't think about being rich or famous anymore. My kids watch television and talk about all the great things they're going to do. Young people think about being great; people my age start thinking about retirement.

When you retired from the railroad, they gave you a lifetime pass. My father always thought of a lifetime pass as something like a credit card you kept in your wallet. Anytime you wanted to go anywhere in the United States, all you had to do was show your pass and they let you ride. He would have his retirement pay, ninety-eight dollars a month; the kids would all be grown and on their own; he would have raised three children and put them through school and out into the world. I imagine him dreaming about that day. He would get his pass and ride. He wouldn't need a house anymore; he'd be a hobo like every hobo who ever dreamed about Heaven must have dreamed; money coming in, a lifetime ticket to ride. Free to go.

The first thing that happened was the pass itself. The pass turned out to be different from what he had imagined. It turned out that to go anywhere, first you had to fill out forms and ask for it. You had to say exactly where you wanted to go, when you wanted the pass for, and when you wanted to come back. You had to do this in advance of the trip and get it approved. My father got to make one trip, to Colorado Springs, to Camp Carson, to visit my older brother, who was stationed there.

The next two things that happened were that the railroads stopped honoring each other's passes; it wasn't possible after 1960 or 1961 to transfer from one line to another on a pass. In about 1962, the IC stopped most of its passenger service, so my father couldn't go anywhere.

Retirement. I've been wondering what I'll do when my two kids graduate and go. What do you look forward to when you're a librarian? I'm a fairly good librarian; I mind my own business and get along with the board and the committee. I raise my kids and I hope they don't grow up to lie or steal. I try to teach them that it is their lot in life to be workers and not freeloaders, and if they learn that, I figure they'll get by. I must confess that I don't have that many plans.

I think sometimes about buying a houseboat and putting it on the Tennessee River. The Tennessee is really a beautiful river. It's fairly safe and I could learn to fish.

My father never took anything for the pain. The cancer in his neck was killing him but he wouldn't take anything. He didn't want to be doped up for his own death and he didn't trust doctors. He went to a free clinic in Jackson for a while, but he stopped going because he thought they were using him in experiments. He endured the pain and the pain affected his mind. In the last few years of his life he was probably crazy. My mother says that he couldn't even remember the railroad at all.

The railroad—people say that the railroads will be back, but I don't think so. Things go on; things even repeat themselves sometimes, but they don't come back. I'm thinking right now about graduation days. I'm thinking about retirement and houseboats, though I've never even been on one. I'm thinking about fishing and I've never caught a fish in my life.

BUNK CAR

Dave Etter

Shoved out on a spur track
across from Petry's Tavern
in East Dubuque
is CB&Q bunk car #212355
salmon colored
peeling curly flakes of paint
muslin curtains at the windows
a tight screen door
a TV antenna jerking in the wind
and a battered kitchen chimney
that looks like a boot gone wrong

Okay now pay attention Clyde
for I'm in pretty bad shape
just bounced out of Petry's
and I have it in my big head
I would like to go railroading
and want to start with a long nap
in old #212355
so can someone
I say can any one of you beer bums
in this here downhill town
fix me up for a stretch on the rails?

New York Public Library Picture Collection

TROOP TRAIN

Karl Shapiro

It stops the town we come through. Workers
    raise
Their oily arms in good salute and grin.
Kids scream as at a circus. Business men
Glance hopefully and go their measured way.
And women standing at their dumbstruck door
More slowly wave and seem to warn us back,
As if a tear blinding the course of war
Might once dissolve our iron in their sweet wish.

Fruit of the world, O clustered on ourselves
We hang as from a cornucopia
In total friendliness, with faces bunched
To spray the streets with catcalls and with leers.
A bottle smashes on the moving ties
And eyes fixed on a lady smiling pink
Stretch like a rubber-band and snap and sting
The mouth that wants the drink-of-water kiss.

And on through crummy continents and days,
Deliberate, grimy, slightly drunk we crawl,
The good-bad boys of circumstance and chance,
Whose bucket-helmets bang the empty wall
Where twist the murdered bodies of our packs
Next to the guns that only seem themselves.
And distance like a strap adjusted shrinks,
Tightens across the shoulder and holds firm.

Here is a deck of cards; out of this hand
Dealer, deal me my luck, a pair of bulls,
The right draw to a flush, the one-eyed jack.
Diamonds and hearts are red but spades are
    black,
And spades are spades and clubs are
    clovers—black.
But deal me winners, souvenirs of peace.
This stands to reason and arithmetic,
Luck also travels and not all come back.

Trains lead to ships and ships to death or trains,
And trains to death or trucks, and trucks to
    death,
Or trucks lead to the march, the march to death,
Or that survival which is all our hope;
And death leads back to trucks and trains and
    ships,
But life leads to the march, O flag! at last
The place of life found after trains and death
—Nightfall of nations brilliant after war.

149

THE LITTLE BLACK TRAIN
(Suggested by a folk song)

Kenneth Patchen

Who hears that whistle blowing?
Who hears that hellish din?
Not the living—but they will.
   Ah, where is it going?
   And where has it been?
Ask the darkness that falls on the hill.

Behind—a ghost smoke flowing;
   Ahead—that quiet inn
Which all may enter—but none come back.
   Ah, where are they going?
   And where have they been?
Ask the thistles that bloom on the track.

The cabman is all-knowing
(They say), and at peace within;
But it must be lonely at night.
   Ah, where is he going?
   And where has he been?
Ask the millions who wait without light.

Black roses need no sowing,
And the soul is born in sin
(We're told)—fouled by that ancient pair.
   Ah, where is it going?
   And where has it been?
Ask the star that touches your loved one's hair.

And now the train is slowing,
And the passengers they grin,
As well they might—a little sly.
   Ah, where are they going?
   And where have they been?
Ask the lanterns that swing in the sky.

TRACK 6: THE SUNSET LIMITED

Shael Herman

Lonnie Barrett mechanic
high school dropout
bronze star for bravery
AWOL a month
when the captain found him home

says he almost killed his sergeant
another kid did it first

what do you call a guy
likes to hurt himself?
Lonnie hammers nails in his arm
shoots anything that moves

we stand at the baggage counter
he grabs his duffel bag
shuffles to the train

his wife waves him off
she aske me do I want a drink

CROSS TIES

X. J. Kennedy

Out walking ties left over from a track
Where nothing travels now but rust and grass,
I could take stock in something that would pass
Bearing down Hell-bent from behind my back:
A thing to sidestep or go down before,
Far-off, indifferent as that curfew's wail
The evening wind flings like a sack of mail
Or close up as the moon whose headbeam stirs
A flock of cloud to make tracks. Down to strafe
The bristled grass a hawk falls—there's a screech
Like steel wrenched taut till severed. Out of reach
Or else beneath desiring, I go safe,
Walk on, tensed for a leap, unreconciled
To a dark void all kindness.
           When I spill
The salt I throw the Devil some and, still,
I let them sprinkle water on my child.

Left: Coming ashore in France, World War II.—*Courtesy of Southern Railway System*

A SOLO SONG: FOR DOC

James A. McPherson

So you want to know this business, youngblood? So you want to be a Waiter's Waiter? The Commissary gives you a book with all the rules and tells you to learn them. And you do, and think that is all there is to it. A big, thick black book. Poor youngblood.

Look at me. *I* am a Waiter's Waiter. I know all the moves, all the pretty, fine moves that big book will never teach you. *I* built this railroad with my moves; and so did Sheik Beasley and Uncle T. Boone and Danny Jackson, and so did Doc Craft. That book they made you learn came from our moves and from our heads. There was a time when six of us, big men, danced at the same time in that little Pantry without touching and shouted orders to the sweating paddies in the kitchen. There was a time when they *had* to respect us because our sweat and our moves supported them. We knew the service and the paddies, even the green dishwashers, knew that we did and didn't give us the crap they pull on you.

Do you know how to sneak a Blackplate to a nasty cracker? Do you know how to rub asses with five other men in the Pantry getting their orders together and still know that you are a man, just like them? Do you know how to bullshit while you work and keep the paddies in their places with your bullshit? Do you know how to breathe down the back of an old lady's dress to hustle a bigger tip?

No. You are summer stuff, youngblood. I am old, my moves are not so good any more, but I know this business. The Commissary hires you for the summer because they don't want to let anyone get as old as me on them. I'm sixty-three, but they can't fire me: I'm in the Union. They can't lay me off for fucking up: I know this business too well. And so they hire you, youngblood, for the summer when the tourists come, and in September you go away with some tips in your pocket to buy pussy and they wait all winter for me to die. I *am* dying, youngblood, and so is this business. Both of us will die together. There'll always be summer stuff like you, but the big men, the big trains, are dying every day and everybody can see it.

And nobody but us who are dying with them gives a damn.

Look at the big picture at the end of the car, youngblood. That's the man who built this road. He's in your history books. He's probably in that big black bible you read. He was a great man. He hated people. He didn't want to feed them but the government said he had to. He didn't want to hire me, but he needed me to feed the people. I know this, youngblood, and that is why that book is written for you and that is why I have never read it. That is why you get nervous and jump up to polish the pepper and salt shakers when the word comes down the line that an inspector is getting on at the next stop. That is why you warm the toast covers for every cheap old lady who wants to get coffee and toast and good service for sixty-five cents and a dime tip. You know that he needs you only for the summer and that hundreds of youngbloods like you want to work this summer to buy that pussy in Chicago and Portland and Seattle. The man uses you, but he doesn't need you. But me he needs for the winter, when you are gone, and to teach you something in the summer about this business you can't get from that big black book. He needs me and he knows it and I know it. That is why I am sitting here when there are tables to be cleaned and linen to be changed and silver to be washed and polished. He needs me to die. That is why I am taking my time. I know it. And I will take his service with me when I die, just like the Sheik did and like Percy Fields did, and like Doc.

Who are they? Why do I keep talking about them? Let me think about it. I guess it is because they were the last of the Old School, like me. We made this road. We got a million miles of walking up and down these cars under our feet. Doc Craft was the Old School, like me. He was a Waiter's Waiter. He danced down these aisles with us and swung his tray with the roll

of the train, never spilling in all his trips a single cup of coffee. He could carry his tray on two fingers, or on one and a half if he wanted, and he knew all the tricks about hustling tips there are to know. He could work anybody. The girls at the Northland in Chicago knew Doc, and the girls at the Haverville in Seattle, and the girls at the Step-Inn in Portland and all the girls in Winnipeg knew Doc Craft.

But wait. It is just 1:30 and the first call for dinner is not until 5:00. You want to kill some time; you want to hear about the Old School and how it was in my day. If you look in that black book you would see that you should be polishing silver now. Look out the window; this is North Dakota, this is Jerry's territory. Jerry, the Unexpected Inspector. Shouldn't you polish the shakers or clean out the Pantry or squeeze oranges, or maybe change the linen on the tables? Jerry Ewald is sly. The train may stop in the middle of this wheatfield and

The dining car in the Florida-bound Silver Meteor.— *Amtrak photo*

Jerry may get on. He lives by that book. He knows where to look for dirt and mistakes. Jerry Ewald, the Unexpected Inspector. He knows where to look; he knows how to get you. He got Doc.

Now you want to know about him, about the Old School. You have even put aside your book of rules. But see how you keep your finger in the pages as if the book was more important than what I tell you. That's a bad move, and it tells on you. You will be a waiter. But you will never be a Waiter's Waiter. The Old School died with Doc, and the very last of it is dying with me. What happened to Doc? Take your finger out of the pages, youngblood, and I will tell you about a kind of life these rails will never carry again.

When your father was a boy playing with himself behind the barn, Doc was already a man and knew what the thing was for. But he got tired of using it when he wasn't much older than you, and he set his mind on making money. He had no skills. He was black. He got hungry. On Christmas Day in 1916, the story goes, he wandered into the Chicago stockyards and over to a dining car waiting to be connected up to the main train for the Chicago-to-San Francisco run. He looked up through the kitchen door at the chef storing supplies for the kitchen and said: "I'm hungry."

"What do you want *me* to do about it?" the Swede chef said.

"I'll work," said Doc.

That Swede was Chips Magnusson, fresh off the boat and lucky to be working himself. He did not know yet that he should save all extra work for other Swedes fresh off the boat. He later learned this by living. But at that time he considered a moment, bit into one of the fresh apples stocked for apple pie, chewed considerably, spit out the seeds and then waved the black man on board the big train. "You can eat all you want," he told Doc. "But you work all I tell you."

He put Doc to rolling dough for the apple pies and the train began rolling for Doc. It never stopped. He fell in love with the feel of the wheels under his feet clicking against the track and he got the rhythm of the wheels in him and learned, like all of us, how to roll with them and move with them. After that first trip Doc was never at home on the ground. He worked everything in the kitchen from putting out dough to second cook, in six years. And then, when the Commissary saw that he was good and would soon be going for one of the chef's spots they saved for the Swedes, they put him out of the kitchen and told him to learn this waiter business; and told him to

Great Eastern Railway: signal gantry at Stratford. 1971—*New York Public Library Picture Collection*

learn how to bullshit on the other side of the Pantry. He was almost thirty, youngblood, when he crossed over to the black side of the Pantry. I wasn't there when he made his first trip as a waiter, but from what they tell me of that trip I know that he was broke in by good men. Pantryman was Sheik Beasley, who stayed high all the time and let the waiters steal anything they wanted as long as they didn't bother his reefers. Danny Jackson, who was black and knew Shakespeare before the world said he could work with it, was second man. Len Dickey was third, Reverend Hendricks was fourth, and Uncle T. Boone, who even in those early days could not straighten his back, ran fifth. Doc started in as sixth waiter, the "mule." They pulled some shit on him at first because they didn't want somebody fresh out of a paddy kitchen on the crew. They messed with his orders, stole his plates, picked up his tips on the sly, and made him do all the dirty work. But when they saw that he could take the shit without getting hot and when they saw that he was set on being a waiter, even though he was older than most of them, they settled down and began to teach him this business and all the words and moves and slickness that made it a good business.

His real name was Leroy Johnson, I think, but when Danny Jackson saw how cool and

neat he was in his moves, and how he handled the plates, he began to call him "the Doctor." Then the Sheik, coming down from his high one day after missing the lunch and dinner service, saw how Doc had taken over his station and collected fat tips from his tables by telling the passengers that the Sheik had had to get off back along the line because of a heart attack. The Sheik liked that because he saw that Doc understood crackers and how they liked nothing better than knowing that a nigger had died on the job, giving them service. The Sheik was impressed. And he was not an easy man to impress because he knew too much about life and had to stay high most of the time. And when Doc would not split the tips with him, the Sheik got mad at first and called Doc a barrel of motherfuckers and some other words you would not recognize. But he was impressed. And later that night, in the crew car when the others were gambling and drinking and bullshitting about the women they had working the corners for them, the Sheik came over to Doc's bunk and said: "You're a crafty motherfucker."

"Yeah?" says Doc.

"Yeah," says the Sheik, who did not say much. "You're a crafty motherfucker but I like you." Then he got into the first waiter's bunk and lit up again. But Reverend Hendricks, who always read his Bible before going to sleep and who always listened to anything the Sheik said because he knew the Sheik only said something when it was important, heard what was said and remembered it. After he put his Bible back in his locker, he walked over to Doc's bunk and looked down at him. "Mister Doctor Craft," the Reverend said. "Youngblood Doctor Craft."

"Yeah?" says Doc.

"Yeah," says Reverend Hendricks. "That's who you are."

And that's who he was from then on.

II

I came to the road away from the war. This was after '41, when people at home were looking for Japs under their beds every night. I did not want to fight because there was no money in it and I didn't want to go overseas to work in a kitchen. The big war was on and a lot of soldiers crossed the country to get to it, and as long as a black man fed them on trains he did not have to go to that war. I could have got a job in a Chicago factory, but there was more money on the road and it was safer. And after a while it got into your blood so that you couldn't leave it for anything. The road got into my blood the way it got into everybody's; the way going to the war got in the blood of redneck farm boys and the crazy Polacks from Chicago. It was all right for them to go to the war. They were young and stupid. And they died that way. I played it smart. I was almost thirty-five and I didn't want to go. But I took *them* and fed them and gave them good times on their way to the war, and for that I did not have to go. The soldiers had plenty of money and were afraid not to spend it all before they got to the ships on the Coast. And we gave them ways to spend it on the trains.

Now in those days there was plenty of money going around and everybody stole from everybody. The kitchen stole food from the company and the company knew it and wouldn't pay good wages. There were no rules in those days, there was no black book to go by and nobody said what you couldn't eat or steal. The paddy cooks used to toss boxes of steaks off the train in the Chicago yards for people at the restaurants there who paid them, cash. These were the days when ordinary people had to have red stamps or blue stamps to get powdered eggs and white lard to mix with red powder to make their own butter.

The stewards stole from the company and from the waiters; the waiters stole from the stewards and the company and from each other. I stole. Doc stole. Even Reverend Hendricks put his Bible far back in his locker and stole with us. You didn't want a man on your crew who didn't steal. He made it bad for everybody. And if the steward saw that he was a dummy and would never get to stealing, he wrote him up for something and got him off the crew so as not to slow down the rest of us. We had a redneck cracker steward from Alabama by the name of Casper who used to say: "*Jesus Christ!* I ain't got time to hate you niggers, I'm making so much money." He used to keep all his cash at home under his bed in a cardboard box because he was afraid to put it in the bank.

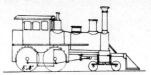

Doc and Sheik Beasley and me were on the same crew together all during the war. Even in those days, as young as we were, we knew how to be Old Heads. We organized for the soldiers. We had to wear skullcaps all the time because the crackers said our hair was poison and didn't want any of it to fall in their food. The Sheik didn't mind wearing one. He kept reefers in his and used to sell them to the soldiers for double what he paid for them in Chicago and three times what he paid the Chinamen in Seattle. That's why we called him the Sheik. After every meal the Sheik would get in the linen closet and light up. Sometimes he wouldn't come out for days. Nobody gave a damn, though; we were all too busy stealing and working. And there was more for us to get as long as he didn't come out.

Doc used to sell bootlegged booze to the soldiers; that was his specialty. He had redcaps in the Chicago stations telling the soldiers who to ask for on the train. He was an open operator and had to give the steward a cut, but he still made a pile of money. That's why that old cracker always kept us together on his crew. We were the three best moneymakers he ever had. That's something you should learn, youngblood. They can't love you for being you. They only love you if you make money for them. All that talk these days about integration and brotherhood, that's a lot of bullshit. The man will love you as long as he can make money with you. I made money. And old Casper had to love me in the open although I knew he called me a nigger at home when he had put that money in his big cardboard box. I know he loved me on the road in the wartime because I used to bring in the biggest moneymakers. I used to handle the girls.

Look out that window. See all that grass and wheat? Look at that big farm boy cutting it. Look at that burnt cracker on that tractor. He probably has a wife who married him because she didn't know what else to do. Back during wartime the girls in this part of the country knew what to do. They got on the trains at night.

You can look out that window all day and run around all the stations when we stop, but you'll never see a black man in any of these towns. You know why, youngblood? These farmers hate you. They still remember when their girls came out of these towns and got on the trains at night. They've been running black men and dark Indians out of these towns for years. They hate anything dark that's not that way because of the sun. Right now there are big farm girls with hair under their arms on the corners in San Francisco, Chicago, Seattle and Minneapolis who got started on these cars back during wartime. The farmers

me and by the time I got to a bar there were ten people on my trail. I was drinking a fast one when the sheriff came in the bar.

"What are you doing here?" he asks me.

"Just getting a shot," I say.

He spit on the floor. "How long you plan to be here?"

"I don't know," I say, just to be nasty.

"There ain't no jobs here," he says.

"I wasn't looking," I say.

"We don't want you here."

"I don't give a good goddamn," I say.

Santa Fe Railway's eastbound "Chief" passes Sullivan's Curve" in Cajon Pass, California.—*Santa Fe Railway photo*

still remember that and they hate you and me for it. But it wasn't for me they got on. Nobody wants a stiff, smelly farm girl when there are sporting women to be got for a dollar in the cities. It was for the soldiers they got on. It was just business to me. But they hate you and me anyway.

I got off in one of these towns once, a long time after the war, just to get a drink while the train changed engines. Everybody looked at

He pulled his gun on me. "All right, coon, back on the train," he says.

"Wait a minute," I tell him. "Let me finish my drink."

He knocked my glass over with his gun. "You're finished *now,*" he says. "Pull your ass out of here *now!*"

I didn't argue.

I was the night man. After dinner it was my job to pull the cloths off the tables and put

paddings on. Then I cut out the lights and locked both doors. There was a big farm girl from Minot named Hilda who could take on eight or ten soldiers in one night, white soldiers. These white boys don't know how to last. I would stand by the door and when the soldiers came back from the club car they would pay me and I would let them in. Some of the girls could make as much as one hundred dollars in one night. And I always made twice as much. Soldiers don't care what they do with their money. They just have to spend it.

We never bothered with the girls ourselves. It was just business as far as we were concerned. But there was one dummy we had with us once, a boy from the South named Willie Joe something who handled the dice. He was really hot for one of these farm girls. He used to buy her good whiskey and he hated to see her go in the car at night to wait for the soldiers. He was a real dummy. One time I heard her tell him: "It's all right. They can have my body. I know I'm black inside. *Jesus,* I'm so black inside I wisht I was black all over!"

And this dummy Willie Joe said: "Baby, *don't you ever change!*"

I knew we had to get rid of him before he started trouble. So we had the steward bump him off the crew as soon as we could find a good man to handle the gambling. That old redneck Casper was glad to do it. He saw what was going on.

But you want to hear about Doc, you say, so you can get back to your reading. What can I tell you? The road got into his blood? He liked being a waiter? You won't understand this, but he did. There were no Civil Rights or marches or riots for something better in those days. In those days a man found something he liked to do and liked it from then on because he couldn't help himself. What did he like about the road? He liked what I liked: the money, owning the car, running it, telling the soldiers what to do, hustling a bigger tip from some old maid by looking under her dress and laughing at her, having all the girls at the Haverville Hotel waiting for us to come in for stopover, the power we had to beat them up or lay them if we wanted. He liked running free and not being married to some bitch who would spend his money when he was out of town or give it to some stud. He liked getting drunk with the boys up at Andy's, setting up the house and then passing out from drinking too much, knowing that the boys would get him home.

I ran with that one crew all during wartime and they, Doc, the Sheik and Reverend Hendricks, had taken me under their wings. *I* was still a youngblood then, and Doc liked me a lot. But he never said that much to me; he was not a talker. The Sheik had taught him the value of silence in things that really matter. We roomed together in Chicago at Mrs. Wright's place in those days. Mrs. Wright didn't allow women in the rooms and Doc liked that, because after being out for a week and after stopping over in those hotels along the way, you get tired of women and bullshit and need your privacy. We weren't like you. We didn't need a woman every time we got hard. We knew when we had to have it and when we didn't. And we didn't spend all our money on it, either. You youngbloods think the way to get a woman is to let her see how you handle your money. That's stupid. The way to get a woman is to let her see how you handle other women. But you'll never believe that until it's too late to do you any good.

Doc knew how to handle women. I can remember a time in a Winnipeg hotel how he ran a bitch out of his room because he had had enough of it and did not need her any more. I was in the next room and heard everything.

"Come on, Doc," the bitch said. "Come on honey, let's do it one more time."

"Hell no," Doc said. "I'm tired and I don't want to any more."

"How can you say you're tired?" the bitch said. "How can you say you're tired when you didn't go but two times?"

"I'm tired of it," Doc said, "because I'm tired of you. And I'm tired of you because I'm tired of it and bitches like you in all the towns I been in. You drain a man. And I know if I beat you, you'll still come back when I hit you again. *That's* why I'm tired. I'm tired of having things around I don't care about."

"What *do* you care about, Doc?" the bitch said.

"I don't know," Doc said. "I guess I care about moving and being somewhere else when I want to be. I guess I care about going out, and coming in to wait for the time to go out again."

"You crazy, Doc," the bitch said.

"Yeah?" Doc said. "I guess I'm crazy all right."

Later that bitch knocked on my door and I did it for her because she was just a bitch and I knew Doc wouldn't want her again. I don't think he ever wanted a bitch again. I never saw him with one after that time. He was just a little over fifty then and could have still done whatever he wanted with women.

The war ended. The farm boys who got back from the war did not spend money on their way home. They did not want to spend any more money on women, and the girls did not get on at night any more. Some of them went into the cities and turned pro. Some of them stayed in the towns and married the farm boys who got back from the war. Things changed on the road. The Commissary started putting that book of rules together and told us to stop stealing. They were losing money on passengers now because of the airplanes and they began to really tighten up and started sending inspectors down along the line to check on us. They started sending in spotters, too. One of them caught that redneck Casper writing out a check for two dollars less than he had charged the spotter. The Commissary got him in on the rug for it. I wasn't there, but they told me he said to the General Superintendent: "Why are you getting on me, a white man, for a lousy son-of-a-bitching two bucks? There's niggers out there been stealing for *years!*"

"Who?" the General Superintendent asked.

And Casper couldn't say anything because he had that cardboard box full of money still under his bed and knew he would have to tell how he got it if any of us was brought in. So he said nothing.

"Who?" the General Superintendent asked him again.

"Why, all them nigger waiters steal, *everybody knows that!*"

"And the cooks, what about them?" the Superintendent said.

"They're white," said Casper.

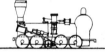

They never got the story out of him and he was fired. He used the money to open a restaurant someplace in Indiana and I heard later that he started a branch of the Klan in his town. One day he showed up at the station and told Doc, Reverend Hendricks and me: "I'll see you boys get *yours.* Damn if I'm takin' the rap for you niggers."

We just laughed in his face because we knew he could do nothing to us through the Commissary. But just to be safe we stopped stealing so much. But they did get the Sheik, though. One day an inspector got on in the mountains just outside of Whitefish and grabbed him right out of that linen closet. The Sheik had been smoking in there all day and he was high and laughing when they pulled him off the train.

That was the year we got the Union. The crackers and Swedes finally let us in after we paid off. We really stopped stealing and got organized and there wasn't a damn thing the company could do about it, although it tried like hell to buy us out. And to get back at us, they put their heads together and began to make up that big book of rules you keep your finger in. Still, *we* knew the service and they had to write the book the way we gave the service and at first there was nothing for the Old School men to learn. We got seniority through the Union, and as long as we gave the service and didn't steal, they couldn't touch us. So they began changing the rules, and sending us notes about the service. Little changes at first, like how the initials on the doily should always face the customer, and how the silver should be taken off the tables between meals. But we were getting old and set in our old service, and it got harder and harder learning all those little changes. And we had to learn new stuff all the time because there was no telling when an inspector would get on and catch us giving bad service. It was hard as hell. It was hard because we knew that the company was out to break up the Old School. The Sheik was gone, and we knew that Reverend Hendricks or Uncle T. or Danny Jackson would go soon because they stood for the Old School, just like the Sheik. But what bothered us most was knowing that they would go for Doc first, before anyone else, because he loved the road so much.

Doc was over sixty-five then and had taken to drinking hard when we were off. But he never touched a drop when we were on the road. I used to wonder whether he drank because being a Waiter's Waiter was getting hard or because he had to do something until his next trip. I could never figure it. When we had our layovers he would spend all his time in Andy's, setting up the house. He had no wife, no relatives, not even a hobby. He just drank. Pretty soon the slicksters at Andy's got to using him for a good thing. They commenced putting the touch on him because they saw he was getting old and knew he didn't have far to go, and they would never have to pay him back. Those of us who were close to

him tried to pull his coat, but it didn't help. He didn't talk about himself much, he didn't talk much about anything that wasn't related to the road; but when I tried to hip him once about the hustlers and how they were closing in on him, he just took another shot and said:

"I don't need no money. Nobody's jiving me. I'm jiving them. You know I can still pull in a hundred in tips in one trip. I *know* this business."

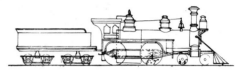

"Yeah, I know, Doc," I said. "But how many more trips can you make before you have to stop?"

"I ain't never gonna stop. Trips are all I know and I'll be making them as long as these trains haul people."

"That's just it," I said. "They don't *want* to haul people any more. The planes do that. The big roads want freight now. Look how they hire youngbloods just for the busy seasons just so they won't get any seniority in the winter. Look how all the Old School waiters are dropping out. They got the Sheik, Percy Fields just lucked up and died before they got to *him,* they almost got Reverend Hendricks. Even *Uncle T.* is going to retire! And they'll get us too."

"Not me," said Doc. "I know my moves. This old fox can still dance with a tray and handle four tables at the same time. I can still bait a queer and make the old ladies tip big. There's no waiter better than me and I know it."

"Sure, Doc," I said. "I know it too. But please save your money. Don't be a dummy. There'll come a day when you just can't get up to go out and they'll put you on the ground for good."

Doc looked at me like he had been shot. "Who taught you the moves when you were just a raggedy-ass waiter?"

"You did, Doc," I said.

"Who's always the first man down in the yard at train-time?" He threw down another shot. "Who's there sitting in the car every tenth morning while you other old heads are still at home pulling on your longjohns?"

I couldn't say anything. He was right and we both knew it.

"I have to go," he told me. "Going out is my whole life, I wait for that tenth morning. I ain't never missed a trip and I don't mean to."

What could I say to him, youngblood? What can I say to you? He had to go out, not for the money; it was in his blood. You have to go out too, but it's for the money you go. You hate going out and you love coming in. He loved going out and he hated coming in. Would *you* listen if I told you to stop spending your money on pussy in Chicago? Would he listen if I told him to save *his* money? To stop setting up the bar at Andy's? No. Old men are just as bad as young men when it comes to money. They can't think. They always try to buy what they should have for free. And what they buy, after they have it, is nothing.

They called Doc into the Commissary and the doctors told him he had lumbago and a bad heart and was weak from drinking too much, and they wanted him to get down for his own good. He wouldn't do it. Tesdale, the General Superintendent, called him in and told him that he had enough years in the service to pull down a big pension and that the company would pay for a retirement party for him, since he was the oldest waiter working, and invite all the Old School waiters to see him off, if he would come down. Doc said no. He knew that the Union had to back him. He knew that he could ride as long as he made the trains on time and as long as he knew the service. And he knew that he could not leave the road.

The company called in its lawyers to go over the Union contract. I wasn't there, but Len Dickey was in on the meeting because of his office in the Union. He told me about it later. Those fat company lawyers took the contract apart and went through all their books. They took the seniority clause apart word by word, trying to figure a way to get at Doc. But they had written it airtight back in the days when the company *needed* waiters, and there was nothing in it about compulsory retirement. Not a word. The paddies in the Union must have figured that waiters didn't *need* a new contract when they let us in, and they had let us come in under the old one thinking that all

Tanks being loaded on flat cars at Wiggins, Miss., for return to their home stations after termination of war games in De Soto National Forest. 3rd Army Maneuvers, Biloxi, Miss., 1938.—*Courtesy of Southern Railway System*

waiters would die on the job, or drink themselves to death when they were still young, or die from buying too much pussy, or just quit when they had put in enough time to draw a pension. But *nothing* in the whole contract could help them get rid of Doc Craft. They were sweating, they were working so hard. And all the time Tesdale, the General Superintendent, was calling them sons-of-bitches for not earning their money. But there was nothing the company lawyers could do but turn the pages of their big books and sweat and promise Tesdale that they would find some way if he gave them more time.

The word went out from the Commissary: "Get Doc." The stewards got it from the assistant superintendents: "Get Doc." Since they could not get him to retire, they were determined to catch him giving bad service. He had more seniority than most other waiters, so they couldn't bump him off our crew. In fact, all the waiters with more seniority than Doc were on the crew with him. There were four of us from the Old School: me, Doc, Uncle T. Boone, and Danny Jackson. Reverend Hendricks wasn't running regular any more; he was spending all his Sundays preaching in his Church on the South Side because he knew what was coming and wanted to have something steady going for him in Chicago when his time came. Fifth and sixth men on that crew were two hardheads who had read the book. The steward was Crouse, and he really didn't want to put the screws to Doc but he couldn't help himself. Everybody wants to work. So Crouse started in to riding Doc, sometimes about moving too fast, sometimes about not moving fast enough. I was on the crew, I saw it all. Crouse would seat four singles at the same table, on Doc's station, and Doc had to take care of all four different orders at the same time. He was seventy-three, but that didn't stop him, knowing this business the way he did. It just slowed him down some. But Crouse got on him even for that and would chew him out in front of the passengers, hoping that he'd start cursing and bother the passengers so that they would complain to the company. It never worked, though. Doc just played it cool. He'd look into Crouse's eyes and know what was going on. And then he'd lay on his good service, the only service he knew, and

the passengers would see how good he was with all that age on his back and they would get mad at the steward, and leave Doc a bigger tip when they left.

WHEN "NUMBER TWO FROM THE SOUTH" PULLS IN

The Commissary sent out spotters to catch him giving bad service. These were pale-white little men in glasses who never looked you in the eye, but who always felt the plate to see if it was warm. And there were the old maids, who like that kind of work, who would order shrimp or crabmeat cocktails or celery and olive plates because they knew how the rules said these things had to be made. And when they came, when Doc brought them out, they would look to see if the oyster fork was stuck into the thing, and look out the window a long time.

"Ain't no use trying to fight it," Uncle T. Boone told Doc in the crew car one night, "the black waiter is *doomed*. Look at all the good restaurants, the class restaurants in Chicago. *You* can't work in them. Them white waiters got those jobs sewed up fine."

"I can be a waiter anywhere," says Doc. "I

know the business and I like it and I can do it anywhere."

"The black waiter is doomed," Uncle T. says again. "The whites is taking over the service in the good places. And when they run you off of here, you won't have no place to go."

"They won't run me off of here," says Doc. "As long as I give the right service they can't touch me."

"You're a goddamn *fool*!" says Uncle T. "You're a nigger and you ain't got no rights except what the Union says you have. And that ain't worth a damn because when the Commissary finally gets you, those niggers won't lift a finger to help you."

"Leave off him," I say to Boone. "If anybody ought to be put off it's you. You ain't had your back straight for thirty years. You even make the crackers sick the way you keep bowing and folding your hands and saying, 'Thank you, Mr. Boss.' Fifty years ago that would of got you a bigger tip," I say, "but now it ain't worth a shit. And every time you do it the crackers hate you. And every time I see you serving with that skullcap on *I* hate you. The Union said we didn't have to wear them *eighteen years ago*! Why can't you take it off?"

Boone just sat on his bunk with his skullcap in his lap, leaning against his big belly. He knew I was telling the truth and he knew he wouldn't change. But he said: "That's the trouble with the Negro waiter today. He ain't got no humility. And as long as he don't have humility, he keeps losing the good jobs."

Doc had climbed into the first waiter's bunk in his longjohns and I got in the second waiter's bunk under him and lay there. I could hear him breathing. It had a hard sound. He wasn't well and all of us knew it.

"Doc?" I said in the dark.

"Yeah?"

"Don't mind Boone, Doc. He's a dead man. He just don't know it."

"We all are," Doc said.

"Not you," I said.

"What's the use? He's right. They'll get me in the end."

"But they ain't done it yet."

"They'll get me. And they know it and I know it. I can even see it in old Crouse's eyes. He knows they're gonna get me."

"Why don't you get a woman?"

He was quiet. "What can I do with a woman now, that I ain't already done too much?"

I thought for a while. "If you're on the ground, being with one might not make it so bad."

"I hate women," he said.

"You ever try fishing?"

"No."

"You want to?"

"No," he said.

"You can't keep *drinking*."

He did not answer.

"Maybe you could work in town. In the Commissary."

I could hear the big wheels rolling and clicking along the tracks and I knew by the smooth way we were moving that we were almost out of the Dakota flatlands. Doc wasn't talking. "Would you like that?" I thought he was asleep. "Doc, would you like that?"

"Hell no," he said.

"You have to try *something*!"

He was quiet again. "I know," he finally said.

III

Jerry Ewald, the Unexpected Inspector, got on in Winachee that next day after lunch and we knew that he had the word from the Commissary. He was cool about it: he laughed with the steward and the waiters about the old days and his hard gray eyes and shining glasses kept looking over our faces as if to see if we knew why he had got on. The two hardheads were in the crew car stealing a nap on company time. Jerry noticed this and could have caught them, but he was after bigger game. We all knew that, and we kept talking to him about the days of the big trains and looking at his white hair and not into the eyes behind his glasses because we knew what was there. Jerry sat down on the first waiter's station and said to Crouse: "Now I'll have some lunch. Steward, let the headwaiter bring me a menu."

Crouse stood next to the table where Jerry sat, and looked at Doc, who had been waiting between the tables with his tray under his arm. The way the rules say. Crouse looked sad because he knew what was coming. Then Jerry looked directly at Doc and said: "Headwaiter Doctor Craft, bring me a menu."

Doc said nothing and he did not smile. He brought the menu. Danny Jackson and I moved back into the hall to watch. There was nothing we could do to help Doc and we knew it. He was the Waiter's Waiter, out there by himself, hustling the biggest tip he would ever get in his life. Or losing it.

"Goddamn," Danny said to me. "Now let's sit on the ground and talk about how *kings* are gonna get fucked."

"Maybe not," I said. But I did not believe it myself because Jerry is the kind of man who lies in bed all night, scheming. I knew he had a plan.

Doc passed us on his way to the kitchen for water and I wanted to say something to him. But what was the use? He brought the water to Jerry. Jerry looked him in the eye. "Now, Headwaiter," he said. "I'll have a bowl of onion soup, a cold roast beef sandwich on white, rare, and a glass of iced tea."

"Write it down," said Doc. He was playing it right. He knew that the new rules had stopped waiters from taking verbal orders.

"Don't be so professional, Doc," Jerry said. "It's me, one of the *boys.*"

"You have to write it out," said Doc, "it's in the black book."

Jerry clicked his pen and wrote the order out on the check. And handed it to Doc. Uncle T. followed Doc back into the Pantry.

"He's gonna get you, Doc," Uncle T. said. "I knew it all along. You know why? The Negro waiter ain't got no more humility."

"Shut the fuck up, Boone!" I told him.

"You'll see," Boone went on. "You'll see I'm right. There ain't a thing Doc can do about it, either. We're gonna lose all the good jobs."

We watched Jerry at the table. He saw us watching and smiled with his gray eyes. Then he poured some of the water from the glass on the linen cloth and picked up the silver sugar bowl and placed it right on the wet spot. Doc was still in the Pantry. Jerry turned the silver sugar bowl around and around on the linen. He pressed down on it some as he turned. But when he picked it up again, there was no dark ring on the wet cloth. We had polished the

silver early that morning, according to the book, and there was not a dirty piece of silver to be found in the whole car. Jerry was drinking the rest of the water when Doc brought out the polished silver soup tureen, underlined with a doily and a breakfast plate, with a shining soup bowl underlined with a doily and a breakfast plate, and a bread-and-butter plate with six crackers; not four or five or seven, but six, the number the Commissary had written in the black book. He swung down the aisle of the car between the two rows of white tables and you could not help but be proud of the way he moved with the roll of the train and the way that tray was like a part of his arm. It was good service. He placed everything neat, with all company initials showing, right where things should go.

"Shall I serve up the soup?" he asked Jerry.

"Please," said Jerry.

Doc handled that silver soup ladle like one of those Chicago Jew tailors handles a needle. He ladled up three good-sized spoonfuls from the tureen and then laid the wet spoon on an extra bread-and-butter plate on the side of the table, so he would not stain the cloth. Then he put a napkin over the wet spot Jerry had made and changed the ashtray for a prayer-card because every good waiter knows that nobody wants to eat a good meal looking at an ashtray.

"You know about the spoon plate, I see," Jerry said to Doc.

"I'm a waiter," said Doc. "I know."

"You're a damn good waiter," said Jerry.

Doc looked Jerry square in the eye. "I know," he said slowly.

Jerry ate a little of the soup and opened all six of the cracker packages. Then he stopped eating and began to look out the window. We were passing through his territory, Washington State, the country he loved because he was the only company inspector in the state and knew that once we got through Montana he would be the only man the waiters feared. He smiled and then waved for Doc to bring out the roast beef sandwich.

But Doc was into his service now and cleared the table completely. Then he got the silver crumb knife from the Pantry and gathered all the cracker crumbs, even the ones Jerry had managed to get in between the salt and pepper shakers.

"You want the tea with your sandwich, or later?" he asked Jerry.

"Now is fine," said Jerry, smiling.

"You're going good," I said to Doc when he passed us on his way to the Pantry. "He can't touch you or nothing."

He did not say anything.

Uncle T. Boone looked at Doc like he wanted to say something too, but he just frowned and shuffled out to stand next to Jerry. You could see that Jerry hated him. But Jerry knew how to smile at everybody, and so he smiled at Uncle T. while Uncle T. bent over the table with his hands together like he was praying, and moved his head up and bowed it down.

crushed ice, it was like he was pouring it through his own fingers; it was like he and the tray and the pot and the glass and all of it was the same body. It was a beautiful move. It was fine service. The iced tea glass sat in a shell dish, and the iced tea spoon lay straight in front of Jerry. The lemon wedge Doc put in a shell dish half-full of crushed ice with an oyster fork struck into its skin. Not in the meat, mind you, but squarely under the skin of that lemon, and the whole thing lay in a pretty curve on top of that crushed ice.

Doc stood back and waited. Jerry had been watching his service and was impressed. He mixed the sugar in his glass and sipped. Danny

A Louisville & Nashville passenger train passes through Kentucky in the 1950's as a young friend waves to the engineer. The L & N's last passenger train ran in 1971.–*Photo courtesy of Louisville & Nashville Railroad*

Doc brought out the roast beef, proper service. The crock of mustard was on a breakfast plate, underlined with a doily, initials facing Jerry. The lid was on the mustard and it was clean, like it says in the book, and the little silver service spoon was clean and polished on a bread-and-butter plate. He set it down. And then he served the tea. You think you know the service, youngblood, all of you do. But you don't. Anybody can serve, but not everybody can become a part of the service. When Doc poured that pot of hot tea into that glass of

Jackson and I were down the aisle in the hall. Uncle T. stood behind Jerry, bending over, his arms folded, waiting. And Doc stood next to the table, his tray under his arm looking straight ahead and calm because he had given good service and knew it. Jerry sipped again.

"Good tea," he said. "Very good tea."

Doc was silent.

Jerry took the lemon wedge off the oyster fork and squeezed it into the glass, and stirred, and sipped again. "*Very* good," he said. Then he drained the glass. Doc reached over to pick

163

it up for more ice but Jerry kept his hand on the glass. "Very good service, Doc," he said. "But you served the lemon wrong."

Everybody was quiet. Uncle T. folded his hands in the praying position.

"How's that?" said Doc.

"The service was wrong," Jerry said. He was not smiling now.

"How could it be? I been giving that same service for years, right down to the crushed ice for the lemon wedge."

"That's just it, Doc," Jerry said. "The lemon wedge. You served it wrong."

"Yeah?" said Doc.

"Yes," said Jerry, his jaws tight. "Haven't you seen the new rule?"

Doc's face went loose. He knew now that they had got him.

"Haven't you *seen* it?" Jerry asked again.

Doc shook his head.

Jerry smiled that hard, gray smile of his, the kind of smile that says: "I have always been the boss and I am smiling this way because I know it and can afford to give you something." "Steward Crouse," he said. "Steward Crouse, go get the black bible for the headwaiter."

Crouse looked beaten too. He was sixty-three and waiting for his pension. He got the bible.

Jerry took it and turned directly to the very last page. He knew where to look. "Now, Headwaiter," he said, "*listen* to this." And he read aloud: "Memorandum Number 22416. From: Douglass A. Tesdale, General Superintendent of Dining Cars. To: Waiters, Stewards, Chefs of Dining Cars. Attention: As of 7/9/65 the proper service for iced tea will be (a) Fresh brewed tea in teapot, poured over crushed ice at table; iced tea glass set in shell dish (b) Additional ice to be immediately available upon request after first glass of tea (c) Fresh lemon wedge will be served on bread-and-butter plate, no doily, with tines of oyster fork stuck into *meat* of lemon." Jerry paused.

"Now you know, Headwaiter," he said.

"Yeah," said Doc.

"But why didn't you know before?"

No answer.

"This notice came out last week."

"I didn't check the book yet," said Doc.

"But that's a rule. Always check the book before each trip. *You* know that, Headwaiter."

"Yeah," said Doc.

"Then that's *two* rules you missed."

Doc was quiet.

"Two rules you didn't read," Jerry said. "You're slowing down, Doc."

"I know," Doc mumbled.

"You want some time off to rest?"

Again Doc said nothing.

Photo: Ronald Shuman

"I think you need some time on the ground to rest up, don't you?"

Doc put his tray on the table and sat down in the seat across from Jerry. This was the first time we had ever seen a waiter sit down with a customer, even an inspector. Uncle T., behind Jerry's back, began waving his hands, trying to tell Doc to get up. Doc did not look at him.

"You *are* tired, aren't you?" said Jerry.

"I'm just resting my feet," Doc said.

"Get up, Headwaiter," Jerry said. "You'll have plenty of time to do that. I'm writing you up."

But Doc did not move and just continued to sit there. And all Danny and I could do was watch him from the back of the car. For the first time I saw that his hair was almost gone and his legs were skinny in the baggy white uniform. I don't think Jerry expected Doc to move. I don't think he really cared. But then Uncle T. moved around the table and stood next to Doc, trying to apologize for him to Jerry with his eyes and bowed head. Doc looked at Uncle T. and then got up and went back to the crew car. He left his tray on the table. It stayed there all that evening because none of us, not even Crouse or Jerry or Uncle T., would touch it. And Jerry didn't try to make any of us take it back to the Pantry. He understood at least that much. The steward closed down Doc's tables during dinner service, all three settings of it. And Jerry got off the train someplace along the way, quiet, like he had got on.

After closing down the car we went back to the crew quarters and Doc was lying on his bunk with his hands behind his head and his eyes open. He looked old. No one knew what to say until Boone went over to his bunk and said: "I feel bad for you, Doc, but all of us are gonna get it in the end. The railroad waiter is *doomed.*"

Doc did not even notice Boone.

"I could of told you about the lemon but he would of got you on something else. It wasn't no use. Any of it."

"Shut the fuck up, Boone!" Danny said. "The one thing that really hurts is that a crawling son-of-a-bitch like you will be riding when all the good men are gone. Dummies like you and these two hardheads will be working your asses off reading that damn bible and never know a goddamn thing about being a waiter. *That* hurts like a *motherfucker*!"

"It ain't my fault if the colored waiter is doomed," said Boone. "It's your fault for letting go your humility and letting the whites take over the good jobs."

Danny grabbed the skullcap off Boone's head and took it into the bathroom and flushed it down the toilet. In a minute it was half a mile away and soaked in old piss on the tracks. Boone did not try to fight, he just sat on his bunk and mumbled. He had other skullcaps. No one said anything to Doc, because that's the way real men show that they care. You don't talk. Talking makes it worse.

IV

What else is there to tell you, youngblood? They made him retire. He didn't try to fight it. He was beaten and he knew it; not by the service, but by a book. *That book,* that *bible* you keep your finger stuck in. That's not a good way for a man to go. He should die in service. He should die doing the things he likes. But not by a book.

All of us Old School men will be beaten by it. Danny Jackson is gone now, and Reverend Hendricks put in for his pension and took up preaching, full-time. But Uncle T. Boone is still riding. They'll get *me* soon enough, with that book. But it will never get you because you'll never be a waiter, or at least a Waiter's Waiter. You read too much.

Doc got a good pension and he took it directly to Andy's. And none of the boys who knew about it knew how to refuse a drink on Doc. But none of us knew how to drink with him knowing that we would be going out again in a few days, and he was on the ground. So a lot of us, even the drunks and hustlers who usually hang around Andy's, avoided him whenever we could. There was nothing to talk about any more.

He died five months after he was put on the ground. He was seventy-three and it was winter. He froze to death wandering around the Chicago yards early one morning. He had been drunk, and was still steaming when the yard crew found him. Only the few of us left in the Old School know what he was doing there.

I am sixty-three now. And I haven't decided if I should take my pension when they ask me to go or continue to ride. I *want* to keep riding, but I know that if I do, Jerry Ewald or Harry Silk or Jack Tate will get me one of these days. I could get down if I wanted: I have a hobby and I am too old to get drunk by myself. I couldn't drink with you, youngblood. We have nothing to talk about. And after a while you would get mad at me for talking anyway, and keeping you from your pussy. You are tired already. I can see it in your eyes and in the way you play with the pages of your rule book.

I know it. And I wonder why I should keep talking to you when you could never see what I see or understand what I understand or know the real difference between my school and yours. I wonder why I have kept talking this long when all the time I have seen that you can hardly wait to hit the city to get off this thing and spend your money. You have a good story. But you will never remember it. Because all this time you have had pussy in your mind, and your fingers in the pages of that black bible.

165

The most powerful steam locomotive used on the Louis-ville & Nashville Railraod was the Class M-1.—*Louis-ville & Nashville Railroad photo*

A POEM WRITTEN UNDER AN ARCHWAY IN A DISCONTINUED RAILRAOD STATION, FARGO, NORTH DAKOTA

James Wright

Outside the great clanging cathedrals of rust and
    smoke,
The locomotives browse on sidings.
They pause, exhausted by the silence of prairies.
Sometimes they leap and cry out, skitterish.
They fear dark little boys in Ohio,
Who know how to giggle without breathing,
Who sneak out of graveyards in summer
    twilights
And lay crossties across rails.
The rattle of coupling pins still echoes
In the smoke stains,
The Cincinnati of the dead.
Around the bend now, beyond the grain
    elevators,
The late afternoon limited wails
Savage with the horror and loneliness of a child,
    lost
And dragged by a glad cop through a Chicago
    terminal.
The noose tightens, the wail stops, and I am
    leaving.
Across the street, an arthritic man
Takes coins at the parking lot.
He smiles with the sinister grief
Of old age.

THE CITY OF NEW ORLEANS

Words and music by Steve Goodman

Ridin' on the City of New Orleans,
Illinois Central Monday morning rail,
15 cars and 15 restless riders,
three conductors, 25 sacks of mail.
All on the southbound odyssey
the train pulls out of Kankakee
and rolls past houses, farms and fields;
passing towns that have no name and
freight yards full of old black men and
the graveyards of rusted automobiles.

Singin': "Good morning America! How are you?
Say, don't you know me? I'm your native son.
I'm the train they call the City of New Orleans.
I'll be gone 500 miles when day is done."

Dealin' card games with the old men in the club
    car.
Penny a point and no one's keeping score.
Pass the paper bag that holds the bottle
and feel the wheels a-rumblin' 'neath the floor.
And the sons of Pullman porters and the sons of
    engineers
ride their fathers' magic carpet made of steel.
And mothers with their babes asleep
are rocking to the gentle beat,
the rhythm of the rail is all they dream.

"Good morning America! How are you?
Say, don't you know me? I'm your native son.
I'm the train they call the City of New Orleans
I'll be gone 500 miles when day is done."

Nighttime on the City of New Orleans,
changing cars in Memphis, Tennessee.
Halfway home and we'll be there by morning,
through the Mississippi darkness rollin' to the
    sea.
But all the towns and people seem to fade into a
    bad dream.
Well, the steel rail hasn't heard the news:
The conductor sings his song again
it's "passengers will please refrain,
this train has the disappearin' railroad blues."

"Goodnight America! How are you?
Say, don't you know me? I'm your native son.
I'm the train they call the City of New Orleans
I'll be gone 500 miles when day is done."

(Repeat chorus for close.)

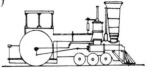

THE WHEELS OF THE TRAINS

W. S. Merwin

They are there just the same
unnoticed for years
on dark tracks at the foot of their mountain

behind them holes in the hill
endless death of the sky
foreheads long unlit
illegibly inscribed

the cars
have been called into the air
an air that has gone
but these wait unmoved in their rust
row of suns
for another life

ahead of them
the tracks lead out through tall milkweed
untouched

for all my travels

This steam-drawn train on the Louisville & Nashville Railroad in 1955 is loaded with coal from mines in eastern Kentucky. The last steam power in revenue service ran on the L & N in 1957.—*Louisville & Nashville Railroad photo*

THE NIGHT TRAIN

Warren Woessner

I grew up next to tracks
and never heard a thing.
Now the engine's horn
and the rattle of iron wheels wake me.

I get on board and am carried past the wrecking
   yard
across the filled-in marsh
into Ten-Mile Woods, faster and faster.
The railings almost brush the wet leaves.
Suddenly I know I am leaving town
on the last passenger train in the world.

SIDETRACK
THE MOVIES

Buster Keaton inspects a cannon with a short fuse in *The General* (United Artists, 1927).

Buster Keaton walks the ties in *The General* (United Artists, 1927).

If anything is as deeply bound to the history of this country over the past sixty years as the railroad is, it can only be the moving picture show, the movies. When the movies and the railroad come together, the sense of adventure and glory is so immediate it almost doesn't require a story line. Even so, when a picture show first told a story it was about the railroad. That was The Great Train Robbery, and it started a long line of movies about trains—and movies about robberies. The trains and robberies were not always in the same movies, but when the setting was the American West they usually were.

It's interesting to compare the movie version of history with the contemporary camera's version. Look at Buster Keaton's flatcar-mounted mortar, for instance, and the real prototype used in the Civil War (p. 47). Hollywood also changed the staging of the spike-driving ceremony at Promontory Point.

—All pictures courtesy of the National Academy of Motion Picture Arts and Sciences

The Golden Spike is driven again in *Union Pacific* (Paramount Studios, 1939).

The perpetrators of *The Great Train Robbery* force the engineer to uncouple the locomotive.

The train and the sheriff wait on George O'Brien (in buckskin) in *The Iron Horse* (Fox, 1924).

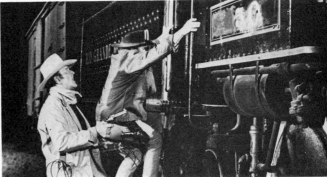

The Duke takes over in *The Train Robbers* (Warner Brothers, 1973).

An iron horse goes down in *Union Pacific* (Paramount Studios, 1939).

PAY DAY HUSSEY'S CAMP B.B & R RR

NOW
AND
AGAIN
1970-Now

AND WHY NOT?

William B. Hart

Christene Gonzales actually operates that 200-ton locomotive shown behind her. She's an engineer with the Atchison, Topeka & Santa Fe Railroad. It's her bare hand with the pink nail polish on the throttle. It's her pay check, up to $1,800 a month. She's been on the job almost a year. She's twenty-two.

When Chris showed up for her first day, back in March 1974, there was no need for the usual new-girl-on-the-job introductions. She hoisted herself into the cab, let out a blast on the whistle and took off while reporters and TV cameras recorded the event. There had never before been a woman operating a diesel locomotive in El Paso, Texas—or anywhere else in the country.

The story went around the world on the news services and the Voice of America. It was translated into forty-six different languages and dialects. She was an item for *Ripley's Believe It or Not.* She appeared on *What's My Line* and *To Tell the Truth,* stumping both panels. Hundreds of letters poured in. All nice. No weirdos.

Christene Gonzales, engineer.—*Photo by J. Frederick Smith*

Everybody seemed to think Christene was great.

Now, a year later, nothing has happened to change that verdict. Despite the world-wide publicity, her life goes on much as before. She still lives with her parents and one of her two brothers. She still hangs around with her old high school friends.

"I can't see any change in her," a fellow railway worker said. "Oh, she may be a little more worldly from all that fuss, but she's just as nice as she always was and she's a *good* engineer."

Chris herself says, "I love what I'm doing. It's exciting. But it will take me maybe ten years to become really good."

That she wanted to be an engineer is easy to understand, she thinks, because of her background.

Her great-grandfather worked in Decatur, Alabama, in the maintenance shop of the old Louisville & Nashville Railroad. Her maternal grandfather, Ernest M. Halbrook, of Ruidosa, New Mexico, was a conductor until his retirement in 1971, on the Sunset Limited, running between Los Angeles and New Orleans. Her father, Frank Gonzales, is a conductor on the Southern Pacific. Betty Gonzales, her mother, is secretary to the trainmaster of the Santa Fe in the El Paso area.

It was her mother who told her that as a result of antidiscrimination legislation, women could apply as fireman-engineer candidates.

"I liked the challenge of it," Chris said, "but I thought about it a couple of months before I could get up the nerve."

After finishing high school in her native El Paso, she had taken an office job with an oil company. She didn't like it; it was too confining. She decided to try college, but after a semester that didn't feel right, either. So she followed her mother's tip and put in her application as an engineer trainee.

Instead of years of apprenticeship, her training was packed into nine months. She started in the yard at Albuquerque, New Mexico, as a hostler, moving the big engines in and out of the roundhouse. Later she was an observer in the cab, hauling freight and learning to take control. The last six weeks were at a locomotive simulator school. The simulator, a mobile unit, teaches locomotive and train operations against a background of authentic sounds, motion, visual panoramas and crisis situations.

At the beginning of her training she was worried about her ability to master the mechanical aspects of the job.

"I've never even held a screwdriver," she told her instructor.

But at the end she passed two exams, one written, one oral, in mechanics. She scored 91.5 in the written test. The oral was tougher, lasting from 8 A.M. to 5 P.M., with some breaks. She scored 100.

Now when she isn't switching in the El Paso yard, she's making up trains bound for Mexico or she's out with a work train laying track, dumping ballast and picking up scrap.

She's still impressed by all that power under her hand.

"You know, it takes about half a mile to stop one of those things, once you're rolling," she said. "It's not like zapping around in my sports convertible."

She works in blue jeans and a shirt in warm weather and adds as many as two ski jackets in winter. She pulls her long, shiny brown hair

back and tucks it inside her shirt to keep it out of the machinery, but she doesn't wear a cap. Nor does she always bother with gloves. Climbing up the ladder into the cab, she says, is the greasiest part of her day. A new rule—no dangling earrings on the job—was added after she came to work.

The men treat her pretty much as they would anyone else, she thinks, taking into account that she's a woman.

"The conversation in the lunchroom is probably censored a little when I'm there," she said. "The ones who've worked with me are used to me. The others may be a little shaky about the idea."

A twenty-year veteran of Santa Fe training crews said this: "Do you know what a hoghead is? Well, that's railroad for 'engineer.' Chris is a real hoghead. She runs that thing like it was a sewing machine."

She doesn't object to being called a hoghead, but apparently the men she works with think it's not quite suitable. Someone coined the word "porkette" for her. Also "enginette." They kid around with her and she hands it right back. As for being accepted, there isn't any doubt. She's proved herself. And why not? Way back to her great-grandfather, she's railroad.

LEAVING NEW YORK ON THE PENN CENTRAL TO METUCHEN

FOR JIM WHITEHEAD

Miller Williams

Go buck, go hiss and the bright bolted works
tremble and turn. Go clank and the car jerks,

grabs at the tracks and moves off underground.
Sealed in a tube of light, we ride the sound

for something to ride. We stare into the black
unsteady glass and see ourselves stare back.

And then we rise. Timetables will tell
that we have risen. But there's no hell if hell

does not receive the leakage of this place.
Nor punishment for sin nor sin nor grace.

A milky head still bounces in the dense
expensive air: closed roads, a gateless fence,

walls of windows, every one gone blind
pass through it like visions through a distracted
    mind.

Here we are she said it's just a room
Gases, like ghosts turned out of a broken tomb,

form faces, halves of faces, ears and eyes
while brimstone burns and jagged slagheaps rise

like bony tumors. Each of us is going
to some green place in sunlight, secure in
    knowing

what schedules tell, what signs go by outside.
She is waiting somewhere while I ride

backward bumping in this trembling crowd
whose hands hold papers and whose heads are
    bowed

as if in prayer, though I imagine not.
More likely they are thinking of a lot

of simple things like is it going to rain
and what to tell her if she meets the train.

The New Yorker, October 7, 1972.—*New York Public Library Picture Collection*

"The diner is back fifteen cars, sir—second car behind yours, just like your wife said." *Saturday Evening Post* April 22, 1950—*New York Public Library Picture Collection*

"Great Scott! *Now* what's happened?" *The New Yorker* December 5, 1965—*New York Public Library Picture Collection*

THIRTY YEARS IN THE DINING CAR

Joe Monroe Talks About How It Was

I left my home in New Orleans when I was a boy. A guy come through there looking for men to go to work, so I put my age up to go with him. We worked off flatcars, throwing steel off on embankments all day long. I worked gandy-dancing—putting steel down and laying track. This guy saw I was willing to work, so he took me off of picking up steel and put me on the flatcar throwing off plates. Then he sent me in the kitchen to help the cook out. Made one dollar a day. Every thirty days, thirty dollars. We slept in boxcars. It was rough. I stayed with them all up in Illinois, all up in Wisconsin. I saved my money. I worked about four months, I had about one hundred some-odd dollars. I got my money up together. I got me a map and hoboed to Denver, where my mother was at. I laid asphalt, worked in a packing house, I was just movin' round. Tried anything once.

I worked for the Soo Line when you had to wash dishes by hand. You had to serve four hundred to five hundred people in a fifty-seat diner with a full crew, six waiters. You served four meals a day, so you had to keep up. At that time the company wasn't furnishin' nothing but a white jacket and a apron. You had to supply your own blue pants. I started working for the Soo Line on the seasons. I worked for them two seasons and then I went to Omaha and I worked awhile out of Omaha. Then I went to work for the Northern Pacific. That was before the Second World War. I worked as a cook. They had very few colored cooks over there because the Northern Pacific advertised a lily-white kitchen. They had colored cooks on private cars but not in the dining cars. I cooked for the vice-president on a private car, and I cooked for some of the big officials on private cars. One time we were comin' out of Chicago, and the chef-cook got left, the second cook got left, the third cook got left, and the steward got left. They said they got locked up in a tavern. Only one left in the kitchen was the fourth cook, and he didn't know how to boil a egg without scorchin' it. I told 'em, I say, "I'll go back there and cook." But a waiter,

English Mickey we called him, say, "No, don't you go back there. They advertised a lily-white kitchen, so we'll just wait for St. Paul to put some white cooks on." And that's what we did. Nobody fixed breakfast. Nobody ate. The steward said later, "Why didn't you go in there, Joe?" I say, "No, y'all advertise in the papers a lily-white kitchen. I ain't got no business in there." After a while they started gettin' these colored cooks out of Florida that could cook rings around all these boys up here. But they never give 'em no chef-cook job. They give 'em third or fourth cook. I remember a guy he was so good he'd say, "Don't you order unless you ready to pick up." And he meant it, too. You didn't order nothin' unless you was ready to pick up. He was that fast. You'd order "French toast"; he'd say, "Well, pick it up, then!"

I remember hauling soldiers in the First World War, and the Second too. We had ten to fifteen cars full of soldiers. We stocked the cars in Seattle and we had so many damn people that when we got to Missoula, Montana, we had to restock the car again. At that time the waiters didn't have no personal space. They had hooks in the walls and a locker at the other end of the diner with beds and cots you took out of there and made your bed every night in the dining car. You never got out of that dining car—no place to go. The train was loaded down; soldiers sleepin' up in the baggage racks. We fed so many that time we didn't have nothin' to eat but some cakes when we got to Missoula in the afternoon. We had a man runnin' jitney; he sold a thousand sandwiches. It was rough. You start early in the morning and don't finish till late at night. Then you tear down the table and make your bed down and hang up your curtain. You had to save all the cans you could get your hands on 'cause there was so many soldiers you couldn't get in the bathroom. You had to be up at six and ready to serve from six-thirty till ten-thirty at night. We slept in the car till the government got on us. Yeah, I'm tellin' you it used to be rough out here. Rough! Inspectors got on and run their fingers along the shelves, lookin' for dust. Instead of gettin' on with everybody else they get on in the baggage car and come through. They didn't allow you to play no funny cards, not on the train. They catch you gamblin', you get some days on the ground or get fired. It was rough. They had a colored inspector. See, they put him on as a inspector but they wanted him to just inspect the waiters, the colored help, and not the cooks. He jumped on the waiters about makin' sandwiches and selling them, then he caught a cook makin' sandwiches and sellin' them through the back door and turned him in. They called the colored inspector in the office and told him, "You stay with them waiters. We'll take care of this." He said, "If that's the way you want it, take your job back. I'm goin' back to the dining car." It was rough.

The service now is a lot different than it was. Back there, you serve breakfast in the morning, you had to serve everybody a demitasse. You had to crumb the tables after the people got through eatin' and before you put down dessert. Then you put down finger bowls after they got through with dessert. They didn't allow you to put down finger bowls while they was eatin' dessert. Used to have mint you put in the finger bowls. And you couldn't top no tables. No indeed. No toppin' no tables. Change the cloth after every meal. Break a glass, you pay for it; you break a cup, you had to pay for it. They had the prices posted. And they had all silver service—finger bowls, teapots, coffeepots, salt and pepper shakers. They had fine service. They gonna come back to it. That's what they was tellin' me . . .

Junction of the Great Western Railway with the London.—*New York Public Library Picture Collection*

SHORT

Irv Broughton

His hair was white but his beard was black. He was wearing a woman's coat—ermine, probably stolen. I met him on a freight train in Cairo, Georgia. It was winter. There was a dead Mexican under the hay in the boxcar. He didn't seem to mind the dead man; perhaps he was his friend. I didn't ask. God, it was cold. His gloves were a pair of socks. They belonged to some athletic department. They said so. His eyes were like clods of dried mud. What a liar he was. He and his years aboard ship, him and his women, him and his fights. He told me a different story every night.

Neither of us had eaten for a week. I *mean* a week. He said, "Whatever your name is, listen: I'm not going to freeze to death, you hear? I only break the law when I have to. I'm not going to starve." His name was Brendan. I never told him mine. I was afraid to.

In the middle of the night, just enough moonlight coming in the old Rock Island boxcar, he would roll up his sleeves and draw on himself. "It won't last long," he told me. He called it *The Skin of Dreams*. What an old fool. He said he could never be evil, could never be a fool, because he had the gift of good humor. He never smiled.

We threw the Mexican off as we crossed a bridge. I wanted to know what river it was we were crossing, but he wouldn't tell me. I wasn't from around there. He smelled like a depot. He talked to me in made-up accents. He asked me questions but he wouldn't answer mine. Like a child, he was able to turn himself into whatever he wanted. During those days I came to adore this—but to adore childhood is to commit heresy. That night, not knowing what river it was that we'd crossed, not knowing what state we were in, I felt him reach down my pants. I really don't think he knew if I was a young man, a young woman. He put his hands over his lips. The bits of tobacco hung there like the markings of dice. "Want to smoke?" he asked me. "No," I told him.

He brought something out of his coat. It flashed. I moved back, afraid. It was a Lifesaver. He'd taken the piece of candy wrapped in tin foil off the Mexican. I put it under my tongue and shut my eyes. He struck a match and held it over my hair. There were ice crystals. A draft put it out. "I found them in the cuff of some old trousers," he told me, pointing to some joints he'd found under the hay. He wrapped smoke around my neck like a scarf. My feet were cold. I seemed to be losing my equilibrium. I took off my boots and shoved my feet into his pockets. There was something cold and hard under his coat. A saxophone. It was like ice to touch it. He brought it out and breathed on it. On this train we were dying, I thought—though it was far from that. I was feeling sorry for myself. I made him play it, expecting a kind of jazz. The music he played wasn't like that, not at all. It was Bach—at least that is what he said. I wouldn't know. *Saint Matthew Passion,* he said. He played the parts for voice and not for voice. He explained. Maybe he wasn't as stupid as I thought he was.

We were found out and put off in Roanoke. There were more trains than I had seen. I'd never been there before. Neither of us had money. They didn't like the idea of a girl with an old bum—he wasn't that old. We took off before they had a chance to ask many questions. In an alley we found an empty refrigera-

tor carton. We holed up there, next to a hotel. There was a can of oysters and red snappers and fish heads which made it smell like the sea. We ate the oysters. One night something was crawling. I thought it was a rat. It was a lobster they hadn't boiled to death.

Each day we thought was our last. We found out the sanitary engineers were on strike. The weather got worse. You could only smell yourself. I told him I was going out to look for something to turn. He hit me in the mouth. It didn't knock me out but sent me into a long, painful kind of sleep. He was gone. He didn't come back for hours. I was ready to leave. Then I saw him running down the alley, a toaster and three loaves of bread under his arms. He'd stolen some electrical wire, too. He said he'd be back in a minute, climbing a fire escape. He found a hidden outlet and ran the extension down into our carton. We toasted the bread. We went through the loaves. "This is the best part," he told me, stuffing tinfoil down the toaster. He made a heater.

It was the worst snow in this country in a hundred years, as far back as anyone could remember. In the paper it said some people were wondering if the government hadn't accidentally caused it. Some special, secret satellite had been launched. People were committing suicide. They say the snow is conducive to it. At night Brendan played music I'd never heard of. Since then, I've heard it in ships, in great halls, in my own home, evenings.

TRAIN WINDOWS

David Allan Evans

one night I am standing on
a high bluff overlooking
the tracks, waiting
for him to leave
once and for all time

suddenly I see his face
in each lighted window
of his train—the face
of a man passing
from darkness into darkness
reading a novel

as I leap I snatch a
white pigeon from the air
and wave with that same hand
going down to my father

177

THE MIDNIGHT FREIGHT TO PORTLAND

Edward Hoagland

Railroads provided the big bones of American industry and of much of the country's mythology, too, until the current containerized epoch of trucks and the small-world era of planes. Children rushed out and waved and their fathers stood alert when a train steamed through town, sometimes crossing at street level, bringing all traffic to a halt, and maybe stopping to let the passengers off or maybe not, though they would look out of the windows ironically, in any case. Part of the privilege of being downtown was to see them and to watch the train, boiling with noise and momentum, the crew ten feet above the ground, detached-looking and far-sighted even as they loafed. Their travels lasted nights and days—even the gandy dancers were legends—and no writer who seriously pursued the chimera of the great American novel could neglect to learn some of the lore of railroading.

Recently I rode a freight train from Island Pond in northeastern Vermont to Portland, Maine, to see how the trains run; there has been no passenger service on the line, or anywhere else in Vermont, for years. This is the last hundred and fifty miles of the famous Grand Trunk international rail route from

A young passenger on Amtrak gathers her own railroad memories.—*Amtrak photo*

Montreal to the ice-free saltwater harbor in Casco Bay, something that the Canadians needed in 1853, when the last spikes were driven with a good deal of fanfare and acclaim. Later, when icebreakers were making more headway in the St. Lawrence, Portland still possessed a thriving year-round port where enormous amounts of Western grain arrived by rail to be shipped abroad. Twenty-six train crews were based in Island Pond to handle the activity; now there are only six. Island Pond is a railroad and sawmill town which does not hide the fact that it has come down in the world, although it's got some dairying going on where the woods aren't too thick and a little tourism. The station is a frowning sooty brick pile with a plaza-sized area left vacant all around. Many of the other local buildings look like old railroad stations too.

Since the 1920s the Grand Trunk's trackage and perquisites have belonged to the Canadian National Railways. Not wanting to go as a hobo, I'd written to the office in Montreal and was received royally. The station agent put me under the wing of Claude Seguin, his brother, the head-end brakeman on the train I rode. Seguin is a loose-cheeked, modest, drawling man with a farmer's emotive hands, an outdoorsman up early for long walks on his days off, who had been helping a neighbor clapboard his house. Like many railroad men, he collects timepieces as a hobby, even buying large restaurant clocks at auctions, cleaning off the grease and putting them up around the house. I asked if he'd seen any hoboes lately. He said not for four or five years, although the crews used to let them ride if they looked decent. "We're just glorified hoboes ourselves, you know."

The engineer was Eddy Boylan, a quick gray active man well past the years when he may or may not have made some mistakes. The seniority system works excellently in railroading, ensuring that nobody who is still trying to prove something will be risking other people's lives. All these men were hefty veterans over fifty years old, with austere, snowy minds and furry, neutral-sounding voices: Joe

Vautour, the fireman; Joe Cargill, the rear-end brakeman; and Donald MacDonald, a judgely, stern but witty man who rides in the caboose ("buggy") and keeps the waybills straight.

I was eager to talk, but when the train pulled in we left immediately, as soon as the Montreal crew stepped off. It was dusk, and a full harvest moon—white, not red, in this cold border country—stood low in the sky toward Portland. The leaves were turning but not yet falling, and we entered fir forests, with low deserted mountains and tamarack bogs and bushy round wild islands posted in a series of lakes. The streams were black and shining; the clouds spread into herringbone patterns. I rode alone in the second of three engines, and Seguin or the fireman paid me visits. The engineer drives from the right-hand side of the front locomotive, controlling the other locomotives from there. The fireman, who nowadays, in the post-steam era, functions as a sort of co-pilot, sits at the left-hand window, looking out at crossings which the engineer can't see. He's there if the engineer gets sick or wishes to eat, in time of hazard, or if the walkie-talkie that the brakemen carry fail and they are dependent upon hand signals. Since he is basically a featherbedder, though, the fireman is mainly supposed to be good company, and Vautour, who has a world-worn face, a furrowed forehead, a buffeted nose, bushy eyebrows and a voice like William Bendix's, fills the bill.

The two brakemen sit watching for sparks, smoke or hotboxes as the train rolls along, one seated facing backwards in the first engine, the other located in the monitor, which is the double-decker compartment on top of the caboose. We were hauling only fifty-two freight cars, considered a light load, because, as it happened, a rail strike was threatened for midnight. I had assumed the President would sign a cooling-off order, but in a pressure play, he was delaying doing that, and since even this spur which angled down from Canada might be affected, the railroad was stripping for trouble.

We ran along the Connecticut River for a while after crossing into New Hampshire. At North Stratford the crew "set off" ten cars; delicately waving his light in signal patterns, Seguin hopped off and on and off to turn the switches and uncouple. Between Groveton and Berlin we skirted the Upper Ammonoosuc River through an expanse of national forest. A deer paused dazzled on the track as we hushed toward it, and Boylan turned off the headlight and tooted. Under the moon, the White Mountains showed themselves in rotund grays and navy blues; lots of empty land, a sense of

A young Southern Pacific brakeman ready to roll out of San Francisco.—*Photo by Ronald Shuman*

calmness. Every station had a telegraph operator usually wearing an eyeshade and a checked shirt, who stepped outside to wave. In Berlin we hitched onto a switching engine that the railroad wanted hauled out of harm's way to Portland, in case there was a strike. Berlin has a big stone station and a round-the-clock paper plant pluming steam and smoke. The crew was quite worked up about the possibility of the strike and how far they should take the train if one was called, whether they shouldn't just leave it standing somewhere on a siding as soon after midnight as they heard. Apparently they assumed the railroad would then have the responsibility of hiring a taxi to take them home to Island Pond.

The shaking and the roar, the rumbling wheels, the amalgam of jolts, hisses and shivers, the rocking and big-bopping over the rails were all as intimately familiar to me as my childhood itself. Though I've never been a railroad fan the way some people are, I sometimes rode at the front window of subways and Toonerville Trolleys as a boy, and admired the figure cut by the engineers on bigger trains as they swept by. Even the track-walker hiking through town on his own lonely schedule intrigued me. Just as a man who has wished to be rich and watched rich men for years is not bewildered about how to behave or what to do when his windfall finally does come, so to be up in that engine myself did not seem novel or astonishing. It was about as I'd expected: the majestic height at which we rode, the swath that the headlight illuminated in front, the diesel fumes, the tilty file of telephone poles, the murky train winding behind. The horn's tattoo was properly pristine. In the moonlight the spruces bulged. There was a breezy, box-shaped chemical toilet perched in among the turbines, a water cooler to drink from, and panels of gauges, gears and levers, with stenciled advisory warnings and small red lights.

Waiting with the ticket.—*Photo by Ronald Shuman*

A pull-rope was attached to the whistle, which Boylan jokingly told me I should pull if I had a question. We sat on upholstered jump seats, not so comfortable that you could fall asleep.

Three hours out we were in Maine, a land of redolent sawmills, clusters of cozy houses with lights in the bedrooms, and a night fog that was gathering across the fields. Chill air, crisp moonlight, gunmetal-colored lakes and tumultuous trees—rollicking, big-topped hardwoods against the sky. At South Paris, a hundred miles from Island Pond, we left off another seven cars, Seguin hopping along the catwalks and the cowcatcher area under the engine's nose. The locomotives revved with the whorling, encompassing sound of a ship's engine—electrical, oil-burning sounds. South Paris is a tranquil little county seat, but it has a shoe-manufacturing plant, a tannery, linoleum and sled-and-ski factories, and a berry cannery. Bouncing along catch-as-catch-can, flying a freight train's white flag on our front, we passed on through Mechanic Falls to Lewiston Junction, and set off two cars which contained cereals and one refrigerator car carrying meat. Because of the projected strike, Boylan and the crew detoured two miles with the meat and placed it at the wholesaler's door, where it could be unloaded promptly. Lewiston has a feed mill, a formica and plastics plant, a factory producing bridge girders, and a General Electric facility.

At Yarmouth Junction we disposed of three more cars, which were to be transferred to the Maine Central, then highballed swiftly towards Portland, brazenly blaring our horn, through dozens of deserted crossings with flailing signals. The extra work and the fact that we had stopped to inquire about strike news at almost every station had made us very late; it was three in the morning. Crossing a drawbridge outside Portland, we ran alongside an arm of the bay. Since we had just emerged from the North Woods, the smell of the salt water stung our lungs. It was a marvelous arrival, a rank, spacious, open harbor. In the yards next to the water, Boylan simply parked the train, and, each man with his overnight kit, we walked away, leaving it right where it was, to be dealt with later.

We slept in a bunkhouse over the terminal

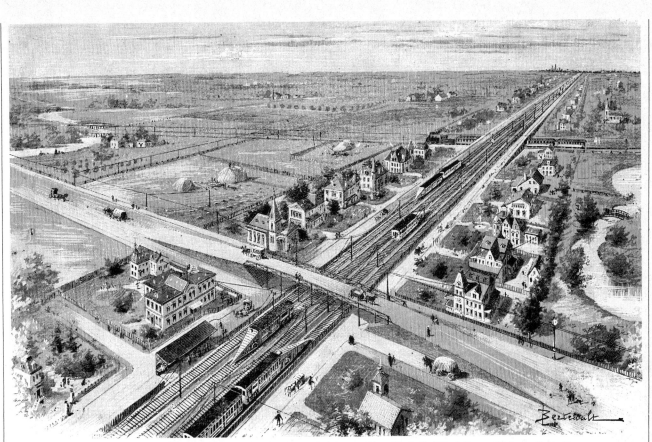

Design of Electric Railroad, from St. Louis to Chicago.—*New York Public Library Picture Collection*

offices, a remnant of Portland's heyday as a port. When I woke up the view was like a Channel town in France, with smudged seacoast weather and Frenchy frame houses spotted on sandy hills. Mewing white gulls had collected on the piers in crowds. Low-rent industry—ironmongeries, beer warehouses and fender shops—was casually clumped about. The groceries featured olive oil. On East India Street a plaque announced that this had been the site of Fort Loyal, built by the English settlers in 1680 and destroyed ten years later by Indians and French. Through the rain I saw an orange-and-black freighter, a lighter and some coastal boats.

Here on the seacoast the crew looked like men out of the woods, slow-speaking, their faces delineated and chunky. They let me look at their noble gold watches, which the railroad inspects every November and May. We breakfasted in a bar where four or five wet prostitutes were having coffee, "too wet to climb on," as the trainmen said. Spread over the wall was a picture of Bobby Orr horizontal in the air after scoring a winning goal, and the talk, perhaps because of me, was mostly of the

heroic era of steam, prior to 1955. The brakemen kidded around, saying they had told the janitor at the terminal that I was a reporter for *Time* and that he was cleaning up like mad, scrubbing cupboards that nobody had even looked into since before the era of steam. MacDonald, the conductor, was trying to think of stories I could use. There used to be contests between the engineers and firemen, he said. If they couldn't manage to get along and the engineer demanded more steam, the fireman *gave* him more steam, until he had more than he wanted, maybe, so that the safety valves were popping, and the fireman would make him figure out how to use it. Putting in more water cooled the boiler, but then the pressure died, or the fire itself might die if there was slate mixed with the coal.

As it turned out, the President had never needed to act, because at the last moment the union limited the strike to three breadbasket railroads in the Midwest, whereupon a federal judge issued an injunction. We left belatedly at 2:10 P.M., pulling twenty-six empty cars that were going to Moncton, New Brunswick, to haul the turnip crop and two that were full of canned goods for Minneapolis and Denver. For a while I was with MacDonald. His desk is the main article of furniture in the caboose, though there are also fold-up beds, a wooden bench, kerosene lamps and an oil stove. Each freight car is in its logical order in the train, and its waybill must give a description explicit enough to help the customs men, who hold the train for an hour after it passes Island Pond.

BACKSTAGE
New York Public Library Picture Collection

MacDonald says he doubts that any of the crews indulge in smuggling now, but back during Prohibition and afterwards, when some of the crews were younger, the Mounties used to hide behind a boxcar in the Montreal rail yards and suddenly jump out and mount the moving engine and search everybody. Luckily there was steam then; they had a firebox where they could throw the contraband.

MacDonald drinks tea from a thermos and carries Preparation H because of the hard benches he sits on and a miniature screwdriver for tightening his glasses. He has a clean, cutting smile that breaks through this methodical exterior, however. His principal avocation

seems to be women, or remembering them. The handsome, slicing smile gives him away, paring ten years off his age. Just as caïque captains on the Ionian Sea flash mirrors at the widows who live on the islands they sail past, so does MacDonald wave and give a high sign to some of the lonely ladies of Maine.

At the Maine Central Railroad's yards at Yarmouth Junction we picked up thirty cars—1,750 tons. Several of these were empty grain hoppers which had carried soybean meal; others had brought asbestos and were going back out West for more. The carloads were either potatoes or else wood pulp or rolled newsprint manufactured to the north in towns like Madawaska; the waybills were from the Belfast and Moosehead Lake Railroad and the Bangor and Aroostook. At Danville, we added on eleven more cars and at Mechanic Falls, another one—now we were hauling seventy. Because of the tangled schedule, our caboose brakeman had been replaced by a fairly young man who had worked fifteen years for the railroad, all of them right in the Portland yards. This was to be his first trip up the line—indeed, the first time he had ever left the state of Maine. Yet he was worrying whether we would reach Island Pond on time so that he could catch the return train and not have to stay over.

The coastal drizzle had preceded us inland, and when the wheels slipped on the track, lights on the panel flashed. I was in the second locomotive again as we began to climb out of the Maine flatlands into the mountains before entering New Hampshire. Westbound, the so-called deciding grade of this particular route is at Bryant Pond, close to the state border. Though each of our engines could pull 2,300 tons on the level ground, their limit for this slope (and therefore for the trip) was calculated at 1,865 tons. Besides being high and steep, it was magnificent abandoned country with forests stretching away for miles, with ducks and herons in all the ponds and lots of creeks—lovely back country, of which we got a view uncluttered by motels.

We acquired nine more cars in Berlin, Seguin adroit and cautious as he moved between them, signaling. A "run-off" is a derailment; a "head-on" is a wreck. The "tell-tales," as he said they were called, used to fascinate me;

they are long strings which hang overhead wherever the tracks near an underpass and slap a man who is on top of a freight car to warn him before he is decapitated. It is the nature of railroading that even a minor goof by somebody means that he has to take a long walk, at the least, maybe the length of a hundred cars.

Because of the rain, night settled down around us much faster. The windshield wipers and heater hissed with enough decibels to have alarmed an ear doctor, quite apart from the roar of the diesels themselves, but I found sitting there in the eye of the roar so soothing that I would have been content for another dozen hours. Railroads are the one exception among our huge machines in that we've finally assimilated them.

Sometimes a hard rain will clean the tracks nicely, but this was a light greasy drizzle. The ponderous train climbed up into Vermont from the trench of the Connecticut River with difficulty, whining around double-reverse curves at five miles per hour, Boylan using his sand

judiciously (each drive wheel of a locomotive is serviced by a pipe from a sand reservoir). The roar had become a lugubrious groan, alternating between two notes like a Parisian police car. It's not the number of cars so much as the load in them, and not the load so much as whether the wheels can grip the tracks. All torments end, however. We followed the Nulhegan River up and out, hooting the horn, regaining speed. White cedars, red spruces, and firs and tamaracks—wild north country. Of course the whole experience was definitive. One wouldn't say that riding a night freight is like driving all night in a mufflerless car across the Texas panhandle, but one might say that driving a mufflerless car across the Texas panhandle all night is somewhat like riding a night freight train. At last, at 9:15 in the evening after seven hours, we pulled into Island Pond again. The Montreal crew took over.

Arkansas Gazette
November 9, 1975

Conrail Born As Congress Fails to Act

7 Northeast Lines

Facing Bankruptcy

Made Into 1 Firm

(c) New York Times News Service

WASHINGTON — By not acting, Congress allowed a sweeping federal plan, that absorbed seven bankrupt Northeast railroads into a semi-nationalized rail system, to become law Saturday night.

The multibillion-dollar plan, embodying the largest corporate reorganization in American history, provides for a federally financed Consolidated Rail Corporation or Conrail, and a government-created private railroad competitor, to take over from the bankrupt private lines next year most of the rail freight-hauling in the populous 17-state region.

Conrail will also take over almost all the 90,000 employes of the absorbed railroads and run the New York metropolitan area commuter rail lines, although intercity trains will continue to be operated by Amtrak, the National Railroad Passenger Corporation.

The plan must now be implemented with legislation.

Under the unusual enactment procedure, Congress had until midnight Saturday to reject the final reorganization plan submitted 60 working days ago by the United States Railway Association, the government agency charged with restructuring the bankrupts.

Lack of Choices Prevented Veto

However it was clear long before Friday's weekend adjournment that the urgency of the Northeast rail crisis made any veto of the only salvage plan unthinkable.

The last possibility either House might block the plan all but vanished Thursday with a long-awaited agreement giving the Chessie (Railroad) System a major part in the restructuring.

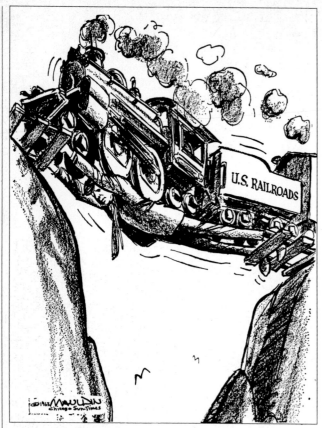

New York *Herald Tribune*, July 21, 1963.—*New York Public Library Picture Collection*

Conditioning his remarks on the expected acceptance, Arthur D. Lewis, chairman of the Railway Association, Friday hailed Congress' enactment of the plan.

"The acceptance is a major step forward in the reorganization process," he said through a spokesman, adding "It is essential now that implementing legislation be adopted as soon as possible."

With the plan adopted, attention focused on emerging House and Senate bills to grant Conrail the $2.5 billion start-up funding the Railway Association called for and to otherwise flesh out the Conrail structure. In addition, the legislation is aimed at reshaping some regulatory powers of the Interstate Commerce Commission to give the new railroads more flexibility to adjust rates.

Under an implementation bill currently undergoing "markup" or revision in the House Transportation and Commerce Subcommittee, railroads would be free to raise and lower their rates each year by up to 7 per cent without prior ICC approval.

Credit Shield Also Proposed

The proposed bill also contains a controversial provision to grant all solvent railroads participating in the reorganization immunity from deficiency judgments. Thus, if a creditor of a bankrupt railroad should file suit claiming the property was sold too cheaply, not the purchaser but the government would be liable for any award. Conrail was originally granted this protection.

The Senate Transportation Subcommittee is expected to start considering its Conrail bill next week. Passage in both Houses, however, is not expected before early next year.

"This is the bill at this point," said Tom Allison, transportation expert on the staff of the Senate Commerce Committee, gesturing over a pile of papers and memos strewn over his desk earlier this week.

Critics of Plan List Objections

Meanwhile, critics of the plan continued to circulate their objections. Pennsylvania and New Jersey expressed concern about the survival of their rail commuter lines under Conrail and Pennsylvania questioned the terms of the deal with Chessie. The Penn-Central complained that its properties were being grossly undervalued by the Railway Association and the First National City Bank, which recently analysed financial needs of the rail industry, saw far greater Conrail expenses than had been anticipated.

Basically, the reorganization plan provides for stripping 5,750 light-density miles from the current 21,000 miles of track operated by the seven bankrupts—Penn Central, Erie-Lackawanna, Ann Arbor, Reading, Lehigh Valley, Central of New Jersey, and Lehigh and Hudson River.

The more lucrative 15,000 remaining route miles will then be divided between a new government-created for profit corporation, Conrail and an expanded private Chessie System. Thus, the railway association felt, it would not be creating a government rail monopoly.

Under the plan, Conrail will account for about 87 per cent of the region's net ton miles annually; Chessie another 32 per cent; the Norfolk and Western, 21 per cent; and smaller solvent lines, 10 per cent.

Conrail to Buy Rolling Stock

Conrail will purchase rights of way and rolling stock from the bankrupts with Conrail stock and certificates of value. However, the railway Association's decision to rate the bankrupts' properties at their scrap value, $621 million, has provoked outrage by the bankrupts. Penn-Central's trustees have valued their own property alone at $7.4 billion.

The dispute really involves different ways of looking at the liquadation and is likely to be resolved only in the United States Court of Claims after years of litigation.

VACATION

William Stafford

One scene as I bow to pour her coffee:—

    Three Indians in the scouring drouth
    huddle at a grave scooped in the gravel,
    lean to the wind as our train goes by.
    Someone is gone.
    There is dust on everything in Nevada.

I pour the cream.

One of the countless sections of track badly in need of replacement. Such a situation causes four to five derailments every hour in the United States.—Courtesy *Construction News,* Inc.

About the Editors

MILLER WILLIAMS, known primarily as a poet and translator, was born in Hoxie, Arkansas, in 1930, and grew up in Methodist parsonages in the state's northern hills. His academic degrees are in biology, which he taught on the university level for several years before moving over to the teaching of literature in 1962. He has been Visiting Professor of U.S. Literature at the University of Chile and Fulbright Professor of American Studies at the National University of Mexico, and was founder and first editor of the *New Orleans Review.* He was awarded the Prix de Rome in Literature by the American Academy of Arts and Letters and the American Academy in Rome. He is currently co-director of the Program in Creative Writing and director of the Program in Translation at the University of Arkansas and conducts the Poetry Workshops at the Arkansas State Penitentiary at Cummins, now in their third year. He lives with his wife, Jordan, on a hillside in Fayetteville.

JAMES A. MCPHERSON, born in Savannah, Georgia, in 1943, received a B.A. from Morris Brown, an L.L.B. from Harvard Law School, and an M.F.A. from Iowa Writers' Workshop. Mr. McPherson is the author of *Hue and Cry,* a collection of short stories, and has been published in the *Atlantic Monthly, Playboy, New York Times Magazine, Harvard Advocate,* and *Reader's Digest.* In addition to teaching at the University of Iowa, University of California, Harvard, and Morgan State University, he has worked as a stock clerk, newsboy, banquet waiter, dining-car waiter, newspaper reporter, and a salad girl. Mr. McPherson now teaches American popular culture at the University of Virginia and is a contributing editor of the *Atlantic Monthly.* He lives in Baltimore with his wife, Sarah. He describes himself as an Omni-American.